Mexican Voices
of the Border Region

In the series *VOICES OF LATIN AMERICAN LIFE*,
edited by Arthur Schmidt

Laura Velasco Ortiz and Oscar F. Contreras,

with translations by Sandra del Castillo

Mexican Voices
of the Border Region

TEMPLE UNIVERSITY PRESS
Philadelphia

TEMPLE UNIVERSITY PRESS
Philadelphia, Pennsylvania 19122
www.temple.edu/tempress

Copyright © 2011 by Temple University
Published 2011

Library of Congress Cataloging-in-Publication Data

Velasco Ortiz, M. Laura.
   Mexican voices of the border region / Laura Velasco Ortiz and Oscar F.
Contreras ; with translations by Sandra del Castillo.
      p. cm. — (Voices of Latin American life)
   Includes bibliographical references and index.
   ISBN 978-1-59213-908-8 (hbk. : alk. paper) — ISBN 978-1-59213-909-5
(pbk. : alk. paper) — ISBN 978-1-59213-910-1 (electronic)
   1. Mexican-American Border Region—Social conditions. 2. Mexican-American
Border Region—Emigration and immigration—Social aspects. 3. Mexicans—
Mexican-American Border Region—Social conditions. 4. Mexican Americans—
Mexican-American Border Region—Social conditions. 5. Mexicans—Mexican-
American Border Region—Ethnic identity. 6. Mexican Americans—Mexican-
American Border Region—Ethnic identity. 7. Social ecology—Mexican-American
Border Region. I. Contreras Montellano, Oscar F. II. Title.
   F787.V45 2011
   972'.1—dc22

                                                            2010030557

Printed in the United States of America

032012P

Contents

Foreword

Arthur Schmidt

Two underlying sources of power interact to shape the early twenty-first-century world. On one hand exists the control of territory, the traditional basis for the recognition of national sovereignty and the operation of the institutions of the nation-state. On the other lies the control over the burgeoning transnational flows of goods, services, information, and people that constitute contemporary globalization. These two forms of power sometimes act in compatible fashion, sometimes in contradiction to each other. The constant dynamic tension between the two has heightened political and academic interest in border areas throughout the past generation. The Association of Borderlands Studies and its scholarly periodical publication, the *Journal of Borderlands Studies,* offer a prominent example of the increased academic focus on borders. The association came into existence in 1976 with an original emphasis on the U.S.-Mexican borderlands region, but since then it has grown and diversified, claiming membership of scholars from over one hundred academic centers, government institutions, and nongovernmental organizations worldwide. Now a quarter century old, the interdisciplinary *Journal of Borderlands Studies* appears three times a year, with peer-reviewed articles on borderlands issues from every region of the globe.[1]

The U.S.-Mexican border is one of the most remarkable anywhere. As Laura Velasco Ortiz and Oscar Contreras explain in their Introduction to *Mexican Voices of the Border Region,* the combination of adjacency, asymmetry, and interaction give the U.S.-Mexican border its particular character. In the words of an earlier book by Oscar Martínez, "Nowhere else do so many millions of people from two so dissimilar nations live in such close proximity and interact with each other so intensely."[2] The border extends nearly two thousand miles, from San Diego, California, and Tijuana, Baja California, on the western end, to Brownsville, Texas, and Matamoros, Tamaulipas, on the eastern end. Altogether the border region contains an estimated 12–14 million residents, with roughly equal totals in Mexico and the United States. Because the border is at once a place and a complex pattern of human interactions, it eludes a simple definition. Some authors employ the term "borderlands" precisely to capture the idea of a geographical zone of influence along an international borderline.[3] In practice, the terms "border," "borderlands," and "border region" are all inexact and shifting. Joan B. Anderson and James Gerber, two economists who specialize in the U.S.-Mexican border, employ the concept of "border region" while they also acknowledge that the border area does not form a "single, geographically and economically coherent region." They emphasize that "what distinguishes our area of interest is the presence of an international border" even though the "border region" consists of several highly distinct areas quite varied in their geographical and social characteristics. "Nevertheless," they explain, "the impact of economic integration and the presence of an international border make it useful to look at the entire border as an area or region of analysis."[4]

The testimonies that Laura Velasco and Oscar Contreras have collected in *Mexican Voices of the Border Region* come from the San Diego–Tijuana area, the largest and most economically powerful urban concentration along the border.[5] One of the busiest international crossing areas in the world, the San Diego–Tijuana gateway processes roughly forty thousand commuters every day for whom the line between Mexico and the United States acts as a "daily border" that they must traverse en route to work. On the whole, about one-fifth of the estimated annual 250 million legal crossings of the U.S.-Mexican border take place through San Diego–Tijuana.[6] The intense linkages between California and Baja California involve two of the three largest Mexican border cities, Tijuana and Mexicali, weaving together webs of activity in agricultural and industrial commerce, border tourism, shopping, prostitution, drug trafficking, low-wage Mexican factory production for the U.S. market, foreign capital investment, undocumented labor migration, money laundering, criminal violence, and a host of other elements. Small wonder, then, that analysts often see the cultural manifestations of the borderlands' population as reflecting a "hybridity" not exemplified by the national cultures of either Mexico or the United States.

As it heads east from California/Baja California, the border between Arizona and New Mexico and the Mexican states of Sonora and Chihuahua exists as an increasingly fortified line in the sand running through the Sonoran and Chihuahuan deserts. At El Paso–Ciudad Juárez, the border changes into the form of a river, the Rio Grande (United States)/Río Bravo (Mexico), for the remainder of its run to the Gulf of Mexico. Over its full extent, the border both connects and divides three binational urban formations, each with a combined population approaching or exceeding a million—San Diego, California

(1,256,000)/Tijuana, Baja California (1,411,000); Calexico, California (36,000)/
Mexicali, Baja California (856,000); and El Paso, Texas (600,000)/Ciudad
Juárez, Chihuahua (1,313,000)—in addition to seven other paired cities, each
with a combined population of well over 100,000: Yuma, Arizona (85,000)/San
Luis, Sonora (157,000); Nogales, Arizona (21,000)/Nogales, Sonora (194,000);
Del Rio, Texas (36,000)/Ciudad Acuña, Coahuila (126,000); Eagle Pass, Texas
(26,000)/Piedras Negras, Coahuila (144,000); Laredo, Texas (209,000)/Nuevo
Laredo, Tamaulipas (356,000); McAllen, Texas (124,000)/Reynosa, Tamaulipas (527,000); and Brownsville, Texas (168,000)/Matamoros, Tamaulipas
(462,000). The size of the Mexican border cities in particular reflects the six-
fold expansion in the population of the border region and even faster urbanization that has taken place since World War II. In 1940, under 17,000 lived
in Tijuana; no Mexican border city exceeded the size of Ciudad Juárez, with
49,000 inhabitants; and no city on either side, other than San Diego (population 203,000), attained even 100,000 residents.[7]

The "internationality and intense cross-border interaction" of the border
region have, more than any other factors, given it a "unique personality and
flavor." As a consequence, some argue, "the borderlands in their entirety constitute a single transnational system" in which human experiences become
defined by "ties to the 'other side.'"[8] The borderlands most clearly manifest
the accelerating process of economic integration that has been taking place
between the United States and Mexico. Mexico, for example, is the leading
market for the exports from the U.S. border states. Arizona and Texas send
close to a third of their international exports to Mexico, New Mexico a quarter
of its international exports, and California (with large markets in the Pacific) 14
percent.[9] The United States is overwhelmingly the largest market for Mexico's
border-area exports—for the commercial agriculture that employs residents of
the San Quintín Valley such as Rosalía, the worker profiled in Chapter 1, and
for the maquiladora manufacturing that began in the mid-1960s with the start
of Mexico's Border Industrialization Program, which today employs hundreds
of thousands of workers such as Elena, who tells her life story in Chapter 2.

Nevertheless, an intensified binational economic and social interaction is
not a social fusion. Although the border may be a "transnational community,"
it is vital to remember that it consists of two interdependent "contiguous geographic entities" that are "inextricably bound to their respective nations." It
would be wrong to regard the border as a distinct "third country" amalgam
of the two societies that abut the international borderline.[10] External national
policies emanating from Washington or Mexico City and globalizing economic
and technological forces provide the framework within which the border functions as a lived experience for those who have told their stories to Velasco and
Contreras. The borderlands may operate as a single transnational system, but
the region does not command the transnational forces that condition its existence. Moreover, the specificities of place and nationality still remain as significant elements.[11] What makes the U.S.-Mexican border so important in the

early twenty-first century is the presence in such a concentrated form of the inherent tensions between national power as sovereign territorial control and transnational power as control over flows of goods, services, information, and people.

The essence of the borderlands is the existence of an international borderline between two countries of notably unequal power. Because the border region is "the only place in the world where a highly developed country and a developing nation meet and interact," it offers "the best-known illustration of the paradoxical continued importance of borders in our globalizing world."[12] The asymmetries between the United States and Mexico have produced what Ramón Ruiz has called "the obsequious nature of the border economy," the dependent character of Mexican economic activity within the borderlands under the overarching superior material power of the United States.[13] The U.S. economy is over nine times the size of Mexico's gross domestic product, and North American per capita purchasing power exceeds that of Mexico by a factor of 3.5. Only slightly more than 1 percent of the U.S. labor force works in agriculture, in contrast with 14 percent of all employed Mexicans.[14] Borderlands communities manifest this inequality in a fashion particular to the region. Income levels on the northern side of the border rank below the U.S. average, while those on the southern side rank higher than the Mexican national average. Thus, the gaps between the U.S. and Mexican income and poverty rates remain generally lower within the borderlands than at national levels. The borderlands gaps tend to fall as one moves from west to east, from the widest levels in the San Diego–Tijuana area to the lowest levels along both sides of the Texas border.[15]

The paradoxes of the present-day U.S.-Mexican border originated in conquest—the military triumph of the westward-expanding United States over Mexico in the 1846–1848 war that followed the U.S. annexation of Texas in 1845.[16] Military conquests like to consider themselves definitive. They establish victors over vanquished, they appropriate territory, and they seek to institute unequivocally the rules of a new order laid down by the triumphant. By the terms of "Manifest Destiny," the expanding United States seized possession of the substantial northern territories that the national government of Mexico had been unable to control. As a result, the U.S.-Mexican border first appeared within a historical narrative that posited an inevitable Mexican decline and an equally inevitable Anglo ascendancy.[17] In the generation after the defeat of Mexico, for example, the American settlers of California thought that they had established a new "Massachusetts of the Pacific," one in which the presence of Mexicans would fade away, leaving only a few "Spanish" motifs behind as cultural adornments.[18] But such absoluteness does not always prevail. The conquered can remain and, over time, however unequally, influence the ways of life of the conquerors. What may result, as in the case of the U.S.-Mexican border region, is a domain of contradiction and ambiguity rather than the total certitude to which conquest aspires.

On one level, borders are intended to separate, to define sovereign owner-
ship, to compartmentalize who belongs where, and to protect one nationality
from another. (As Gael García Bernal drives southward across the border in
Alejandro González Iñárritu's film *Babel*, he responds as follows to his young
North American passengers' comment that Mexico is dangerous: "It is. It's full
of Mexicans.")[19] Those in the United States today who want to build physical
and electronic fences to "secure the border" with Mexico simplistically focus on
this function of borders. They fail to recognize that another purpose of borders
is to join. As Timothy Henderson has noted in the preface to his history of the
war between Mexico and the United States, "American interest in Mexico has
been conditioned by Mexico's ability to benefit or menace the United States."[20]
Under this dual vision, the border must both seal off and connect Mexico and
the United States. Thus, the border has acted as an entryway into Mexico for
U.S. tourists, investors, and products. At the same time, it has operated as a
set of gateways into the United States for the flow of not only the Mexican
laborers on whom sectors of the U.S. economy heavily rely but also shipments
of Mexican goods (with Mexico currently serving as the third-largest trading
partner for the United States, behind only Canada and the People's Republic
of China).[21]

The paradoxes of the present-day U.S.-Mexican borderlands arise from
the contradictory functions of the border as separation and as connection in
the midst of the socially integrating forces of labor migration, mass communications, and tourism on one hand and the economically integrating forces
of trade, production, and investment on the other. Since neither the citizenry
nor the institutions of either Mexico or the United States are fully prepared to
cope with the contemporary experience of economic and social integration, the
border is obliged to respond simultaneously to forces of attraction and forces
of rejection. In short, what Velasco and Contreras call the "structural border"
operates as a filter, screening out some aspects of the Mexico–United States
relationship while letting others pass.

The de facto definition of the U.S.-Mexican border as a filter emerged at
the time of the Mexican Revolution and World War I. Until the late nineteenth
century, a relative isolation and autonomy characterized the areas that today
make up the borderlands. By the 1880s, U.S. economic forces began to dimin-
ish the border region's peripheral isolation. In 1881, the first transcontinental
railroad to pass through the borderlands tied the region to the East and West
Coast markets and investors. By then, Mexico had abandoned the dictum of
former president Sebastián Lerdo de Tejada—"between the strong and the
weak, the desert"—and at the end of the century a significant rail network,
built mostly by means of U.S. capital with subsidies from the Mexican government, linked the cities of central and northern Mexico with the United States.
Rail transportation encouraged the growth of mining, petroleum production,
commercial agriculture, and livestock raising in various parts of northern
Mexico. By 1910, a quarter of all foreign investment in Mexico was located

in Chihuahua, Coahuila, Nuevo León, and Sonora. Economic development and private American investments transformed the states of northern Mexico from the frontier into the "border." The five states and one territory adjacent to the United States increased their share of the country's population from slightly under 8 percent in 1877 to slightly more than 11 percent in 1910. Cities on both sides of the border became transit routes for a flourishing commerce between the two countries.[22]

Integration of the borderlands into wider economic patterns involving the United States and Mexico ended the region's relative isolation and brought greater prosperity. Over the course of the twentieth century, the "group of small, scattered outposts along the international boundary between the United States and Mexico" would evolve into "one of the most economically and demographically dynamic regions of the world."[23] With the growth of both U.S. power in the world and U.S. investments in Mexico, dominion over the local economics and politics of the borderlands increasingly rested in the hands of distant financiers, corporations, politicians, and bureaucrats in Mexico City, New York, Washington, and elsewhere. During the most violent years of the Mexican Revolution, 1910–1920, when as many as 1.4 million Mexicans may have died, communities along the international borderline acted as both battlegrounds and places of refuge.[24] The battle of Ciudad Juárez in 1911 brought the downfall of the dictator Porfirio Díaz, and Pancho Villa's attack on the town of Columbus, New Mexico, in 1916 led to General John J. Pershing's unsuccessful Punitive Expedition, a futile search for Villa that lasted eleven months. Washington's influence over the ability or inability of different contending forces to secure arms across the border in the United States became an important strategic element in the dynamics of Mexico's internal revolutionary warfare. Between 1915 and the U.S. entry into World War I in 1917, events in south Texas created security concerns for Washington. The abortive Plan of San Diego, named for a small Texas town, called for an armed uprising against the U.S. government. Continued Mexican American unrest met frequently lawless repression by the Texas Rangers and local vigilantes. Germany issued unsuccessful overtures to the Mexican government of Venustiano Carranza for the formation of a secret anti–United States alliance.

Even as security matters reinforced the border's function as an international line marking the separation of sovereign nation-states, its role as a connecting route for transnational commerce and labor migration increased. Both facets of the border's character required an augmented and more formal federal presence to regulate transborder movement of goods and people. The border now became a filter that defined the difference between not only legitimate merchandise and contraband goods but also permitted and prohibited Mexican labor migration. The value of trade between the United States and Mexico during the Mexican Revolution tripled between 1911 and 1920. While some of the commerce between the two countries took place by sea, the border nevertheless participated significantly in the "export boom of the Mexican Revolution" through the transit of a variety of mineral, agricultural, and livestock products destined for the United States.[25] The Mexican Revolution also increased the movement of Mexicans seeking work in the United States. Although figures are notoriously unreliable, Mexican migration to the United States probably numbered at least several hundred thousand persons between 1900 and 1930 and may have exceeded a million. Labor shortages during World War I brought a demand for Mexican workers, who crossed the border to find jobs as far away as the rail yards, steel works, and meatpacking houses of Chicago; the steel furnaces of Bethlehem; and the sugar beet fields of Colorado and Michigan.[26] In an era of strong anti-immigrant public sentiment along with virulent racial hostility toward African Americans and Asians, Mexicans became the preferred migrant labor force for the substantial expansion in agriculture and mining taking place in the economy of the southwestern United States.

A formal but flexible administration of the U.S.-Mexican border proved instrumental in accommodating racist hostility at the presence of Mexicans in the United States to the economic demand for their labor. Powerful agricultural and mining interests in California and Texas continually secured legal loopholes for cross-border Mexican laborers, exempting them from the numerous immigrant exclusionary measures enacted at the federal level between 1917 and 1929. Using the same demeaning racial stereotypes as anti-immigrant restrictionists, employers defined Mexicans as unambitious and docile, an ideal stoop labor force that could be returned next door, across the border, when no longer needed in the United States. In the words of Mae Ngai, "During the 1920s, immigration policy rearticulated the U.S.-Mexican border as a cultural and racial boundary, as a creator of illegal immigration. Federal officials self-consciously understood their task as creating a barrier where, in a practical sense, none had existed before."[27] Instituted in 1924, the U.S. Border Patrol came into existence to provide the policing of Mexican labor migration, allowing the passage of Mexicans through the border "barrier" and obliging their return in accord with the fluctuating needs of agricultural, mining, and railroad employers in the Southwest.

Contrary to the image of the sovereign border as a firm barrier, the history of the U.S.-Mexican border as a filter since the 1920s has inevitably been one of contradictory and often arbitrary policies. During the Great Depression of the 1930s, local authorities in various parts of the United States expelled Mexican laborers—perhaps as many as half a million—only to experience an even greater demand for their labor a short time later, with the outbreak of World War II.[28] In 1942, the U.S. and Mexican governments signed a formal contract labor agreement—colloquially known as the Bracero Program—meant to harmonize U.S. labor demands with Mexico's need for an orderly, humane treatment of its laborers. Originally intended as a temporary wartime measure, the Bracero Program evolved into a series of renewed agreements that lasted until 1964. Although it was created as a measure to control a legal flow of laborers and promote humane administration, the Bracero Program led to a considerable amount of undocumented labor and often descended into a legalization of the exploitive.[29]

The enormous growth of economic activity between the United States and Mexico over the past several decades has made the filtering mission of the border increasingly difficult. Since the inauguration of the North American Free Trade Area in 1994, trade between the United States and Mexico has increased more than three and a half fold and private U.S. direct investment in Mexico has expanded by a factor of nine.[30] The filtering function of the border has had to absorb the contradictions inherent in the policies that the U.S. and Mexican governments have pursued in the midst of this dynamic economic integration. The examples of Mexican labor migration and narcotics trafficking, two prominent issues associated today with the U.S.-Mexican border, demonstrate the enormous strains that national factors in both Mexico and the United States place on the filtering function of the border.

In the view of many analysts, the economic policies that the Mexican government has pursued since the 1980s have generated out-migration more than they have created successful economic development.[31] Over the same period of time, the U.S. policy toward Mexico has assumed that increased economic activity could take place between the two countries without generating further labor migration, an assumption that simply flies in the face of the historical experience of United States–Mexico relationships and that of labor migration elsewhere in the world. Various pieces of U.S. immigration legislation, including the Immigration Reform and Control Act of 1986, have vastly augmented the exclusionary police functions of the border without having achieved any measurable success in deterring undocumented Mexican labor migration to the United States. In fact, "securing the border" has contributed to transforming the movement of Mexicans to the United States from a predominantly circular migration into a settlement migration. While the numbers of Mexicans migrating to the United States has not increased substantially over the levels of previous decades, the numbers of those remaining more or less permanently has. In other words, tightening the border filter by the increasing militarization of the borderlands has acted less as a deterrent against migration from Mexico and more as an incentive for immigrants to remain within the United States once arrived. Currently, Mexicans constitute about six of every ten undocumented immigrants in the United States.[32]

In recent years, high levels of violence associated with the cartels that struggle for control of the shipment of narcotics to the United States have plagued border cities in Mexico. The demand for illegal drugs in the United States generates an enormous flow of money—some say an annual $10 billion and others considerably more—to Mexico.[33] Efforts by the Mexican government, with U.S. support, to use the army to suppress the cartels have seemingly only widened the circle of violence within Mexico.[34] Meanwhile, loose gun laws in the United States allow the Mexican cartels to readily obtain ample high-powered weaponry across the border. By some accounts, more than sixty-six hundred licensed gun dealers exist along the border in the United States, making the borderlands a virtual arms supermarket for violent crime in Mexico.[35] The Mexican government receives equipment, training, and judicial reform assistance from the United States through Plan Mérida (alternatively known as Plan Mexico), but many analysts doubt the efficacy of this aid and fear that it may make conditions even worse.[36] The United States has failed to reduce its domestic demand for drugs. At the same time, in the face of the gun lobby and court decisions regarding the Second Amendment, U.S. authorities have been unable to combat the flagrantly open sale of lethal weaponry that makes its way across the border into Mexico. As a result, the ability of the border to function as an effective filter has been undermined, and violence has increased in the borderlands.

As the testimonies in *Mexican Voices of the Border Region* illustrate, residents of the Mexican borderlands experience in their everyday lives the paradoxes and strains of the border as an international filter. The "lived border" creates a climate of uncertainty that surrounds their existence whether or not they ever cross the border. The border region is a terrain of both movement and settlement, and during the past two generations many have migrated there in hopes of a better life. For women workers such as Rosalía and Elena, "the border never crossed" has dashed their hopes. The selective filter of the border blocks them from the possibility of benefiting from the greater earning opportunities of U.S. labor markets. Despite their creative and energetic capacity for survival, conditions assign them, as unskilled female workers, to permanency at the bottom levels of an unequal binational labor chain. Others for whom the border may never be crossed or for whom it is a "backdrop" may experience its filtering functions differently. Through its power of exclusion in a context of binational inequality, the border assigns some activities to the Mexican side of the line. Border tourism brings generally wealthier (although not necessarily wealthy) U.S. tourists to Tijuana for an excursion to "the other side." Some may engage in innocuous pursuits, such as the purchase of inexpensive craft goods of the sort sold by Ofelia, the Mixtec street vendor from Chapter 5. For Ofelia, the informal street economy of Tijuana tourism has provided a creative outlet for her leadership capacity and has brought her earnings. Other activities "across the line" may be less savory. Ever since the time of U.S. Prohibition, Tijuana has been an entertainment haven for U.S. tourists seeking legal gambling, drinking, and prostitution. Rosa, from Chapter 3, finds that the "border never crossed" generates work for her as a prostitute, a legal if undesirable niche within the local entertainment economy that has been transnationally relegated to the Mexican side of the border.[37] Juan, in Chapter 4, has spent a life involved in the shady trades made possible by the underground economies of the border, growing marijuana, dealing in "hot" cars, and selling drugs.

Underground markets come into existence when the legitimate economy cannot provide for persistent genuine or perceived needs. The Panther from Chapter 8, like Juan, supplies the illegal market for addictive drugs, but unlike

Juan he crosses over the international line, taking up the long-standing border role of a smuggler. Since demand for narcotics and for Mexican laborers exists in the United States, the Panther specializes in transporting both to the other side. Eloísa, from Chapter 6, and Porfirio, from Chapter 7, both cross over in order to provide the lower-cost labor that segments of the U.S. economy require—Eloísa in elder care and Porfirio in the construction trades. Although these two border crossers live lives defined by two worlds, they are not fully at home in either. For Eloísa, the earning opportunities in the United States are vital to her hopes for entering graduate school in Mexico. Porfirio, the border-jumping acrobat, however, has spent much of his life in pursuits that have led him nowhere. The border is a region of ambiguity and uncertainty, and their lack of legality in the United States has remained an obstacle for both Eloísa and Porfirio, as it has for so many Mexican migrants to the United States.

Emilio and Julius, the final two subjects profiled by Velasco and Contreras, exemplify the successful fulfillment of one version of the hopes that the border evokes for many Mexicans. Each represents the transgenerational social mobility that legal residence in the United States, the hard work of immigrant parents, and successful educational experiences make possible. For both Emilio and Julius, the border filter has encouraged the personal traits most likely to promote assimilation—the acquisition of fluent English and new cultural perspectives and the inclination to envisage Mexico as heritage. Emilio, a college student who aims to study European history on the East Coast of the United States, and Julius, an officer of the Border Patrol, have permanently crossed the border to become Mexican Americans for whom Mexico is a heritage more than a continuously lived reality.

Emilio and Julius do not stand at the end of a continuum. The ten border voices that Velasco and Contreras present exist as a collage, not as a linear progression. In contemplating the life stories in this book, readers will come to appreciate the borderlands as a complex binational society whose aspirations, ambiguities, and contradictions embody, in particular ways, those of the two nations that meet on that two-thousand-mile line from San Diego/Tijuana to Brownsville/Matamoros. In a time of rapid economic and social integration between Mexico and the United States, these stories underscore the importance of approaching the complex issues of the United States–Mexico relationship not with narrow nationalism, intolerance, or demagoguery but with a humane intelligence.

Acknowledgments

We thank all the individuals who invited us into their (sometimes clandestine) homes and recounted their life stories. Without their willingness to open their lives to us and their eagerness to be heard, this book would not exist.

This volume is the product of an ongoing dialogue between the authors and the series editor. Over a period of years, we had the opportunity to exchange ideas with Arthur Schmidt and to observe, with gratitude and admiration, his patient yet galvanizing efforts in support of the writing of this book—from project design to text editing.

Contacts that we had established previously helped us compile the diverse biographical profiles that are the framework of this book, but our efforts would have been incomplete without the assistance of people such as Gerardo Medrano, our guide in the field and an extremely knowledgeable source on border life in Tijuana. With his help, we were able to approach areas and people who would otherwise have been beyond the reach of even these two researchers, who felt that they knew Tijuana well. We also thank Professor José Moreno Mena, of the Universidad Autónoma de Baja California and a human rights activist on the border, who guided us through Mexicali's subterranean migration network. And we thank Father Luiz Kendzierski, director of the Casa del Migrante, for opening the center's doors and allowing us to listen to the life stories of the people who find shelter there.

This book was originally written in Spanish, and thanks to the expert pen and literary sensibility of Sandra del Castillo, our translator, as we read the

English translations, we encounter the same rhythm and tone that were present in the life stories as we received them. Her enthusiastic comments on the texts also accompanied us throughout our writing process.

We are grateful to El Colegio de la Frontera Norte and El Colegio de Sonora, which provided us with a supportive and flexible environment as we nurtured the evolution of this project.

And, finally, for his critical readings and support in the field, we thank our son, Oscar Contreras Velasco.

Mexican Voices
of the Border Region

Introduction

Lived Borders

The Two Faces of the U.S.-Mexican Border: Mobility and Settlement

One summer afternoon, as Don Fernando sat on the patio of his home to escape the day's heat, he remembered that his "laser visa" (border crossing card) for entering the United States was about to expire. Memories of times past filled his mind as he recalled the days when he had harvested cherries in the orchards of the Santa Clara Valley in the embrace of the California summer sun. Fifty years had passed since he was last deported and had decided he would not return to "American soil" but would remain in the border city of Tecate, where his parents had established a tortilla business.

Some days later he went to the U.S. immigration office in Tecate with his wife, Consuelo, and his oldest daughter, Angeles, to renew his visa. A week later he received a phone call notifying him of an appointment at the immigration office. Don Fernando was consumed with worry. What could be the matter? Perhaps he had failed to submit all the required paperwork or had not demonstrated sufficient income. On the day of the appointment, the family rose early, confused and worried that their visa renewals would be denied. They ultimately learned at the immigration office that immigration records showed Don Fernando had been deported in 1959. Fifty years had passed since he had last crossed the border to work as an undocumented laborer in rural California. In the intervening years he had built a small business, first a general store and then a stationers' shop, and had been crossing the border legally for many years using his border resident visa and, later, his laser visa. Now, at age seventy-five and somewhat bewildered by the immigration official's questions about the deportation incident, he tried to recall the details the official sought, but he remembered only the sunny afternoons he had spent up a ladder, picking apricots or pruning peach trees. Meanwhile, Doña Consuelo and Angeles looked on, alarmed by the possibility that their visas would be denied. Then the immigration official called Doña Consuelo over and questioned her about the incident. She tried to remember but was unable to recall any details about where they'd been detained or where on the border they'd been deported. Her only recollection was that her second child had been born two months later. On hearing her few memories, the immigration official smiled and said, "So the two of you were detained together, already married. How romantic!" The interview ended then, and a few minutes later they were called over to have their documents stamped and to receive their laser visas, now valid for another ten years.

Don Fernando and his family are part of a subset of residents of the Mexican border region who have visas to cross into the United States. This family drama recurs throughout the border area, given that a permit to cross the border is a coveted object among border residents, and to the extent that it is issued selectively, it serves to differentiate and socially stratify the region's inhabitants. This differentiating mechanism operates among border residents, but also among people to the south of the border. For them, it is a powerful magnet that attracts flows of people to the border zone year after year, people who either settle on the Mexican side or cross into the United States as undocumented migrants.

The course that Don Fernando and his family have followed illustrates Zygmunt Bauman's conceptualization of the differentiating power of geographic mobility as a characteristic feature of modern-day globalization. The borderlands of nation-states have been transformed into spaces where diverse human flows converge with exceptional intensity. Nevertheless, while goods and capital enjoy an ever-increasing freedom of movement, people remain subject to an assortment of economic and legal restrictions. This means that mobility is not a homogenizing factor among the population but is instead a process of differentiation (Bauman 1999). Both the motivations and the conditions under which human mobility occurs express hierarchies linked to class, ethnicity, and gender: For some, itineraries are planned, predictable, and safe, while for others, movement is subject to risk and uncertainty, to the contingencies of passage. Among the differentiating factors that derive from mobility, gender has particular relevance due to the persisting association of the "feminine" with the domestic arena. A focus on gender uncovers the violence that exists within the intimate spaces of the home but that is also present in mobility and border crossing. Along with the construct of ethnicity-race, gender decisively influences the configuration of risks and opportunities in the life experience of the border.

When mobility connected to the search for employment reaches massive proportions, uncertainty and risk seem to transform into a social constant that spills beyond the protagonists themselves to encompass their family members, the ones who remain behind and the ones who receive the migrants, as well as contacts and observers along the way. Paradoxically, this transposition of people that separates and uproots migrants from their homes arises out of a search for stability and security, generally via a better job and better living conditions. Therefore, we must look at not only mobility but also the processes of settlement, the mechanisms that accord stability to a population and create relatively anchored communities and that eventually can provide support to the influxes of new immigrants in border regions.

The U.S.-Mexican border, and especially Tijuana–San Diego, is an iconographic space for the movement of people between south and north and for the formation of new, culturally diverse border communities. This space allows us to reflect on the factors that afflict border regions linking asymmetrical country pairs in other parts of the world.

Three elements define what can be described as the structural condition of the border: adjacency, asymmetry, and interaction. A key moment in the history of asymmetry occurred in the nineteenth century, when Mexico lost nearly half its territory to annexation by the United States. Geographic contiguity facilitated the continued maintenance of commercial and family ties in the new border region, establishing the social bases for the intense cross-border interaction seen today. Over the course of the twentieth century, differences in the two countries' economic development, combined with their physical proximity, set in motion an unstoppable migratory flow from south to north. Perhaps the most telling indicator of the asymmetry of this interaction is the fact that more than five hundred migrants die and an unknown number simply disappear each year in their attempts to cross the border and find work in the United States.

Despite strong U.S. government restrictions on entry, tens of thousands of migrants succeed in crossing and merge into the army of undocumented workers who undertake the most onerous and poorly paid jobs in the United States. Others remain and settle on the Mexican side, find jobs, establish families, educate their children, and pursue lives that apparently are unattainable in their places of origin. Still others find a niche in the flourishing but dangerous activities that are emblematic of border areas: prostitution, human trafficking, and drug smuggling. The intense economic and social interactions across the border underpin the livings of millions of people who have made this border their home and the terrain on which they construct their life projects. The dialectic between mobility and settlement, between setting down roots and being uprooted, gives the region a sense of vitality, of constant renewal.

As the life stories contained in this book demonstrate, this structural framework is the milieu in which an extensive array of life options unfolds for the region's inhabitants. The structural frontier seeps into the life of each person differentially, depending on his or her particular circumstances, life trajectory, and capacity for agency as they are linked to the structuring effect of social class, ethnicity, and gender.

Given the ample existing literature on what we term the structural condition of the border, in this book we explore a second dimension of the border, what we call the *lived border* or the *experienced border*. Drawing on the phenomenological concept of life experiences, which stems from reflections on life itself (Dilthey 1994, 41), the *lived border* encompasses the subjective experience of the border, its key referent the meaning of the border crossing between the two countries. In this subjective dimension we also find expression of the structural elements that historically have defined the border: adjacency, asymmetry, and interaction. Crossing experiences can be diametrically opposed to one another depending on the direction of crossing (northward or southward), legal status (legal or undocumented), and motivation (entertainment or employment). For example, illegality in border crossing is visible and problematic when the crossing is from south to north, but not so if it is in the opposite direction. According to Michael Kearney (2008, 81), crossing the border is a transformative experience because it alters the crossers' worth as they enter a classification system that changes the value of their attributes. That is, moving across this dividing line breaks the spatial continuity of life and repositions the subject in the social scheme, changing the value of his or her attributes and requiring the individual to adapt. The discontinuity and constant repositioning that occur in relationship systems with differentiated hierarchies become routine, and the region's inhabitants assimilate this discontinuity and incorporate it into their daily lives.

Within this fluid system of classification and hierarchization, a sharp shift occurs in the ethnic position of crossers into the United States as they are inserted into a set of relationships in which "national" becomes "ethnic" and influences one's position and value in the new society. In contrast, gender position seems to remain largely constant because "feminine" continues to be linked to the domestic and reproductive realms, though with important nuances depending on the ethnic-national configuration that predominates on each side of the border. In Mexico, ethnicity is associated with the indigenous-mestizo duality that took root during the period of Spanish conquest and colonization, while in the United States, ethnicity connotes race and is primarily based on national origin, a reflection of the importance of population displacements and migrations over the past two decades (Velasco 2010).

The Structural Border: Adjacency, Asymmetry, and Interaction

The border that separates Mexico and the United States runs for just over two thousand miles and is the most transited border in the world, with 350 million legal crossings each year. It is also the international frontier manifesting the greatest contrasts, given the profound asymmetry between the two neighboring countries. A practical definition delineates the border region as the area that includes the thirty-eight *municipios* (akin to U.S. counties) that lie along the border on the Mexican side and the twenty-five U.S. counties that abut the border with Mexico. This vast borderlands region contained some 12.2 million inhabitants in 2000, distributed almost evenly on the two sides of the border: 5.9 million on the Mexican side and 6.3 million on the U.S. side (Anderson and Gerber 2008).

In addition to historical and cultural differences that stem from the contrasting colonization processes in the two nations—one Protestant, the other Catholic—there are economic differences between the two countries, which have deepened over the course of the twentieth century. While the United States consolidated as the world's dominant economic power, the Mexican economy grew only modestly for forty years and then stagnated beginning in the 1970s, at the same time as inequality and poverty were on the rise. On the border, these differences are expressed tangentially as economic, social, and territorial discontinuity, a reality the border population encounters every day. This is why the descriptor that best defines the border zone is "the adjacency of difference" (Alegría 1989).

In large part because of this asymmetry, relations between the two nations were close during the final decades of the twentieth century. Economic relations advanced at a steady pace beginning with World War II, intensified with Mexico's economic liberalization in the early 1980s, and deepened even further with the implementation of the North American Free Trade Agreement (NAFTA) in 1994. Under NAFTA, United States–Mexico trade rose substantially, to reach a value of US$350 billion in 2008.

For Mexico, the rise in trade with the United States is explained in part by the growth of exports from transnational companies with operations in Mexico. These companies increased their industrial output by making major investments in their installations. Foreign direct investment (FDI) in Mexico, which totaled US$2.6 billion in 1990, exceeded $250 billion in the period from 1994 to 2008, and 47 percent went to the manufacturing sector (Contreras 2010). But there was also a sizable investment in agricultural exports, which dramatically altered Mexico's agricultural sector. Whereas Mexico was previously self-sufficient in food production and a food exporter, it was transformed into a food importer, now needing to purchase abroad 40 percent of the grains required for national consumption. In contrast, production and export of fresh fruits and vegetables accelerated to such a degree that in 2006 these products accounted for half the value generated by the agricultural sector and 93 percent of agricultural exports, most destined for the U.S. market (Echánove 2009). In sum, as Mexico tightened its economic ties with the United States, both its industrial and agricultural sectors underwent a radical transformation, privileging the external over the domestic market. These figures signal a relationship of dependency in both sectors, compromising not only Mexico's human resources but the nation's natural resources as well.

The principal point of contact between the two countries is the border region, the area where most transactions and interactions are concentrated. But interactions are concentrated even further at one extreme end of the border zone, in the Pacific coast states of California and Baja California. Forty-four percent of the border population of the United States lives in San Diego County, and 41 percent of Mexico's border population lives in the *municipio* of Tijuana (Anderson and Gerber 2008). Together Tijuana and San Diego form a binational zone of high economic, social, and population density, an area that typifies life along the border.

The city of Tijuana, with nearly 2 million inhabitants, is the largest urban concentration on Mexico's northern border. It has been called "the border of Latin America," given its position at the extreme geographic edge of the Latin American region, with the Pacific Ocean to the west and California, the most prosperous state of the world's richest nation, to the north. Tijuana is a young city, whose growth has been tightly linked to the California economy and the proximity of San Diego County.

Throughout the second half of the twentieth century, the vigorous California economy enabled Tijuana to develop a vibrant economy based on services linked to tourism, along with an expansive industrial sector devoted to the assembly of products for export. Tijuana also became the most important entry point on the border with the United States, not only for legal visitors and migrants but also for those entering clandestinely. Most recently, Tijuana has also been transformed into a primary arena for the illicit drug trade and the accompanying violent exchanges between drug cartels vying for control of the market—in addition to the bloody war that the Mexican government is waging against these criminal syndicates.

The establishment of maquiladoras (in-bond assembly plants) in Tijuana beginning in the 1970s brought a number of consequences, including a sizable expansion of the labor market, especially jobs for women. Between 1985 and 2000, the maquiladoras, most of which are subsidiaries or subcontractors of transnational companies, emerged as one of the primary sources of employment on Mexico's northern border. In Tijuana, more than eight hundred of these plants were employing nearly two hundred thousand workers at the end of 2000. Despite the decline in industrial activity caused by the economic crisis of 2008–2009, these assembly plants continue to be a major source of jobs in the city. Some of these positions are formal jobs with salaries above the national average,[1] but many *maquila* jobs are unstable and precarious, particularly those in small workshops or done at home.

Along with the expansion of its industrial base, Tijuana became the most visited city on the border and, in fact, one of the most visited cities in the world, with 22 million international visitors in 2006 (Bringas and Gaxiola 2010). In that same year, 29.4 million people entered the United States from Tijuana, for a total of nearly 50 million border crossings through Tijuana in 2006.

A characteristic feature of the tourism that comes to Tijuana is its short duration, a time frame that reflects the legendary local permissiveness regarding the sale of alcohol to minors and the diversity and dynamism of the sex trade. This kind of tourism has been part of Tijuana's history since early in the twentieth century and was even present at the city's founding. Over the last decade, and especially since the terrorist attacks of 2001, tourism activity has waned, a decline visible in the pervasive emptiness of the fabled Avenida Revolución.

On the other hand, in the final decades of the twentieth century, Tijuana also became the most important crossing point into the United States, not only for tourists but also for migrants, with or without documents. Estimates suggest that in the early 1990s more than 40 percent of undocumented migrants entering the United States from Mexican territory were crossing via Tijuana–San Diego. In later years, heightened border enforcement led to a diversification in crossing points, shifting them eastward along the border. Domestic political pressures and a new urgency in the fight against terrorism combined to translate into an expanded presence of Border Patrol personnel and the emergence of new anti-immigrant groups in the borderlands.[2] This prompted migrants to alter their routes, which made the crossings riskier and more costly, but it had little or no effect on reducing undocumented migrant flows.

Despite the drastic measures implemented to dissuade illegal entry to the United States, Tijuana continues to be the chosen crossing point for a third of undocumented migrants and the most transited point for traffic in both directions. Part of this flow is accounted for by the fact that most migrants deported from the United States are returned to Mexico at Tijuana.

Finally, the surge in narco-trafficking in the region beginning in the 1990s reflects the new power of Mexican drug traffickers following the Colombian and U.S. governments' successes against the Colombian cartels. By the late 1990s, Mexican syndicates dominated the markets for cocaine, marijuana, and methamphetamines, giving them virtual control over the trafficking of drugs into the United States. The U.S. market for illicit drugs is enormous, with a value of between US$6 billion and $25 billion annually (Chabat 2002; González-Ruiz 2001). Though the Tijuana cartel has suffered severe setbacks in recent years, it continues to vie with the Sinaloa cartel for control of the city and to clash with the Mexican army, which has stationed soldiers in Tijuana on a permanent basis.

In contrast to the situation just two decades ago, Tijuana is no longer only a point for smuggling drugs over the border; it is now also a point of consumption, with a local market whose strength depends on the fluidity of cross-border drug traffic. In part because of rising drug production in Mexico but also because of the increasing difficulty of smuggling drugs into the United States, the cartels have moved to expand the local market, and domestic drug consumption in Mexico has risen accordingly. It is no coincidence that the main drug-trafficking areas are also those with the highest rates of drug use. A 2006 study found that 14.7 percent of Tijuana's population between the ages of twelve and sixty-five had used an illicit drug at some time, a rate three times higher than the national average of 5.3 percent; next was Ciudad Juárez, at 9.2 percent (Brouwer et al. 2006).

These are the global, national, and local forces that have shaped the borderlands and the lives of the people whose narratives appear in this book. Thanks to the border region's asymmetrical integration, these forces coexist in contradictory fashion, as suggested by Lynn Stephen (2007, 311). Underpinning the research that gave rise to this book is the hypothesis that the structural border socially and politically differentiates and stratifies the population that lives in and passes through the region, precisely because of the juxtaposition of the three elements that best define this border—adjacency, asymmetry, and intense interaction—with historical roots that reach back far beyond the twentieth century. The book documents the different experiences of border life, depending on one's relationship with the border crossing, and postulates that the daily event of crossing sustains specific ways of life and subjectivities. The border crossing can be conceptualized as the nucleus of a tangled skein of events and social relationships that constitute an individual's life. Not all border residents cross the line, yet their lives are all constantly influenced by the structural factors associated with the presence of this political-administrative divide.

The Lived Border: Crossing from One Side to the Other

Experience of the border crossing can be analyzed using the concept of transit in three dimensions—temporal, spatial, and social—which assume meaning in a biographical framework. The time of crossing holds meaning in someone's biography depending on his or her life stage. The spatial dimension, like the temporal one, has a broad referent and assumes meaning in a person's biography in his or her itineraries of mobility—that is, places where the person has been or visited but especially where he or she has lived or resided. The social dimension ties the biographical frame to the individual's social attachments. In this way, the experience of transiting or crossing the border is framed within the biography of the individual as part of a social class or specific social category, as a man or woman, with a specific ethnicity, in a temporal and spatial dimension that extends outward to one's ancestors, one's contemporaries, and one's successors through a web of social relationships.

In the life histories in this book, the concept of transit refers to the life-experience itineraries involved in crossing the border, which individuals experience differentially depending on legal status, intensity of crossing (frequency and duration), and motivation for crossing. Not all who come to and reside in the Mexican portion of the border region cross the border. In Tijuana, more than half the city's population lacks documents to cross to the U.S. side, and though some individuals may attempt to cross clandestinely, it is clear that many Tijuana residents have never crossed. Yet the possibility is always present as a more or less accessible option. Moreover, the flows of people and goods in both directions over the border are a prominent referent in the array of life options on the Mexican side and perhaps, though with less intensity, on the U.S. side as well.[3]

Viewing the border from the Mexican side as an opportunity, yet not crossing, is an irrefutable sign of the structural asymmetry that exists between the two countries. The perception that the U.S. side offers advantages not present on the Mexican side has structural foundations that are well documented and well established in shared understandings and in the narratives of the region's inhabitants. For example, current salaries in Mexico's maquiladoras are just a tenth of the industrial wage in the United States, and the quality of life is generally better in the United States as well. Alejandro Portes and Rubén G. Rumbaut (2006) note that international migration to the United States in some sense represents the triumph of a lifestyle. The narratives in this book reveal a kind of fascination with this lifestyle and the possibility of crossing the border and approaching that imagined well-being, but also a disenchantment stemming from the unattainability of these realities.

The book presents a set of ten life narratives by individuals whose common characteristic is living at the western edge of the border between Mexico and the United States. Most live on the Mexican side, in Tijuana. Yet, as these various cases reveal, these individuals' life trajectories are tied to both sides of the border. The heterogeneity of border lives is echoed in Pablo Vila's (2000) questioning of the viewpoint that dominated Chicano studies in the 1990s regarding the hybrid nature of border crossers, postulating a more complex heterogeneity in identities in the U.S.-Mexican border region. As portrayed in the narratives in this book, the border is not lived the same way if one lives on the northern versus the southern side, or if one crosses legally versus illegally. Crossing the border is not something that is generalized among all the region's inhabitants. While there is a fraction of the population whose lives unfold in a constant coming and going across the border, on both sides there are segments of the population whose lives are determined by the reality of the border but who live on only one side and rarely if ever cross the line.

The Schema for Presentation of the Cases

The presentation of the narratives follows a classification based on personal experience of the border crossing. In this set of cases we find a diversity of life experiences that can be organized along a continuum extending from people who live in Mexico and have never crossed the border to those who live on the U.S. side and also do not cross, even when crossing the border is a future possibility for some of them or, alternatively, an option now relegated to a nostalgic and distant past.

Our first step in selecting the cases was to construct a set of "ideal type" profiles based on the literature and on our previous fieldwork on the Tijuana–San Diego border, the goal being to accurately represent the cultural diversity and varied social spheres that define life along this border. Once the profiles were drawn, we employed our extensive network of contacts to identify appropriate cases in the field and then conducted biographical interviews. Several cases were collected for each profile, and the most illustrative one was ultimately selected for inclusion. In addition to reflecting specific *types* of border experience, the chosen cases are significant because of the interviewees themselves, whose tremendously compelling life stories are incarnations of a drive to survive, of creativity, and of resilience across a range of social environments.

The logic that determines the presentation of the biographical texts conforms to the idea of narrative coproduction, in which the narrator coproduces his or her story jointly with the interviewer in a human and social interrelationship (Tierney 2000). Each chapter unfolds around the protagonist's recountings, organized with a series of questions that function as a connecting thread running through the narrative fabric. Other authors have employed this strategy (Gay 2005), which yields a life story reached through dialogue between the narrator and the listener and which acquires meaning within the specific context of each biography. Each narrative is preceded by a two-part introduction, which first traces the historical context for the respective life story and then sketches the specific situation in which the narrative was produced.

We have made an effort to go beyond the stereotypical images of Mexico's northern border, especially regarding the city of Tijuana, which is commonly portrayed as a point of passage dominated by insecurity, narco-trafficking, and the aimless wanderings of deported migrants. Admittedly, these phenomena are present, and they exert a significant impact on the history and current reality of the border, as is evident in the biographical narratives presented here. Nevertheless, it is essential that we take note of the ways of life that exist beyond the clandestine activities that are becoming increasingly widespread under the current economic conditions affecting both countries. By highlighting the other ways of life that are being pursued—within the law—in these same domestic, neighborhood, and city spaces permeated by clandestine activities, we are able to grasp the complete tapestry of border life. Our objective is to introduce the faces and the viewpoints of the people who live in the region and re-create it day by day as their place of residence, as a zone of daily crossings, as a mythical and determinant referent, as a space of aspirations, achievements, and tragedies.

In order to ensure the inherent unity of the narrative that each individual recounts of his or her life, we do not interrupt with our own interpretations. Even so, the stories as presented are not the original versions; they have been edited to enhance their accessibility to a broad audience and organized according to literary dictates that confer thematic and chronological coherence.

The Structure of the Book: Diverse Ways
of Living the Border

The Border Never Crossed

The life experience of the border never crossed relates to residents on the Mexican side who have not crossed into the United States but whose lives are imprinted by the region's border identity. The three narratives that accord with this characterization are of migrant women, female heads of household, who work, respectively, in the agricultural, industrial, and service sectors. None of the three has crossed the border, but their lives are influenced by the effects of the adjacency and asymmetry characterizing Mexico's border with the United States through their participation in economic activities (agricultural and industrial exports, sex tourism) that are directly linked to the consumer market in California and the low cost of labor on the Mexican side. Migration is a constant in their lives, and the process of settlement, the attainment of housing for their families, emerges as a driving force in each case. As their narratives demonstrate, their jobs are not free from the traditional construct of the feminine ethic or the erotic/sexual ethic associated with the feminine in Mexico. At the same time, the migration of these women is linked with domestic and gender violence through a devaluation of the feminine and networks of sexual exploitation. The gender-ethnicity-race triad responds to the Mexican ethnic configuration in which indigenous people are devalued vis-à-vis mestizos or whites, and this correlates with the marginalized position of these women in the social structure. Rosalía's awareness of her indigenous identity contrasts with the lack of ethnic awareness we find in Elena and Rosa, whose origins place them outside the indigenous world.

Chapter 1 presents the life story of Rosalía, a thirty-eight-year-old Mixtec woman who is the head of her family.[4] Her life is conditioned by her work in export agriculture. For Rosalía, the border emerges as a structural more than a subjective framework, given that the consumer market in California exerts a strong impact on the conditions of her work and, therefore, on her life and the lives of her family members. At the same time, the fact that she is a female indigenous migrant finds expression in her ethnic subordination. The exploitive conditions of agricultural work carry over into the lives of her children, and there appears little likelihood that their situation will change. Her hope is to return someday to her community of origin, ending her odyssey of migration to the agricultural fields on the border and her years of residence in workers' *colonias* (residential areas). In her narrative, a discourse of suffering and uncertainty is a matter of everyday life and is tied to the exploitive conditions of agricultural work and of migration itself.

Chapter 2 offers the narrative of Elena, a forty-nine-year-old woman.[5] Her migration from southern Mexico marks the beginning of a family life linked to

Tijuana's urban growth and work in the maquiladoras, in the factories them-selves and as an industrial homeworker, that is, someone who works in her own home but as a piecework employee for a maquiladora. The border is inher-ently present in the region's employment opportunities, the origin of industrial investment, and interactions with U.S.-origin managers and entrepreneurs. These are not the large maquiladoras linked to the huge foreign investments flowing into the region, but rather small workshops with limited numbers of employees, where women are employed for short periods or on a piecework basis. Maquiladora employment is situated against a backdrop of family life permeated with separation and abandonment, from infancy onward, yet this work, though unstable, remains a source of motivation and hope.

Chapter 3 presents the life story of Rosa, a forty-seven-year-old woman who has worked as a street prostitute for nearly twenty years.[6] Behind the pro-fession of prostitution we find a young woman who migrates from Texcoco, Puebla, a semiurban community in southern Mexico, fleeing domestic violence and reestablishing a family with herself as household head. The border that emerges in this narrative is sexual in nature, involving the clients who cross from north to south to obtain sex services. Work as a prostitute coexists with motherhood and the economic support of a family but always under the violent shadow of temporary partners. This double family life in the North and South, with sons in southern Mexico and daughters in the North, is cross-cut by a past in the place of origin and a present in the receiving destination. Solidarity among friends serves as an accessible resource with which to counteract the weakening or absence of family and community ties.

The Border as Backdrop

The second type of life experience of the border pertains to individuals who cross the border only occasionally but whose lives are structured around com-mercial transactions typical of border zones or who have transborder fam-ily ties. The narratives in this section correspond to two individuals, both migrants, who have crossed the border at some point in their lives but whose work trajectory is not defined by a daily crossing of the border. Nevertheless, their occupations depend on the context of transborder markets—in one case, U.S. tourists' affinity for Mexican curios and, in the other, the consumption of illicit drugs on both sides of the border. In both cases, family life is a source of worry and sadness but also a source of confidence and conviction. In these narratives, we once again find that the gender-ethnicity-race triad acquires special meaning within the Mexican context and in connection with the indig-enous-mestizo distinction, in which being indigenous shapes the narrative of a woman street vendor while ethnicity is of minor importance for men. Vio-lence permeates these narratives in different ways. In the case of the man it is because of the illegal nature of his work and the high risks associated with it; for the woman, violence has been present since childhood via discrimination directed against her because she speaks an indigenous language and later, on the border, because of her indigenous identity, contrasted with Mexican and U.S. identities.

Chapter 4 portrays a lifestyle that is increasingly common worldwide, especially in border zones. Juan is a man in his forties involved since childhood in the cultivation of hallucinogens and with a job history of trafficking drugs and stealing cars.[7] In his case, the border is a place for illegal employment in a dual marketplace, satisfying local demand on one hand and operating within the transnational logic of the worldwide narco-trafficking network on the other. This network, which generally exists outside the participants' awareness, orders the conduct of the drug trade above and beyond the narrow local and regional narco-trafficking networks, where our protagonist is a small player who tries to survive by contending with the logics of business, market, and government control.

Chapter 5 tells the life history of Ofelia Santos, an indigenous street vendor in downtown Tijuana who shows a marked ability to "read" the political environment, possibly because of her leadership position in the street vendors' association and her role as intermediary between her street-vendor colleagues and government officials.[8] Like the other narratives presented in this book, her story involves migration from southern Mexico as well as settlement in a poor colonia, which she is able to achieve thanks to family and home community connections. The border emerges in diverse forms in her story—through the tourists with whom she interacts and through her husband's situation as a cross-border commuter working in greenhouses in California, and later through her children, who gradually make the move to California to work in agriculture, repeating a pattern common among this ethnic group, which is closely identified with fieldwork on both sides of the border, in the San Quintín Valley and in California.

The Everyday Border

The third type of life experience on the border incorporates individuals who have made the border crossing their primary means of economic survival and the stage on which their daily activities play out. This is the paradigmatic transborder experience: The crossing is the strategic resource that shapes these people's lives. Crossing the border, whether for legal or illegal employment, is a way of life. In these cases, the border is seen as an opportunity, not just for better earnings but also for a better life. The border displays two faces—the legal and the illegal—and both appear permeable thanks to mechanisms of corruption and collusion on both sides. Official policies on employment, immigration, and narco-trafficking are mere fictions in the lives of these individuals.

In Chapter 6, we find a life testimony in which the structural inequality that exists between Mexico and the United States translates into a life opportunity for Eloísa, a twenty-six-year-old woman whose family is dispersed on the two sides of the border.[9] In this narrative, the border becomes an opportunity for someone with the skills to take advantage of the salary differential between the two countries and with the specific gender and ethnic characteristics that lead Mexican women to be viewed as appropriate employees for certain kinds of personal care. Behind the central theme of the story, we also see the border as a way to escape gender abuse and domestic captivity. At the same time, this narrative reveals some of the workings of the vast web of narco-trafficking that exists in the border region and highlights the vulnerability of people who do not enjoy regularized immigration status in the United States.

Chapter 7 presents the life story of Porfirio, a forty-year-old undocumented migrant who moves constantly from one side of the border to the other.[10] The experience of the border plays a central role in his life. The concrete act of crossing is matched in importance by the vigilance and patience he must practice in order to identify an appropriate crossing opportunity. His condition of being doubly undocumented, without legal status in either Mexico or the United States, keeps him in the interstices of the two nation-states, and he is subject to abuse in both countries. The border appears as a region of shadows and risk, where anything can happen to an undocumented migrant. Being inside Mexican territory offers no protection from police abuse, and the border zone is revealed as a space where human rights are suspended. Different legal statuses among members of the same family ultimately erode the social fabric: the inability to reunite with loved ones for lack of a border-crossing document, and obstacles to communication caused by differentiated meanings of gender roles.

Chapter 8 displays the reverse side of the undocumented immigrant coin, but entwined in the same youth culture in which young people seek life options that offer possibilities for maturity and fulfillment. The Mexicali Panther is a thirty-three-year-old with a transborder life history, having been born in Tijuana and raised in California.[11] Since childhood, he aspired to be a people smuggler, and a close relative later lured him into the drug trade, just like thousands of youths around the world. For the Panther, the border is in constant movement, and he must pursue and negotiate it in parallel with the eastward shift of the Border Patrol along the line. A people smuggler must always stay one step ahead to outsmart the border's enforcers. From another perspective, the border presents an opportunity for survival through the clandestine activities that flourish there thanks to border enforcement efforts themselves. Here the migrants are merchandise, "little chickens," to be sold, handed on to others, traded, or lost.

The Border Traversed

The fourth type of life experience of the border includes those who have traversed the border and established themselves in the United States with relative success. The final narratives in this book relate the lives of two people—one a second-generation Mexican immigrant to the United States and one from the 1.5 generation (raised in the United States but not born there)—who are embroiled in a constant struggle to integrate into U.S. life, with its emphasis on legal status and advancement through effort. For these men, the border is the Mexican border they left behind, whether through their parents' crossing or in their own childhood years. For them, the border is cultural and political in nature and holds ambiguous valences for things such as personal warmth and systemic political corruption. The narrative of the process of regularizing residency and citizenship shifts between the state's legitimate use of violence in controlling national borders and the "patriotic conversion" of the individual. This conversion contradicts the nativist interpretation about the difficulty an immigrant confronts when adopting the vision of a U.S. national common good. Such a view is evident in the justifications these men offer about the benefits and rights accruing to newly minted citizens. On the other hand, it nonetheless supports the thesis inherent in a transnational focus, which holds that a sense of origin persists not only because of the nostalgia of one's emotional ties to one's ancestors but also because place of origin remains an element that defines one's existence when one is being classified as "Mexican-origin" or "Latino" in censuses and government offices.

Chapter 9 recounts the life of Emilio, a twenty-two-year-old member of the 1.5 immigrant generation, born in Mexico and raised in the United States.[12] His father is the U.S.-born son of a Mexican-origin family, and his mother was born in Mexico. His is the typical case of the successful young son of immigrants, with a promising future and a present of rapid assimilation to the values of American society. His border is the dividing line between backwardness and progress, and he holds a very negative view of the grime and corruption in Mexico, at the same time idealizing Mexican patterns of personal relationships infused with emotion and warmth. This young man's border, seen rising from the U.S. side, is infinitely fluid. Because of his U.S. citizenship, he can cross the border at will. The border is fluid in terms of mobility, but it is highly differentiated culturally.

In Chapter 10, we encounter the life story of Julius Alatorre, a Border Patrol official who was serving as his agency's spokesperson at the time of our interview; we can imagine, therefore, that we are listening to an official narrative of border enforcement.[13] He is thirty years old and the California-born son of Mexican immigrants. This immigration official's border has two sides. On the Mexican side, people want to cross in order to achieve the American Dream. On the U.S. side, the official himself is part of that American Dream. His narrative is grounded in the machinery of order and the application of U.S. law on the border. His is not a fluid border; it is rock solid. His mission is to stop migration because it is illegal. He views the Mexican side of the border as dangerous, in part because of the drug cartels and kidnappings but also because his identity as a member of the immigration police makes him vulnerable. Yet the tone of his narrative reveals affection for all that is Mexican. This fondness emerges from his interaction with his parents, and it filters into his view of undocumented migrants as "working people."

The Conclusion situates this book's contribution within the context of border studies, following Michael Kearney (2008) on the importance of exploring the relationship between geopolitical borders and sociocultural borders. Based on the thesis that the border constitutes a force for differentiation and social hierarchization, the typology outlined here is employed to order the individual cases in terms of their life experience of the border crossing. This analytical tool permits us to distinguish ways of life that are molded in various ways by the structural processes that constitute an asymmetrical border.

In the midst of the worldwide economic crisis, we have begun to discern some changes in the life dynamics of the borderlands. The economic recession in California and its effects on employment and housing can be traced in the return to Tijuana of some border residents who had taken mortgages and purchased homes in California. The economic crisis has also cast its shadow on the Mexican side, where some families fear they will be unable to put food on the table and would-be migrants continue coming to the border because the situation in Mexico is no better than in the United States. In the depths of this recession, illegal activities become an attractive alternative for thousands of people who want to work and earn, even given the risks and uncertainties that such endeavors imply. Crossing the border continues to be a recourse, a way to flee the crisis in a developing country even if it means one must then survive the crisis in a developed country.

1
Living on the Agricultural Frontier

Farming in Northern Mexico

The San Quintín Valley lies in the state of Baja California; its primary economic activity is agricultural production for export. The region's population growth since the 1960s can be attributed to seasonal migrants who work in agriculture. In the last decade of the twentieth century, the valley witnessed the permanent settlement of thousands of these immigrants, along with the technologization of agricultural production, which nevertheless continues to rely primarily on the hiring of seasonal fieldworkers.

The 2000 population census counted 74,427 residents in the San Quintín Valley.[1] Just over half (52 percent) were born in other Mexican states: Oaxaca (39 percent), Sinaloa (14 percent), Michoacán (9 percent), Guerrero (6 percent), and Veracruz (4 percent). Sixteen percent of residents over five years of age speak an indigenous language, such as Mixtec, Triqui, or Zapotec (COESPO-COLEF 2003b).[2] And even though the number of people employed in agriculture declined in the 1990s, 55 percent of the regional population was still employed in this sector in 2000 (COLEF-CONACYT 2003).

Local agricultural production, which specializes in fresh fruits and vegetables for export, imposes its rhythm on the migratory flows because of fluctuations in the intensity of agricultural tasks and the varying number of field hands required at different times of the year. Even though technology has lessened the gap between

Illustration: Women at work, San Quintín Valley. *(Photograph by Laura Velasco Ortiz.)*

*the highly labor-intensive spring and summer seasons and the relative inactivity of
fall and winter, certain high-intensity tasks still demand a large concentration of
manual laborers, especially from May to October.*

*According to Roberta Cook (2006), Mexico provides 65 percent of U.S.
imports of fresh vegetables, and the San Quintín Valley is one of the regions
actively involved in this commercial relationship. In 2003, 57 percent of a set of
interviewed agribusinesses in the region[3] reported that they had planted tomatoes;
12 percent were cultivating cucumbers; 8 percent, strawberries; 7 percent, onions;
and 7 percent, brussels sprouts (COESPO-COLEF 2003c).[4] Just four of these
companies accounted for 66.3 percent of the total cultivated land in the area, and
they employed 77.7 percent of the agricultural labor force. Notable among these
large agroenterprises is Seminis Vegetable, a transnational established in 1985.
According to Esther Grávalos and Alejandro García (2001), Seminis is the world's
largest producer of vegetables and stone fruits. Another regionally prominent company is Los Pinos, founded by Luis Rodríguez Aviña, a pioneer immigrant from
Michoacán who arrived in San Quintín in the 1940s. But regardless of their size
or their origin (local or extrinsic), the majority of these firms sell to the international market through a distributor. Since the implementation of the North
American Free Trade Agreement, most use the services of international certifiers
to gain approval of their products for the U.S. market.*

*Technological advances are visible in the uptick in yields by year and by agri-
cultural cycle. In the 1990s, drip irrigation and plastic coverings on furrows were
introduced, enhancing the per-hectare yield.[5] Additional improvements in the late
1990s included the introduction of greenhouses for growing cucumbers, tomatoes,
and chilies. In 2000, Seminis built 23 hectares of greenhouses, which employed
seven hundred workers from June to December.[6] In 2005, growers cultivated a
total of 287 hectares in shade-cloth installations, in which computers regulate
climatic conditions.[7]*

*The region's growers use a variety of methods to recruit workers. Thirty-one
percent of them hire workers from among those who arrive at the companies' fields
independently. Thirty-eight percent have agreements with contractors who gather
workers from nearby colonias. And 31 percent employ long-distance contractors
who bring workers from states such as Guerrero, Oaxaca, and Veracruz.*

*These recruiting strategies reflect local residential patterns that existed at the
beginning of the twenty-first century. In 2003, there were seventy residential colonias in the valley's two most populous precincts (delegaciones): Vicente Guerrero and San Quintín. That same year there were thirty-four camps for seasonal
migrants, most of them clustered at the valley's two extremes: at Lázaro Cárdenas
in the south and in Punta Colonet in the north. Of these, only twenty-six sites
were inhabited at the height of the season, and the number fell to twenty-one in
the off-season. The third type of housing is rental cuarterías (bare-bones rooming
houses) concentrated in certain areas of the San Quintín and Camalú precincts.[8]
These cuarterías have replaced migrant camps to some extent in recent years,
largely through direct arrangements with growers.[9]*

The Establishment of Nuevo San Juan Copala

Nuevo San Juan Copala is a popular colonia in the Vicente Guerrero precinct.[10] Its name commemorates the place of origin of many of its residents: San Juan Copala, Oaxaca, a small Triqui community in the Mixteca region.[11] The Nuevo San Juan Copala colonia was founded in 1997 by Triqui Indians and a few Mixtecos, agricultural workers who left migrant camps (primarily the Aguaje del Burro camp) and cuarterías *with the dream of having a piece of land of their own. In the gloom of early dawn, the colonia's men, women, and children, all carrying white buckets, follow its ochre-colored dirt roads to the trucks that will carry them to the strawberry and tomato fields that still lie shrouded in coastal fog.*

Rosalía J.'s home has a small wooden door that opens onto the street. Her family is one of the few Mixtec families that live in this Triqui colonia. The patio is furnished with the white buckets that are used in the tomato harvest. After a long workday, Rosalía washes her feet while her three children circle the patio, entering and exiting the wooden structure in the back: a single room illuminated by only a bare light bulb hanging from the ceiling. Darío, her eldest son, washes his hands in an attempt to dissolve the sticky residue left by a day of picking strawberries. It is April, and the heat in the valley indicates the optimal time for harvesting. Rosalía offers her visitors upturned buckets to sit on and, with a smile, begins to recount the story of her life.

Leaving Home: Childhood and Work

I'm thirty-eight years old. I was born in 1968 in San José de las Flores, in the municipality of Putla Villa de Guerrero, in Oaxaca State. My mother spoke an indigenous language [Mixtec], my father also,[12] though they came from different towns. My mother was from San José de las Flores, in Oaxaca, and my father was from Chilpancingo, in Guerrero. There were two of us—me and my sister, who is three years younger than I am.

I've had a rough time ever since childhood. I left San José after my father died; I was only six years old. In my hometown, they would kill one another with rifles and machetes, but because they could never find my father, they used witchcraft on him, and we couldn't cure him. They put a curse on him . . . and he began to waste away. . . . We couldn't do anything for him, and he died. He loved me very much, but my mother doesn't care much for me; I don't know why. I was very close to my father.

After my father died, I left to work, first in Putla [the seat of the municipality], in the same house where my father had worked. Later I went to Acapulco, Guerrero, to work as a domestic. In Putla, I sold bread in the plaza. I worked for a woman while I was also going to school. I started school when I was ten years old, thanks to help that my employer gave me because she had known my father.

And your mother?

My mother? Well, she was there in the town. But since she didn't know how to support us, I went to work, and she . . . she stayed there alone. Even now she's still all alone there in the town.

When I left Putla, I went to Acapulco with my uncles. . . . I worked as a nanny; I washed and ironed clothes. I liked the way people treated me . . . and I continued working. That's how I got ahead . . . working and studying. . . . I got only as far as fifth grade; I couldn't go any further. They asked for a lot of things in primary school, especially in fifth grade, and I didn't have enough money. Furthermore, the woman who was taking care of me, the woman I worked for, mistreated me. She wouldn't allow me time to study, so I focused on work and dropped out of school.

Returning Home to Be Stolen

When my uncles returned to Putla [in 1983], I came back as well. When I was fifteen, I had a boyfriend and planned to marry him, but it didn't work out that way.

It happens that, there in my town, there is a custom of "stealing" a wife. Men can come from other places, and if they like the local girls they can steal them and make them their wives. That's what happened to me. A man from Santa María Zacatepec stole me, and they married me off to him.

I knew that girls in my hometown could be stolen, but I didn't imagine that someday it would happen to me. This is how it was: Every community holds sports competitions, and the locals invite a crowd of people. Competitors come from all around. I was still in school, in fifth grade. I was fifteen years old, and I went to play basketball with a women's team called Born to Lose.

Then some men arrived, and we thought they were members of a sports team, so we said hello. We got acquainted, got to know one another, and we liked them, and that was that. They didn't know who our parents were, or even who we really were.

It happened on the road, when my aunt and I were going out to shop in the plaza. They carried us both off by force. My aunt was eighteen, and I was fifteen. They grabbed us on the hillside and took us off in their car. There were several of them and only two of us, so we couldn't defend ourselves. We tried to defend ourselves; we ran and they caught us; they threw stones at us. . . . They were injured, and my aunt and I were hurt as well. We thought they were going to kill us because we'd heard rumors that they were killing people.

I had never seen this man before. I didn't even know his name. He took me to an isolated house and told me, "I want you to be my woman. And my friends here are going to help me." . . . My aunt and I were in a daze; we didn't even know how to respond.

Afterward I could tell that they didn't want me back home. I telephoned the woman I had worked for as a domestic in Putla, and she came and brought me to Pinotepa Nacional, where we went to the municipal authorities. My family didn't want me to come back home, because I was no longer a virgin.

My uncle told the man, "Well, you stole her and now you're going to marry her." And we married, but he was thirty years old and I was only fifteen. He was much older than I was. I said that I didn't want to marry, that I wasn't ready. I never imagined that I would be getting married. Nor did I know what it meant to have a husband.

I felt awful; I told my uncle not to leave me with that man.

When my father died, my uncle, my father's brother, took his place. . . . My mother did everything my uncle told her; she would listen only to him, nobody else.

My mother worked in the fields. She went with the workers to harvest chilies, corn, whatever needed picking. What she earned she kept for herself, and we had to work to pay for school. So she never got involved.

So we married and we went to live in my mother-in-law's house in Santa María Zacatepec, Putla. He [my husband] worked in a factory. He really liked to work, but he was a terrible skirt-chaser. Several years went by before I had children, but I finally became pregnant. When I was six months pregnant, he cheated on me with another woman. My life was very ugly and very difficult, because I didn't love him. . . . I was in love with the boyfriend I'd had before he stole me.

What happened to your boyfriend?

He came looking for me, asking me to leave my husband . . . but I couldn't because I was married. I told him, "Go find another woman, make a life, because I can't go with you. I don't want them to kill you." And yes, he found another woman, but things didn't go well. They killed him.

Abandoned in Sinaloa and Arriving in the San Quintín Valley: El Aguaje del Burro

I got pregnant when I was nineteen years old, and my husband said that he was very happy. Before I became pregnant, he would say that I was a crazy girl . . . because I didn't live with my mother and I was working outside my hometown . . . so they said that I was running around like a crazy person.

I gave birth to my daughter in my mother-in-law's house, with help from my mother-in-law, my father-in-law, my husband, and my uncles. My mother-in-law treated me well—she was very fond of me, she was very kind to me. We named the baby Antonia Victoria.

After Antonia was born, in 1989, we went to Sinaloa.[13] We didn't even stay there a month, because after two weeks my husband ran off with another woman and left me stranded there. I joined up with some women friends I'd made in the fields. They saw that I was alone, and they invited me to come to Ensenada. That's how I ended up here, in San Quintín.

We arrived at the Aguaje del Burro ranch, owned by the Garcías.[14] When we got here, there were no rooms; they were all full. So we had to build our own little house with plastic sheets and cardboard, there, where there was some open space. The camp boss helped us ask the owners for some cardboard, wood, and plastic.

Later they built more rooms and gave one to us. . . . We dismantled our little plastic house and moved into the room. The room didn't have a kitchen; it didn't have anything. We had to build a kitchen; we cut wood on the hillside to make a cooking fire. It was a struggle much of the time, and we suffered. . . . Sometimes the truck picked us up when we had to go to distant fields. . . . Other times we walked because the work was nearby. We would leave home around six-thirty in the morning in order to catch the ride to work in the strawberry fields.

Back then some strawberries went to the cannery. For these we had to trim off the leaves from the base of the fruit and put the berries in plastic boxes. But the berries that would be sold as fresh fruit in the market, these we picked and put into cardboard boxes.

After I'd been in the camp about a month, a young man fell in love with me. I didn't want to be with him. I got along very well with the older women in the camp, so I told the young man that he had to ask permission from my aunts[15]—that is, my friends. At first he didn't tell me where he came from, but later he told me that he was a Triqui from Tierra Blanca, near San Juan Copala in Oaxaca. But I didn't care for him. . . . I thought I didn't want to get married yet, but he kept insisting. I told him, "If you really care for me, don't drink any alcohol for fifteen or twenty days, and then I'll marry you, but you have to ask my aunt for me." He agreed, and he asked my aunt for me, so I went with him. When I was living with him, I found that I was pregnant with Darío [her second child].

Two years later, in 1992, I had another son, Misael. In those days life in the camp was nothing but work. . . . If you didn't work, they evicted you from your room. . . . We had to get up at three in the morning to make our lunches and get to work by five. . . . On longer days,[16] we get back in time to prepare a meal, eat supper, and, if there's still time, wash clothes. . . .

The children stayed in the camp, cared for by some neighbor. . . . That's how we helped one another. When the children were very little, I stopped going to work in the fields for a while. . . . My husband wouldn't let me go to work. . . . Only he worked. That's when I started raising pigs and chickens. . . . The camp boss let us build a small corral on the hillside. . . .

Two years after Misael was born, I got pregnant with Maricela. But things weren't going well between me and my husband. We fought. He said I ate too much or that I was giving food away. But I was eating a lot because I was breast-feeding the children and that made me very hungry. . . . I had to eat. My babies grew very chubby; they never got sick. But he thought that I was giving food away or that I had a lover who came to eat with me. His family put these ugly ideas in his head.

I told him, "Well, fine, stay with your family. I'm leaving." That's when we split up. I didn't take any legal action or anything; I just left. I told him, "If you're not happy with me, I couldn't be happy with you." I shared all my happiness with him, but he didn't understand. So I said, "No, this is as far as it goes. I was your wife, your lover, whichever, but we end here. I'm leaving." He said he'd let me visit my children, but I told him, "I'll die first, because as long as I'm alive I'm not leaving my children." I moved to a different room and continued to live in Aguaje del Burro.

Around this time my husband wanted to cross the border to the "other side," but he didn't want me to get pregnant or, if I did, he wanted me to abort the baby. I didn't like the pill [contraceptive] because it made me feel sick, and I ended up pregnant without realizing it. That caused a lot of trouble; he hit me a lot because he wanted me to abort. He didn't want another child. He wanted me to stay here and didn't want me pregnant so that I wouldn't have to suffer alone. I did want another child, though, and I didn't want my husband to go. I wanted him to stay with me.

He left in 1993. He wasn't here for the birth of his daughter. He stayed in the United States about a year and then returned. That's when he learned that I'd had a little girl, but he didn't come back to us. He went south. Supposedly he was going to build a house and then come back for us. He said, "I'll build a house and come back for you," but he never returned. He found another woman in his hometown.

In the meantime, what did you do with your children here in San Quintín?

My baby girl was born by cesarean section, and it took six months of rest for me to recover. That was a rough time. . . . I suffered a great deal. I asked the religious brothers for assistance, and they helped me for a while but later they criticized me. . . . First I went to Puerta Abierta, but then they invited me to a missionary church. There one of the brothers claimed that my children were taking the food out of his children's mouths and that I was not behaving appropriately. I felt very bad. I like to be on friendly terms with people, and this brother said that I went from one man to another . . . and that I drank alcohol . . . but this wasn't true. I didn't drink. They were judging me, and I said some awful things to them because they aren't really religious people. I have nothing to hide; I have a clean conscience because I didn't do anything wrong. I told them to get lost and I went back to work. I left their religion and returned to my own [Catholicism].

I left the migrant camp and rented a place in the Maclovio Rojas colonia and went to work in the fields. I enrolled Darío in kindergarten, but they treated him badly so I took him out. From then on, the three children stayed at home, looked after by a neighbor.

What happened to Antonia, your first daughter?

One of my uncles came to visit me in the valley, and he told me that my mother was all alone in the town. Antonia was six years old—this was 1994—and they took her to keep my mother company. Antonia said, "Yes, I'm going with my grandma." My mother enrolled her in school in San José de las Flores.

I felt very sad staying here with just the three children. Darío, the eldest, took care of the little ones while I went to work in the fields. It was harder now because I had to send money to my mother to pay for Antonia's studies there in Oaxaca.

One of my brothers-in-law saw me here alone with my children, and he offered to help. . . . He said, "Rosalía, there's going to be an opportunity to get a little plot somewhere; I don't know exactly where, but we'll see." He'd go to the meetings, and I'd go to work in the fields. . . . Every time there was a meeting I'd have to pay him 20 pesos to get him to tell me what had happened. . . . Then one day he told me, "You know what? On May 5, they're going to go and occupy the land. So tomorrow afternoon, get ready to go." I said that was fine . . . but I sent my son Darío, who was ten years old. . . . That's how we got here. . . . It was 1997.

Living in Nuevo San Juan Copala:
Settlement and Family Life

What were the lots like when you first arrived?

Well, everything was just vacant land . . . lots of thorns and cow pies. There were even tarantulas and scorpions—dangerous animals! We settled at the edge of the highway; that's where we were living. In the beginning, there were little cardboard houses that we roofed with blankets, and we used tarps and nylon sheeting to protect us from the wind. The children were still small; the oldest was ten and the youngest, four.

That's when I started getting acquainted with them [the community leaders] because I really wanted to get a little plot.[17] . . . They even went to beat up my *compadre!* Because he was organizing people. . . . We became friends here; I didn't know him before.

My brother-in-law and I were involved in the struggle [for land]. . . . We had to go to Ensenada because that's where they were going to allocate the plots. They [the leaders] already had our names on the list . . . but there were also rumors that they were going in with tractors to get us out of there. I had to go alone with a group of all men to Ensenada [to the government offices]. . . . We wanted a plot; that's why we came here   to have something of our own. It's not like at the ranch. . . . At least a little plot is your own property. We prayed a lot, and we succeeded, and here we are—not so good, not so bad, but surviving. But yes, we endured a lot.

We stopped going to work because our employer didn't want to send the truck here to take us to the fields. Once we had our plots, a group went to the boss to ask him to send the truck. . . . And he did agree to send the truck, but it doesn't come all the way here. It goes to the Triqui colonia or to Trece de Mayo. We have to walk there to catch the truck that takes us to the fields.

Later one of the Christian brothers came and told me, "No, this house is no good." My house was made of canvas. They built one out of wood. Since then, they've invited us to their church. But we don't want to abandon our [Catholic] religion. So we tell them we'll go later, but that's all.

My neighbor told me that when the brothers came to bring materials to build her house, she asked them, "What do I have to do if you build me a house?" They said, "Look, in all sincerity, we invite you to attend our church, and if your heart accepts, you can come. And if your heart doesn't accept, no problem. Your heart is free. Your house will be built, and we're not going to tell you afterward that you have to go to our church. Other religions may require you to do that, but we don't." "That's good," she told them. "The truth is that I don't want to be obligated."

I still practice the religion that my father gave me when he brought me into the world, when I first opened my eyes. I have no desire to say, "I'm going to stop going to the Catholic church." . . . Moreover, we know only the religion we're baptized in, and we don't know which one is the real truth. Whether this one is the truth or that one is the truth. We don't know!

After the brothers constructed the house, there were some very heavy rains . . . and the house was damaged. Then the Agricultural Day Laborers Program [Programa de Atención a Jornaleros Agrícolas] arrived.[18] They started building houses in 1998. I already knew the promoter from when I'd been a promoter in Rancho del Aguaje, and I told him about my need. And he said, "Well, I'll give you a hand." And he's the one who helped me get this little house. It's only one room, with two beds. I sleep in one with my daughter, and the two boys sleep in the other one, but it's better than we had before.

I decided to stay unattached, to help my children get ahead. Their father doesn't come to see the children, he doesn't help me . . . and he doesn't send money. I learned through the grapevine that he goes regularly to the United States, but he doesn't come through here; he goes straight south [to Oaxaca].

Since you separated from your husband, how have you supported your children?

Working. Yes, I work. Sometimes I had to pay someone to care for the three children while I went to work. They'd charge me 50 or 60 pesos a week. I'd take them to the house of the person who was going to care for them. It was the same as in Camalú when I left my children in the daycare. They grew up there in the daycare. When we came here, they were already older . . . so I had to take only the little girl. The two boys stayed home alone. I thank God that I was able to bring them up strong and start them on their way.

What have you worked at?

Always in the fields. From the very beginning I've worked for a single employer, and I'm still working for the same one. I've been with Juan Antonio García for twenty-two years.

He grows strawberries, tomatoes, and cherries. I'm comfortable working for this employer, because when I need some help, I can go to him. . . . He used to help us more before, because I used to go to him and I'd say, "You know what, Don Toño? My daughter is very sick and I need an advance." He'd loan me money, and I would go to the pharmacy and buy injections or whatever my daughter needed. And at the end of the week, he'd deduct the loan. And when I needed firewood, he'd give it to me. But no longer. . . . I think it's because we don't live on the ranch any longer; that's why. Because he was the owner of the Aguaje del Burro ranch. When the ranch was dismantled, the people scattered. Most of them came here, and the rest went to Militar colonia.

Life on the ranch was hard. There was no electricity; we had to use candles for light. It's true that we had plenty of water, though. That's why the owner refused to send the truck to take us to work when we moved here. . . . He said, "If we had everything here—at the Aguaje del Burro ranch—why did we want to go there, to the colonia?" But we fought hard, and we finally got him to send the truck to take us to work in his fields.

The work changes throughout the year. For example, in November there might be tomatoes, and the strawberries are just going in or they're preparing the fields. That's the time of little work, and generally the work is by assigned tasks.

What is a task like?

The task is, say, they give you a stretch of furrows. They assign some to each person. "You're going to do that furrow, and that one, and that one." You can determine when you do it, but they pay you for finishing the whole task. They might give you fourteen furrows for 90 pesos. . . . And you have to hustle because if you fall behind, others—not you—will do your task, and then they pay you only for what you managed to finish, not the entire task. It comes out to more or less 5 pesos a furrow.

Because the people are together in this, they help me with my task. Someone who finished early, a friend who is working close by, gives me a hand, and we all come out ahead.

They treat us women well at work, but sometimes they humiliate us because, well, we're not equal to the men, who do more work. And then, because we're single women, if we talk to the boss or to the men, they say that we're going with them. We've experienced all of that . . . but I say that we should just let it go [*she laughs*]. There are many women on their own who are working in the fields. . . . Their husbands have gone off with another woman or they've gone across the border . . . and the women are left on their own.

I like working the cherry and strawberry crops. It doesn't feel like such heavy work. . . . But the plastic and cardboard tasks make for heavy going . . . because we have to pull the plastic off the furrow . . . pull with all our strength so that the plants come out with the roots intact. . . . You pull the nylon off as you run from one end to the other, and you roll it up as you go along so that you end up with a ball at the end of the furrow.[19]

Putting down stakes is also hard work. . . . Well, it seems really hard to me. They give us bunches of stakes and we have to distribute them . . . putting one here, another there, and so on, putting the stakes down along the furrows. . . . Fifty meters takes two rolls. . . . Then you have to go back with another two rolls and finish placing the stakes. . . . They're the sticks that support the tomato plants as they grow. Behind us comes a team of men, and they plant the stakes. This task is an all-day effort, sometimes lasting into the night. . . . It's the same when the tomato harvest is over. We have to collect the stakes, carry them to the edge of the field, and bundle them together. Oh, it's very tiring!

Have you already paid for your house lots?

Some have paid, and others of us haven't paid. I've not been able to pay. I've not done well because the harvest is very bad. Now that my son—Darío—left school, he comes to work with me every day. And not even the two of us together earn enough to cover expenses. During the slow season, each worker gets only half a task. We each earn 45 pesos a day, or 90 pesos between the two of us . . . beginning work at six in the morning and ending at eleven or midnight. . . . In contrast, strong men are assigned a whole task.

Things get better at the height of the season. . . . Then we're able to catch up a bit. . . . We can earn double . . . but it doesn't last long.

How much does it cost to get the property title to a plot?

At first it was . . . 7,990 pesos, in installments. I paid some, but we couldn't keep up because my children were very young and then I started them in school, and I couldn't make the payments. Some people finished paying, and all they need is the title to their property. . . . I paid a little, but now I can't remember how much I paid. I put in the water supply and electricity, and that's as far as I got. . . . It was really hard for me because all my children were in school. I barely paid off one debt before I had another one.

You are a health promoter. What does that job consist of?

I go from house to house advising them to care for their children, to keep their houses clean, and to feed their children healthy foods. I also visit pregnant women, to see how they're doing, to find out if they've seen a doctor. I have a list of how many pregnant women there are, how many diabetics, how many elderly, how many are ill.

The children are malnourished. They're very thin; they don't gain weight. . . . I recommend soy products . . . but they don't use them. . . . They don't like them. They like fried eggs, beans, and lentils.

It's hard working with the mothers because they don't get checkups. They don't want to have an operation [tubal ligation] because their husbands don't want them to have one. They want to have more children. If the woman doesn't want any more children . . . she knows that her husband will leave her to marry someone else [*she laughs*]. The men don't take any precautions. They say, "Here's where you married me, here's where you're going to have the children that we can have, without any birth control." And we have a hospital here in San Quintín. . . . I had my children here in the boss's hospital, in the Social Security hospital.[20]

I've been in this job for six years. In the beginning it was a volunteer position. Now they pay me a compensation of 300 pesos a month. There's no place else to earn money; that's why I could leave only two of my children in school. They're still in elementary school. One is in fourth grade, and the other is in second grade. The eldest, Darío, already left school. . . . He reached only the first year of the distance-learning middle school, and now he works with me. But they don't give him very good jobs because he's still a minor. He just turned fifteen. One day he told me, "You're killing yourself working, Mama. Better for me not to study." He said, "Better for me to help you work."

Between Homeland and Life
in Nuevo San Juan Copala

I took Darío out of school because I just couldn't let him study any longer. There were too many expenses . . . buying him a typewriter, uniform, everything he needed, the books they were using, and everything. And the inscription fees—I just couldn't any longer. My earnings all go to support my family here and those in the South, my mother and my daughter.

And it's a heavy burden for me because I was the only one working and I was supporting five people. And I still support them, now six of us, six including myself. Because I still send them money.

In the slow season, when Darío and I work six days, together we earn 400 and something pesos a week . . . and I send her money. When the harvesting is best . . . in April or May . . . we earn more and I send more home. I send money home every two or three months, because I can't do more [she laughs].

I make contributions to the *cundinas*.[21] I limit myself to 300 pesos for my three children who are here, and the 100 or 150 that are left go to the *cundina,* and there's where I get the money to send south.

Is Antonia, your eldest daughter who is in your hometown with her grandmother, in school?

She only went as far as the third year of middle school. She got pregnant last year and had her baby at eighteen years of age. That's why I stopped helping her. . . . I used to send her money . . . I supported three here and two over there. . . . I didn't send a lot, 800 or 1,000 pesos every month or two . . . but it was a lot for me. . . .

She got pregnant and they never told me. When she was about to give birth, they told me to send 3,000 pesos for expenses. I didn't want to send her the money. I didn't want to help her.

Who helped her out?

My sister was the one who helped her. She paid the hospital; she paid for everything. I didn't want any part of it. I felt so bad because I gave her the best at the expense of those I have here. I entered into the *cundinas* and made sacrifices because I had to send money so that she could go to school. She was able to dress better than these here, and now I'm really hurt by what she did, because she didn't appreciate me. My son's also going around like a bum; he likes to go out with his friends. I tell him that I'm going to kick him out one of these days. Because I already told them, "If you don't appreciate me, you'll never amount to anything. What I've done for you, giving my life for you, wasn't worth anything."

I spoke with her when I went to the South. . . . Last September I went south with my three children. I wanted to show my husband that even though he was with another woman, I was going to go to my in-laws. My brothers-in-law were behind me in this. First I visited one of my brothers-in-law, and then I went to see my mother.

My daughter told me that I wasn't her mother any longer, that my sister was her mother now. Because my friends told her, "Your mother's arrived," and she said, "What mother? That woman [meaning me]? She's not my mother; my mother's across the border." She spoke to me, but she never called me Mother. She ignored me.

What was the problem?

Her problem with me was that I hadn't raised her, I hadn't been with her. I told her, "Look, I wasn't with you because your grandmother demanded that I send you to her. That's why you came here, but if you hadn't wanted to come, I would never have let you go. I'm not to blame here. Your grandma is the one at fault, so don't reproach me. I gave you everything I had. And I devoted myself to giving you more money than I gave to the others."

But she claimed that when I wasn't around, my mother and sister would hit her and that when she told me they were mistreating her, I scolded her instead of helping her.

She behaves very badly; she's still running around with that guy, the father of her daughter. I wanted her to marry him, but she didn't want to. That's why I can't forgive her.

You were in your hometown for three months, from September to December. What happened with your children, and how did they get along with their father?

The three kids were very upset when they found that he was with another woman. I didn't expect him to give me such a warm reception. He was with us for the three months we were there. I stayed at his mother's house, but I didn't want anything to do with him. He would come to spend a few days with us. The children called him "Sir." They didn't call him "Father." They asked him for money . . . and he gave it to them.

I already had plans for our return. I couldn't stay long because I had asked for only three months off from work. The children's father said, "Why don't you leave one of the kids with me?" And I told him, "Talk to them to see who wants to stay. I can't take them with me if they want to stay. The decision is theirs." He chose the two who were in school: Maricela and Misael.

And what did the children say?

They said, "Yes, we're going to stay with you, but don't think that we're going to stay forever, because we're going to go back with Mama." I felt bad; I told them, "Are you determined to stay?" They said yes. I said, "Okay, it's your decision." I took them to my mother-in-law's house; she's going to take care of them. Their father has three children with the other woman.

Before I left to come back here, to San Quintín, my parents-in-law took

me to the plot they own . . . and they handed it over to me as an inheritance.
That's where I'm going to live with my children, there in the township.
Because I'm the first wife of their youngest son, the land comes to me as an
inheritance. They told me that even though we're not married, it's still valid
because I've struggled so hard to raise my children

He continues going to work in the United States, but he doesn't come
through San Quintín anymore. . . . That's why we went there. People had told
me that his woman lives very well, and I said, "Let her enjoy it, because I'll be
arriving soon." Sooner or later I would go there. And I did it; I went to the town.

*You didn't have enough money when you were preparing to come back.
Is that why the children stayed, or was it because their father decided
they should stay?*

If I'd had enough money, I wouldn't have left them.
I took 8,000 pesos with me. I thought it would be enough, but it wasn't.
The bus tickets cost 800 pesos each, plus the expenses on the road. . . . Food
is very expensive. We spent nearly 1,000 pesos just getting there. Then we
had to take another bus to his hometown. And my hometown is even farther
away. Bus fare isn't that expensive, but there are four of us, and if it's 50 pesos
per person, well, that's 200 pesos just in bus fare for the four of us. And then
add in the food.

I joined the *cundinas* in order to put that much money together. I put
in 200 pesos every week. Among the ten members, we managed to scrape
together 4,000 pesos.

*So you came back with only Darío. What did he think when his brother
and sister stayed behind?*

He felt so bad; he said he didn't want them to stay. But if they wanted to
stay, he said, there was nothing to be done about it. He wanted to stay too,
but he was worried about his chickens. A woman was supposed to take care
of them, but she didn't come . . . so we lost some of them. They also broke
into our house . . . and some things were taken. . . . That's why Toño, my
brother-in-law, got a family to stay and take care of his house. They are from
Sinaloa; they came to work the strawberry crop and had no place to live. They
don't pay rent; they just help pay for electricity and water.

*You have been working with the same employer for twenty-two years.
Suppose you decide to return to your home in the South. Would your
boss pay you some severance for all those years?*

Who knows? I've seen them fire people and not want to give them
anything. They have paid out in some cases, but only when the worker has

died. They gave 15,000 pesos to the family of a guy who died two or three months ago after working here for fifteen years. He was poisoned. . . . Sometimes they fumigate, and this fellow was elderly.

In 2003, I joined the IMSS [the Mexican Social Security Institute] . . . and enrolled only Darío . . . because the other children didn't have birth certificates. When I went to San José de las Flores, I registered my youngest daughter.

When Darío was born, I wrote that I was a single mother on his birth certificate, using only my maiden name, because I wanted to continue studying. But I didn't want to register my daughter because her father said he would register her with his surname.[22] . . . They used to change our Social Security numbers every so often, but ever since the late Don Bonfilio went on a hunger strike, they've enrolled us correctly. He went on a hunger strike in support of the people of San Quintín, who were being mistreated. That's when they began enrolling the workers. People say they shot him to death in his home.

Darío, the Second Generation
in Agricultural Labor

Darío dropped out of school. Does he now just work in the fields?

Yes. He leaves for the fields at five in the morning and comes back at five in the afternoon. He comes in, he eats; sometimes I prepare a meal for him. When I stay late at work, he prepares the meal. Then he bathes, sometimes he goes to the ball fields to play, and he comes home after dark. . . . But they tell me that he doesn't really go to play ball, that he's going around smoking and hanging out on the street with his friends.

I don't like his friends, because they use drugs. That's why I don't want him hanging around with them. He can be friendly with them, but not hang around with them, even though they're from here, from the neighborhood.

Some days they work; some days they don't. When they go to work, he comes back with them, and how am I to know if he's telling the truth? The neighbors say he's using drugs. One day he smelled really bad. I said, "You'd better pray that I don't catch you, because the day I catch you I'll knock your teeth out with a rock, and you'll have a big gap in your teeth and you'll remember me for the rest of your life."

He doesn't spend his pay; he gives it to me. Right now he's picking strawberries piecework and earns 1,000 pesos a week. They pay him 14 pesos a box, and he does some fifteen, twenty, maybe twenty-five boxes a day. But that's just for the season, April and May, that's all.

Then comes the tomato season. . . . Darío hardly works then, because he can't earn much working in tomatoes. He doesn't like it. He says he gets confused working tomatoes. Since he's just learning to work that crop, he puts too many tomatoes in a container, and the buckets fall. Darío works four or five days a week.

What would you like for Darío in the future?

What I'd like is for him to think, to not run around doing things he shouldn't do, not get involved in drugs. If he wants to get married someday, that he would say, "Mom, I like this girl. Will you ask for her for me?" I'd be willing to do that, but if he just went ahead without my permission, I don't think I'd like it.

And would you want Dario's future to be working in the fields?

No, I wouldn't like that. Because the bosses humiliate us. If somebody is not doing good work, they're mistreated, and I wouldn't want that for him.
My idea is to go back south with him and work my own land. That's my thought. To work for ourselves.

You have land there?

Yes. My mother is taking care of it, even though she's seventy-eight years old, plus the land that they're going to give me as an inheritance.

Do you think Darío wants to go to Oaxaca?

Sometimes he says yes, and sometimes no. I tell him, "Son, we're going because I don't want to be buried here; I want to be buried near my father." Then he says, "Yes, I'll take you."

Darío was watching us from a corner of the patio. He was sitting on a crate while he scrubbed his hands with water and a brush, trying to remove the sticky residue from the strawberry harvesting. The next day Darío was sick with a sore throat. It was very cold and he didn't go to work; this gave us an opportunity to spend some time with him, talking about the chickens. They're full grown; some already have chicks. Rosalía and Darío agreed to let us tape our conversation. She asked us to talk about drugs, saying that he needed some direction. . . . Darío sits down and we begin the interview. His replies are short and to the point, but as we continue talking about his life at school and with his friends in the colonia, his voice catches fire and his words flow easily.
Darío is clearly conflicted when he recalls the trip to Oaxaca, when his siblings remained with their father. He continues talking about life in the colonia, repeatedly distinguishing between "them" and "us." . . . When we ask him who "they" are,

*he mentions "traditional" adults and says that "we" are the young people . . . he
and his friends. Regarding the idea of returning to Oaxaca, as his mother wants to
do, he seems unsure. He was born in San Quintín. His perspective on the family's
hometown and their current residence differs from that of his mother.*

Would you like to go to live in Oaxaca?

D: No, this is where I belong, where my place is. Why should I go there?
I grew up here on my own; I'm going to find myself on my own here. Here I
know everyone, I know them all. . . . Not over there, because they all stare
at you . . . and ask, "Who's that?" It's really different there. If you talk to the
girls, they take you to the municipal office. . . . They make an issue of it.
That's why they wanted to do things here just like in their hometown; that's
why the people here didn't like them. . . . They wanted to create their own
precinct, deal with problems in their own way, according to the rules of their
town. . . . That's why there was a problem with the name of the colonia. About
four years ago, they wanted to call the colonia Nuevo San Juan Copala,[23] but
the name on some of the property titles is Las Misiones. San Juan Copala
sounds like the name of one of their hometowns, but we're not in Oaxaca.
We're in Baja California. They want to continue the traditions of their town,
but we're not in their hometown. . . . They want to change the name of
the church, but the church's name is fine as it is, and they can have their
fiesta without changing the name of the church. They speak in their own
languages. . . . What they ought to do is speak in Spanish and then have
someone translate into their own language. . . .
We're supportive of their fiesta. And we get along with them, but
they don't take our experience into consideration. Because what they've
experienced is all out of date, while our experiences are really fantastic.

What have been your experiences?

D: We've gone to school, and they haven't. Some of them don't know how
to read, like those who have just arrived [he points to a family returning from
work in the fields and carrying their buckets]. . . . Some say they know how to
speak very well, but they don't know. . . .

Do you speak Triqui?

D: No.

Would you like to speak it?

D: No, I'm fine like this.

Does your mother speak Mixtec?

D: Yes.

And do you speak Mixtec?

D: No.

Would you like to be able to speak Mixtec?

D: No, why do we have to be just like them? Can't we speak neither one or the other language—that is, neither one? We have many ideas that are different from theirs. . . . They do everything their way, to suit themselves, without taking everybody into account, like us, the young people.

2
Home, Sweet Industrial Home

The Border and the Maquiladora Industry

Toward the end of the 1960s, major cities on Mexico's northern border began an industrialization drive based on export assembly plants called maquiladoras or maquilas. These plants would import raw materials or components, along with the machines needed to process or assemble them in Mexico. The finished products would then be exported, with import taxes charged on only the value added in Mexico.[1] Mexico's border region held a number of attractions for manufacturing firms, most of them U.S. owned, that were interested in establishing offshore assembly operations. Principal among them were Mexico's low labor costs and the border region's proximity to the United States. At the same time, jobs in Mexico's interior were becoming increasingly scarce, and many thousands of migrant families flowed to the border in search of work. They came to fill jobs in the border region itself or to wait on the border for an opportunity to cross into the United States and obtain work on the other side.

In the years that followed their initial appearance, maquiladoras became ubiquitous on the border and came to define much of the social and economic contours of the cities where they took root. Most of these cities had no important industrial history, nor did they possess a working class or an entrepreneurial class with ties to the secondary sector. Further, they lacked an urban infrastructure suf-

Illustration: Staircase made from tires, Colonia Sánchez Taboada, Tijuana. *(Photograph by Alfonso Caraveo Castro.)*

*ficient to accommodate the newly arriving residents. These workers had to con-
struct their own improvised housing on the cities' outskirts, often invading land
with support from civic leaders, and they began to coalesce into a new border
working class (Barajas and Kopinak 2003).*

*From 1965 to 1975, the maquiladoras created more than sixty thousand new
jobs, most of which were filled by young women who lacked previous work experience and were not affiliated with a union. From this period forward, the number
of new jobs doubled every five years, and male workers' share in this labor force
rose, though only gradually, while women continued to constitute the bulk of
people employed in the sector. Job growth in the maquiladoras peaked between
1985 and 2000. At the close of 2000, there were 3,703 maquiladora plants, with
the majority located in the border region. They employed just over 1.3 million
workers, and employment was rising at 13 percent annually, far faster than in
any other sector of the Mexican economy, making the maquiladoras the primary
source of industrial job creation and the second most important source of foreign
currency earnings in Mexico (Contreras 2000).*

*Maquiladoras are one of the principal sources of employment in Tijuana,
even though the city's labor market is extremely diverse and dynamic owing to its
strong economic links with Southern California. This close relationship is directly
responsible for a large proportion of employment in tourism services and business
in Tijuana more generally. The maquiladoras made a substantial contribution
to job growth in Tijuana from 1985 to 2000, with 810 maquiladoras employing
199,000 workers by the end of 2000. This figure represents one-fourth of the economically active population in a city that would soon reach a population of 1.5
million inhabitants (INEGI 2009; COESPO 2008). Since then, and especially
following the attacks of September 11, 2001, in the United States, both maquiladora employment and the total number of maquilas have dropped considerably.
By December 2002, 320 plants had closed and 61,000 jobs had been lost. Some
of these jobs were recovered beginning in 2003, but employment in the maquiladoras has never again reached the peak levels attained in 2000.*

*During their first twenty years in operation, the maquiladoras' workforce was
overwhelmingly female and young. However, as available young female workers
became increasingly hard to find, the composition of the labor force gradually
diversified with the inclusion of more male workers and of women over the age
of thirty-four (Carrillo 1993), including large numbers of married women and
female household heads (López 2003).*

*The majority of the maquiladoras produce electronics and auto parts, and the
electronics industry alone accounts for most maquila plants and maquila jobs in
Tijuana. Nevertheless, alongside these more formalized and modern enterprises,
such as brand-name television manufacturers,[2] there has been a proliferation of
less stable, more precarious businesses, typically small workshops producing clothing or furniture. These businesses rely heavily on industrial homeworkers. They
operate through formal and informal subcontracting chains, and they follow a
strategy of externalizing social costs and responsibilities from the companies to*

the workers, most of whom are women. In the prevailing pattern, formal plants are linked with informal production structures that subcontract simple assembly tasks to homeworkers. Industrial homework is characterized by flexible hours, low salaries, and piecework, and this type of work is done only by women, though the women are frequently assisted by other family members (López 2005).

Studies of women's participation in the maquiladora labor force, especially as industrial homeworkers, have shed light on the nature of this work. On one hand, these jobs carry additional workplace risks: Worksites are often inadequate for the tasks being performed, workdays tend to exceed standard work hours, and it can be difficult to combine work and family life within a single space (Alonso 2002; López 2005). On the other hand, industrial homework allows women to earn an income, which increases their ability to make decisions concerning their own lives, and it offers more flexibility in their use of time than a factory job would (López 2005). Though these jobs are generally routine and tiring, the women undertake them not only as workers subordinated to capital but also as part of a personal strategy that favors the interests and concerns they have outside the world of work (Contreras 2000).

Elena, Mother to All

The Infonavit Latinos housing complex lies to the south of Tijuana and is flanked by two major roads that cross the city from north to south. This residential complex was constructed in the 1980s by Infonavit,[3] the government agency responsible for building worker housing and providing workers with affordable credit so that they can purchase these homes. The two broad avenues are not visible from inside the barrio, partly because the neighborhood is tucked into a twisting landscape and partly because of the intricate interweaving of its streets, named for the peoples of Latin America (Argentines, Cubans, and so on). From the outside of the barrio, the dull four-story buildings appear to be symmetrical, impersonal blocks, but once inside, one finds crowded, bustling streets, even during work hours on a weekday.

Locating Elena's house is a challenge because all the buildings look alike, there are no street signs, and neighbors either do not know the names of nearby streets or have no desire to give directions to strangers. When we finally reach the correct building, Elena is waiting for us on the patio of the house next door, along with two neighbors: María (who is fifty-four years old, a native of Veracruz, and the daughter of fishermen) and Selene (thirty-three, born in Sinaloa, and the daughter of a farmworker). Both have lengthy work histories in Tijuana maquiladoras that produce electronics, clothing, and medical equipment.

After talking awhile with us, the neighbors leave and we are left alone with Elena. She is a plump woman with a broad face, short hair, and an easy smile. She tells us that today is her forty-ninth birthday. Inside her apartment, preparations are under way for the family celebration that will begin later, but first she tells us her story as the afternoon fades.

A Wagon, a Hammer, and a Crowbar: Coming to Tijuana

I was born in Mexico City on July 8, 1959. I'm the daughter of a single mother; I don't know what my mother was doing at the time I was born. What I do know is that forty days later we went to Poza Rica, Veracruz, and my mother worked there. Doing what? I don't know that either. She went there with one of her sisters, the one who raised me, my Mama María Luisa.

I suspect that my Mama Socorro had always worked at men's jobs. She always wore men's pants, men's boots. . . . She's eighty-one years old now.

I remember that when I was about two or three years old we were living in Gutiérrez Zamora, Veracruz. Mama Socorro was a fisherwoman; she fished. I remember that we were poor, very poor. We didn't have shoes or clothes, just underwear, and it was really hot. My aunt who lived in Mexico City was my Mama María Luisa; she would send us clothes. My mother wasn't the feminine type. . . . What can I tell you? She dressed like a man. Did she cook? No, she didn't cook! Did she wash clothes or change? Never! None of that! But she did struggle to make a home for us. She cut wood; she cut tree trunks; she hauled the huge branches. I have a brother four years younger than I am, and my mother would carry him while she climbed trees to cut down the branches. That's my mother, a real workhorse! But she was more man than woman.

Why did you go to live in Gutiérrez Zamora?

Well, they said there wasn't work in Poza Rica anymore. There was no work, and my mother always liked to fish. And fishing was good there because of the river.

We didn't know anyone there, nobody, but my mom was like that. She'd just get a notion and . . . "I'm off," and she'd go, just like that, and that's how she'd arrive at a new place and start from zero. She went and bought a piece of land in Cerro de la Cruz; that's where she built our little house. I remember that we'd go with her to gather wood, me and my brother.

And when it was raining and the fishing was bad, I'd run errands and that's what fed us. I earned about 4 pesos a day. One peso's worth of beans, one of this, one of that, and I've been at it ever since. My mother would take care of the house, and I'd get money for food, and that's how we got along because I couldn't go to school. . . . There was no money for school, no money for uniforms, no money for anything. I remember being envious when I saw women with their children on the way to school, and I said, "I want to go to school," and she'd say, "No! You're not going to school." "Then what am I going to do?" "You're going to fish." But I didn't like fishing; I liked to walk around the streets, so I was better off running errands.

But then my mother came here to Tijuana after the boyfriend she had at the time raped me. I was five years old. My brother and I stayed behind in the care of a godmother, and after about a month Mama Luisa [the aunt] came for us and took us to Mexico City. We went to live with her. She enrolled us in school; she stopped working in order to take care of us. . . . She had worked as a domestic, cleaning houses, but she stopped working.

She enrolled me in a private school; it was a drastic change. The school was run by nuns. I took ballet classes, because there was a fine arts extension program there, and also catechism class. So my life was very different. My Mama Luisa didn't know how to read, but she wanted us to go further in school than she had. And she stopped working in order to care for us. She rented one room and then a second room for us. I stayed with her until I was eleven. . . . I completed first, second, and third grades.

My Mama Luisa had two daughters, my sister Rocío and my sister Carmen. When Carmen divorced and came to live in Tijuana, my Mama Luisa said to me, "Your sister's going to Tijuana. Would you like to go there with your mother or stay here with me?" "Well, I'll go to my mother in Tijuana."

I would always ask my mother, "Why don't we live with you?" And she'd tell me that it was because she didn't have a house and didn't have a job. But I was now eleven years old, and my mom had a place to live, a little room downtown, and she had a job, and I said, "I'm on my way!" When I got to my mother's, she was really angry: "What are you doing here?" she said. "Well, I saw that you have a place to live and you have a job, so I came." And she said, "No! Go back; here you're just in the way. Why do I want you visiting me here in Tijuana?" I just stared at her. . . . Well, a week later she rented a place in Colonia Libertad, and that's where I went to live, twelve years old, all by myself in a big house. Well, it seemed really big to me; there were two bedrooms, a living room. It was one of those American-style houses, very pretty.

She stayed in her little room. The problem with my mother was that she never wanted us to live with her. I don't know what problems she had; I still don't. We lived in the same city, but she lived in a different part. I stayed in Colonia Libertad for three months, and then she came to get me and said, "Come with me; I've got a plot of land."

So we started over again! What we did was this; she bought one of those little red wagons, a hammer, and a crowbar. In those days in Tijuana, they'd throw the trash out in big wooden crates. The stores threw their trash away like that, so we'd pry the crates apart and throw the wood in the wagon . . . and that's how she built the house in Colonia Lázaro Cárdenas, where she had the lot. That was our job every day; we'd start at four o'clock in the morning. First we'd buy some copies of the *El Mexicano* newspaper and deliver them all around the Zona Norte. We'd deliver the newspapers and finish at five-thirty or six in the afternoon. Then we'd go help out at the terminal. My mom worked in the Tres Estrellas de Oro bus terminal, cleaning bathrooms and selling things. She sold everything: cosmetics, clothing, everything. . . . We'd finish there at ten o'clock at night, every bloody day, and we'd go for the wagon, the hammer, and the crowbar and take crates apart. . . . That was our life. I was so sorry I'd come!

Between School and Work

When I came here from Mexico City, I was in fourth grade, but my mom wouldn't give us money for school. . . . That's why when my Mama Luisa came, I said, "I'm saved!" My mom didn't have a stove, so she never made food for us. She'd go and buy bread, and that's what we ate . . . bread in the morning, bread at noon, bread in the evening . . . but not my Mama Luisa; she's a cook. We went with her to Colonia Lázaro Cárdenas, my brother and I. My mom stayed in her little room downtown; she's never left there. That's when I was able to go back to school, there in Lázaro Cárdenas. I worked in the bus terminal in the morning, from six o'clock until one, and then I'd go to school. And when it wasn't a school day, I'd work from six in the morning until ten at night. I worked a double shift.

I cleaned bathrooms at the bus terminal; I managed our stand. . . . We earned most of our money from sales; everybody who was headed south who didn't already have some memento would buy it there . . . and that was my life, from fourth grade until sixth grade, going back and forth to work and from work to school. When I was in sixth grade, I told my mom that I wanted to go to junior high school. "What for? Take sewing classes, study dressmaking, hair styling. You're a woman, and that's what women are for!"

I remember that I cried from May until June . . . because my teacher told me that I could get a scholarship for junior high. All my mother had to do was sign a permission form, because I was going to work as an intern teaching at a preschool called the Future of Man. But my mom said no. Then my teacher told me, "Do you know what my sister did when they wouldn't let her continue her studies? She told her boyfriend to ask for her hand in marriage, and the next day they enrolled her in school." I had a boyfriend then, and I went and told my mom, "Mama! Guess what? Pancho wants to talk to you. . . . His parents have come and they want to talk to you." Her response was "But don't you want to continue studying?"

So it worked. But not for junior high school, because there were too many expenses. Instead, they enrolled me in a technical academy that's well known here in Tijuana, with Professor Mauro. He taught classes in accounting; there was a bilingual secretarial program, a business secretarial program. . . . It was downtown, on Second Street, and that's where I went because he didn't require junior high school or anything; and after two years Professor Mauro offered me a scholarship to a high school in San Diego. He told me I could go to high school and teach Spanish classes. But my mom said no, and if she wouldn't give her permission, what good was the scholarship? No good at all, and so that's why I didn't go to school anymore. I got married when I was sixteen.

Family Life: Living with Three Husbands, Working without Pay

We went to San Luis Potosí to get married because that's where he was from. Five months later we came back to Tijuana. He didn't want to come because he wanted to be with his mother. But I told him, "You want to live with your mother? Then stay." And I came back to Tijuana alone. He arrived three days later, with my mother-in-law. At first we stayed with my mom in Colonia Lázaro Cárdenas, and a year later we moved into a little room, just big enough for a bed and a tiny kitchen. That was in 1977. We were living there when my mother came to visit one day. She made herself comfortable, lay down, and there she stayed. She stayed with us for more than twelve years.

We lived in that little room for a year. My second son was born there, eleven months after my first. I moved out because it was such a little room and we didn't fit . . . my mother, my brother, my children, and us; we couldn't all fit. Then we rented an apartment, also downtown. There near Negrete Street; it had two bedrooms, a living room, kitchen, and a private patio.

With my mom in the house, I didn't have just one spouse, I had two . . . and when my brother came to live with us, then there were three. My husband would tell me, "Hey, when's your mother leaving?" But I didn't say anything; I was always very quiet; I just put up with it.

I never asked her why she came to live with us. She had her own place, her room downtown. We never talked about it! I just came to see myself as mother to all of them. Ever since I was little, if there wasn't anything to eat I'd go do some errand and bring back money for tortillas or for beans. And when we came here to Tijuana, I was the one who handled the money at our stand in the bus terminal. I was the one who washed the clothes, ironed, cooked, and I kept on doing it even after I had the children. It was always the same.

My brother never married. He had his first child when he was forty years old, but he never gave my mom a nickel. He never helped out. That's how she raised him, and that's why he thinks he doesn't owe anybody anything. Now he's into drugs, and my mom pays his water bill, his electric bill, and she's still taking him food.

You didn't look for a job for yourself?

No, I couldn't. How could I leave my mother all alone at her job? But I didn't get any salary; she kept all the money. She said that's the reason she'd had children, to support her, to take care of her. I'd take my son

Javier, and after Jesús was born, I'd take both of them. I'd get the stroller, put my two kids in it, and take them to work, starting at five o'clock in the morning. I'd take the two of them with me, and when the third was born, I'd take him to the bus terminal with me as well. But when my first child started kindergarten, I did leave my mother's job to her alone. We had a big fight. "What do you mean you're not going to work? What's stopping you? You can take the kids." But I couldn't open up at five-thirty, come back and drop off my son at kindergarten at nine, and then come back at two. . . . I've always worked for her, ever since I arrived in Tijuana and all the time I was married . . . always. After I got married, I returned to Tijuana and went straight to the bus terminal, all day, every day. No days off, no salary, no nothing. I worked in the terminal until 1983, when Antonio, my third son, was born.

When I got married, all I gained was that I didn't have to work in the bus terminal until ten at night, only until two in the afternoon. When I was going to school at the technical academy, I'd start work at five in the morning, and I'd leave at ten minutes before ten because school started at ten o'clock, and at one o'clock I'd go back to the terminal to work my shift until four-thirty. But that's because my Mama María Luisa was here. She fought hard so that they'd let me go in the afternoon and I wouldn't have to work two shifts. She's the one who fought to provide us a house, food, clothing. . . . When we were in elementary school, before Mama María Luisa arrived, our meals were just a piece of bread with pickled chilies. Now when my brother and I get together we say, "How was it possible that she didn't even know whether or not we were getting something to eat?" We'd take ten cents out of our bus fare and use five cents to buy a piece of bread and three cents for chilies, and that was our meal. On Saturdays and Sundays, we'd wish for Monday to come. We hated vacation days. My brother says that it wasn't so bad for him because he'd walk around and find food somewhere. But me?

She didn't know; she never wondered whether we were eating or not. My mom kind of kept her distance, like she was living her own life; I don't know. By then she was secretary general of the Shoe Shiners' Union, part of the Confederation of Mexican Workers. For her, the union was her life. If you wanted to talk to her, you had to talk about the union. If you didn't, there wasn't any conversation, nothing; the conversation would end. If we wanted to talk about ourselves, about how we were doing, nothing. "How's it going in the union? What are you going to do? Do you need me to do something for you?" Then, yes, my mom would be very talkative. When she'd go to the union meetings, the workers would invite her to share a meal. But she didn't worry or even remember whether we ate, and that's always been a sore spot with us. When she tells us, "I worked, I slaved for you," my brother and I look at each other and he says, "Your mother's talking to you!" and I say, "She's your mother!" My poor mother.

In 1983, I moved to Colonia Guerrero when the owners asked for my apartment back. The new place had only one room, a big bedroom, along with the kitchen. So we had a living room and a kitchen, everything in just those two rooms. Antonio, my third son, was born there. So was Aaron, my fourth. I remember that my mother came to visit a week after we moved in. It was nine o'clock at night, and when I saw her I said, "She's going to want to stay; she's not going to leave. Just like the first time!" My mom said, "Daughter, I've come to see you! Open the door!" I was pregnant, and I told her, "I can't open the door, Mom; I've hung a rug over it, and I can't open it until Pancho comes home and cuts the rug down." She answered, "But open up, child, it's nine o'clock at night!" "Yes, Mother, but I can't open the door; I can't cut down the rug to get it down. It's too heavy." She left then but she came back a week later and she stayed. She didn't leave. "Daughter, may I stay?" Bloody hell, I thought, because I'd have to wash her clothes for her, do her ironing, prepare her food, everything. She never did anything for herself. I had to do everything for her; I had to wash her clothes, I had to wait on her. And I was never brave enough to say, "No, Mother." Or to say, "Leave, Mother; let me take care of my own house." I was never that brave—until we moved here.

A House of One's Own, a Salary of One's Own

In 1985, we moved here. My husband was working at the Tres Estrellas de Oro bus terminal too, as a janitor. He was a staff employee, so he had benefits. When they offered him this house,[4] he didn't want to take it. His dream was to go and live with his mother in San Luis Potosí. I told him that he should go with his mother but also take the house. By then I was working again. My husband told me that the owners of the Tres Estrellas de Oro bus company were coming from Mexico City and they wanted someone trustworthy to iron for them, so they hired me.

When my husband took me to their house, I remember that I was crying, crying, and I said to him, "You wouldn't let me work as a secretary; you wouldn't even let me work as a receptionist; you didn't let me do anything, and now you're bringing me here to iron." My eyes were swollen. "Why should I do other people's ironing if I'm capable of doing other things? I know how to do other things! Why do I have to iron?" But at bottom I was grateful to him, because when I started doing their ironing I began earning some money of my own. The lady of the house liked my work, and she hired me to do the housecleaning. Then her other two daughters came to Tijuana, and I worked in all three houses.

So when we moved to this house, when he didn't want to buy the house, he said, "You're never happy!" And I said, "Go to San Luis, but let me have the house. Sign the loan papers and leave me the house." We got into a real fight that time; we knocked each other around. But he signed the loan papers for the house. And I said, "Now go, and I'll stay here in my house." When I moved here, I didn't bring my mother's things or his things. But then, of course, my mother arrived, and then he came, and they both stayed. But I didn't do their laundry or their ironing after that.

One day I ran them both out because I heard them talking about some woman my husband had gotten pregnant. My mother told him, "How can you leave that woman alone and pregnant?" My mother said, "I know what that's like. That's how it was when Elena was born. It's awful when they leave you, alone and pregnant, with no money." I felt so bad. Why didn't my mother defend me? Why didn't she? I didn't say anything right then; I just went out. But the next day I made them leave the house.

They both left, but he came back a year later . . . and there I go again. I let him stay, and I got pregnant again. I had a daughter. I had two daughters, one in 1987 and one in 1991. But my mother never came back to live here in the house. . . . I'd like to bring her here now, because she's eighty-one years old. She doesn't work. I don't know; I think I'll bring her here. . . . I can see that she can't fend for herself. She's old, and I tell myself, "What do I gain if I tell her what I heard that day?" I don't think it would do me any good. In any case, I don't live with him anymore. I have a different partner now, so I don't see any point in mentioning it.

When I ran them out of the house, my life changed, because before, I couldn't go out without the two of them coming along. I was always with my mother, or with him, or with both of them. I could never go out by myself, and there was always an argument if I said I wanted to go out alone. But I was also terrified of getting on a bus. I didn't even know how to cross the avenue. That's why he'd tell me, "What are you going to do? You can't do anything; you don't know how to do anything. You don't even know how to cross the street. You'd die without me; you'd starve to death." But no. When I got the house, when I ran them off, that's when I was able to fix the house up a bit with my own money. I worked for those people who came from Mexico City, and I used my earnings to buy things for the house. I had furniture made, I put in flooring, I had the interior plastered, they made closets, beds. I had everything made, everything. I bought a living room set, a water heater, everything new. I was better off without them, very content. I learned how to cross the streets, because sometimes that scared me. Oh, that was really awful. It's horrible when somebody's got you under their heel.

But like I'm telling you, I was a fool and I took him back, even after I had all of this. I'd already bought all of this, and he came back. But it was different then, because I didn't put up with anything anymore. Things changed after I'd been on my own, and I started doing new things. For example, there was no school here, and my children didn't have a school to go to. . . . So we women organized; we started by taking a census, we asked for teachers, and they loaned us some buildings so they could begin teaching classes. I was on the board of directors, and I started lobbying for a piece of land to build a school and then to level the lot and begin to build. . . . And I didn't let anything stop me. I'd go out, I'd come and go and accomplish things.

And that little school there is one of my proudest achievements because it came about thanks to the struggle we waged here in Infonavit Latinos. And then there was none of the "You have to stay home; you can't go out." I'd just say to him, "I'm going out; I'll see you." Or I'd leave a message: "I went to such and such a place; I'll be around there." And then they'd know that I was busy with the school issue and things like that, but I was never their servant again. I wouldn't sacrifice myself for them anymore; no more of that.

Working in the Maquiladoras

During all that time, I was working part-time for the family of the bus company's owners. But I was looking for another job, one that would pay more but still let me take care of my family, so that I wouldn't have to leave my children alone. My daughters were still very young. My next-door neighbor was working in a factory, and she said to me, "Elena, there's work we can do at home, and it pays good money." "What would we be doing?" I asked. "We'd be painters," she said. "Painters? But what would we paint?" "Well, lawn and garden plaques, decorated signs for Halloween, for Christmas." "But I don't know how to paint," I said. "Well, they'll teach you."

That's how I started painting, and I liked it a lot because I was earning good money; I was making 1,200 pesos a week.[5] We'd paint signs like the ones you see in yards and gardens on the other side of the border . . . the ones that say, "Welcome" or "Home, Sweet Home" and things like that. And the signs for Christmas, and Halloween, and springtime; those were the ones I liked most, and that's what we painted.

They paid us 79 or 89 cents each for the hanging signs. The pay varied depending on the kind of sign. The ones with stakes paid US$1.17, $1.19, or $1.15; I started out painting the signs with stakes. First they gave me ten signs to paint, then twenty, then thirty, and then forty. . . . After six months they'd give you your order to complete and say you were now a part owner. That was a lie, because we weren't really partners. We just became regular employees, and we got social security and benefits. Then they'd give us an order for ninety signs to finish in ten days. You'd have to deliver them all at the end of ten days, but the problem was that they didn't give us all the signs on the same day, so we'd have to keep going back for more. . . . Today they made staked signs or today, hanging ones. By then we were going to the factory three or four days. The good thing was that we always delivered our work on time. . . . There were two of us here [in the same building], three across the way, and another woman behind us. We'd all go together in one truck. What we'd do was this: We'd have to produce a copy of the sample sign. So some of us would get in line for paint, others would line up for wooden signs waiting to be painted, and the rest of us would get the samples and the molds. We'd paint from a sample. We'd get a sample of what we were going to paint and we'd make a copy of what it was supposed to look like. Then we'd all take some of the work; each of us would do our share. Sometimes ten of us worked together on a single order. We'd work like this: You do this, you do that, and you take that, and we'd finish the job up fast. They'd lend us the sample, and we'd make a copy of it on our first sign.

The factory was called Gran Tenochtitlan, even though it was a U.S. company. All the workers were Mexicans, but the owners were from the United States, and everything we made was for sale over there. Rubén was the one who gave us our jobs; he's the one who contracted us, and he's the one we delivered our work to. And if we had a problem, we took it up with him directly. I liked that job because we got turkey at Christmas; we got a holiday dinner, benefits, profit sharing, a Christmas bonus. . . . We even had a savings program. I listed my son Javier as well, so that I could earn more, so they would give me two orders to do and everybody would help me complete the work. Everybody in the house worked on it. Somebody would sand the wooden signs, others would paint, and still others would do the measuring. I did all the painting myself, but they helped me with sanding and tying stuff.

I always had to have the sample in front of me to look at while I worked. But I always added something to it. When I first arrived, Rubén said, "You're going to make your signs, and you're going to put your name or a pseudonym on them, whatever you want, so they know who painted them." I said, "Wow! Where are the signs going, to Poland?" Because on the back it said, "Handmade by . . ." Ever since then, I tried very hard to do good work because each sign had my name on it so that they'd know who'd made it, and I always added something in addition to what was on the sample design. And I was lucky enough that when I turned in my first ten signs, they used them as samples, which means they liked my work. They presented it as an example of the very best work, to show the others how to do it well. Because I always used a lot of color, or more foliage, more stars, I don't know, something extra. That's how I liked it; I painted the signs to suit my own taste, and I never had any problem. And we earned a good income; between my son's order and mine we'd make nearly 2,000 pesos a week.[6]

I did that job until 2000. Apparently sales were dropping, and they switched to a lower-quality paint. Before, a single coat of paint was sufficient to produce a good finish, but now we had to apply four coats of paint because the paint was of such poor quality, really thin. The brushes weren't what they should have been either, and the wood was of lower quality too. . . . But that wasn't our fault; it was their fault. They started giving us smaller orders. I went from earning about 1,800 pesos a week to only 1,600, and then 1,400. When we dropped to 800 pesos a week, we held a meeting and asked them to buy better materials or, if they didn't, they should at least stop returning the work to us to be done over. Instead of painting a sign once, we had to paint it five times. We told them it wasn't our fault. It was their fault, because they were the ones buying poor materials, and we wanted to earn what we had before.

So then the American owner, Johnson, told us that if we didn't want to accept his terms, he'd move the work to Brazil, where people were willing to make the signs for just a bean taco. "Well, make them in Brazil then. We won't do it; we earn this amount of money, and it's our jobs" . . . and he moved to Brazil. He left us stranded. We already had orders ready to go. The factory was jam-packed with signs everywhere.

There were meetings in the factory. They told us that we didn't have social security coverage anymore because they couldn't pay for it, and that anyone who wanted could claim severance pay. "We lost this buyer, but we could find another one. The space belongs to you, and you'll have to decide what you're going to do with it or what kind of work we'll do." A year earlier they'd bought some lots to build a painting factory, and there were people who kept that land. The factory was going to be located in the middle, with painters all around it. . . . They paid for the land out of their salaries; the money was deducted from the workers' salaries. I couldn't take part because I'd been working there only a short time. The factory had been in operation for twenty-seven years, and there were people who'd been working there their whole lives, and that's why some claimed the land without paying. . . . Anyway, when the factory closed, many of the workers decided to stay on as partners and try to find other clients for their paintings, and I was one of them. I said, "I'd rather have this place and a space to work; all we need to do is find a new client, so I'm going to go look for one." I was so confident; I thought it would be easy. . . .

I wanted to stay on as a worker. Those who quit got nothing; they paid them a little something, but very little. But now there were no clients and no work, and we weren't earning any money either. They told us, "Take whatever you want." So then we divvied up everything that was in the factory: machinery, sewing machines, lots of fabric, a lot of paint, a lot of wooden boards. I asked for the boards. I took boards home and some paint, some fabric. . . . I took a lot of stuff. I still have some fabric left. I sell it by the yard at Christmas and for events with dance music, like on November 20 [Mexican Revolution Day] and all that. My neighbor Elvira still makes tablecloths, curtains, napkins, chair seat covers, and skirts for dances, so she's also still making some money from the materials we took.

Did you have other jobs after you worked in the maquila?

I was working for INEGI.[7] I'd already worked for them in 1995, and they hired me again in 2000 for the census. That's where Alfonso Mesa met me; after the census work was done, he hired me to do survey work. I started working as a recruiter, and I began putting my team together. I got a lot of people to do market research and other kinds of research. Because I had already put a team together, people from Mitofsky and Gallup[8] sought me out, and now the companies that we'd worked for hire me directly. I worked for

Mitofsky covering all of Baja California. I had 150 people in the study, and I was getting paid very well. I liked that. Ten thousand pesos. Who can earn that much money in three days? I'd take my truck and get some other cars. I felt really good, working really hard, me and my friends. . . .

But that's when I first got involved with Factor X.[9] That's where I started to learn about labor laws and obligations, and I realized the risks to uninsured people, and it scared me. I started looking into workers' rights, and I got scared and I started easing out of that work. But when I left that job, I got another one. Gallup offered me a job recruiting people for market studies and, later, for focus groups, and my job was to take the people to the office: "We'll pay this much to the people you bring and this much to you." I think this is better because I didn't want to run any more risks, so I started to work at that. And that's what I'm still doing today, for several companies.

But sometimes there aren't any studies, and that's why I returned to work in the maquila in 2003, making piñatas. I combined the two jobs, making piñatas and recruiting for research studies. Making piñatas was a homework job. They paid us US$1.49 for each piñata, but I had to buy my own materials, so in effect I was selling each piñata at a $1.00, because I bought the cardboard, newspaper, all the materials. I ended up earning about 500 pesos a week, but that helped because it brought in a steady income for the household when there weren't any focus studies. Besides, everybody in the house did something; everybody participated in making the piñatas. But I had to leave that job last year when I had health problems with my liver and gall bladder, and I couldn't make the piñatas anymore or even do housework. . . . I didn't have any strength, and I had to leave the job. I lost it.

How do you see yourself in the future?

When I joined Factor X, we took trips to get to know women workers in Central America, Brazil, Chile. . . . I didn't see myself as an industrial homeworker, just like the women I was going to survey. "And what do you do?" "Well, nothing, I'm just here at home, though I do some work that I bring home and then deliver back to the factory." Then I began to see the world in a new light, and I realized I could do more for my community, for myself. My outlook had changed so much.

That's why I have no interest in talking to my mother anymore, or to the father of my children, because my life is different now. My outlook isn't just one of sorrow, of suffering, anymore. Now I see myself in a different place, and my goal is to work in the community, to help women do better, or at least help them to realize, to understand what's happening, the causes that underlie violence and low self-esteem. . . . That's why we established Latinos[10] six years ago. Its full name is the Industrial Homework, Latinos Group. We have psychologists, training workshops in human rights. . . .

The core element is the psychological support services, because women

come to us suffering, crying, with low self-esteem, with their husband's foot
on their neck, with children bumming around and using drugs, and we don't
realize that sometimes we share the blame because we don't take off the
blindfold; we let them keep walking all over us. We help women coming from
violent, abusive homes, women who are suffering in the factories. . . . The
first thing is psychological support, and from there we direct them toward
other services they need—legal help, training. . . .

We've been in operation since 2003. We've already produced three or
four generations of promoters, and they are now working on their own in the
community. That gives me so much satisfaction. My daughters are grown up
now; one is in her fifth semester of junior high, and the other one is getting an
undergraduate degree in social work. And when they finish school, I intend
to become even more involved in community work. I think I'd like to work for
an institution because I'd gain more knowledge. They give people additional
training so that they can better help others. Working alone, we can't do as
much. When we started working with women doing industrial homework,
we saw that it wasn't just a matter of informing them about their labor rights.
Lots of other issues come into play. This one has one problem, another one
has a different problem, and you have to help all of them. But what I tell them
is "I can't help you with everything, but I'm going to take you somewhere
where they can help. You're the ones who are going to do this; all I can do is
to go along with you."

We've made progress; we don't hold meetings at my house anymore. We
fought for months to get a community center, and now we have it. I could
see that it wasn't a good idea holding meetings in my home. The kids were
there, and they had things to do, and me, always with people and with my
meetings. That's why we promoted the idea of a community center, and we
got it a month ago. Now we receive the women there, and we'll be able to
offer more services, to help more people. The next step might be to establish
a nongovernmental organization and have a location, an office, a space for our
group, so that we don't have to use family spaces. That's how I see myself in
the future.

3

Sex without Kisses, Love with Abuse

A Century of the Sex Trade in Tijuana

On September 27, 2004, a group of women sex workers in Tijuana handed a letter to a representative of the city government. The letter concluded with a verse by Mexico's nun poet, Sor Juana Inés de la Cruz:

Silly, you men—so very adept
at wrongly faulting womankind,
not seeing you're alone to blame
for faults you plant in woman's mind.
(Qtd. in Rea 2004)

These women were not seeking moral approbation for their profession, only respect for a work space to which several generations of prostitutes had laid claim through the practice of their trade. Having conducted business in a "tolerance zone"[1] on Coahuila Street for years, the women were protesting a local government initiative to relocate them to the bars of the Zona Norte. The women denounced the pressures being applied to "attach" them to the bars, where they would be required to drink and smoke and would be vulnerable to the lure of drug dealers.[2]

Public authorities had repeatedly expressed concern about the visibility of these women in the city's downtown. Sex work—or "sex services," as the women

Illustration: Plaza Santa Cecilia, Tijuana. *(Photograph by Laura Velasco Ortiz.)*

call it, echoing its institutional label—is a core element in Tijuana's urban history and image. Prostitution is tolerated in the area known as the Zona Norte, both in clubs and on the street, but always with some degree of regulation and health oversight. According to data from the municipal office charged with regulating prostitution, the health registry listed only seventeen hundred sex workers out of the approximately seven thousand men and women working in prostitution in the city (Salinas 2008). This same source acknowledges that the majority of women entered in the health registry practice their trade in the Zona Norte and that they represent a mere fraction of the people involved in prostitution in Tijuana. The registry includes very few of the women who work in bars and massage parlors, where prostitution is also practiced. According to one study, nearly 80 percent of sex work in the city occurs in the Zona Norte,[3] home to nearly 45 percent of Tijuana's "unclassified" hotels (Secture 2008, cited in Bringas and Gaxiola 2010).

In many Mexican cities, urban space is organized around a central plaza dating from the colonial period. Buildings around the plaza house the municipal government offices, and the plaza is also the hub of business and tourism activities and, ultimately, of prostitution. In Tijuana, these activities are all concentrated at the city's northern rim, in the Zona Norte, mere blocks from the U.S.-Mexican border. This pattern reflects the beginnings of the city, arising as it did on the border line and extending south, east, and west from there, so that Tijuana's historic "center" actually lies on the city's northern edge. Traces of the Zona Norte's streets were already visible in the early decades of the twentieth century, and it was along these arteries that the first businesses were established, most of them selling entertainments and pleasures to the multitude of visitors coming from the United States.

Prostitution held a peculiar position among these businesses from the very beginning because of its association with the sale of alcohol and, more recently, narcotics. The fact that certain types of behaviors that are prohibited on the other side of the border are tolerated in Tijuana is tightly linked with the emergence of this city, whose earliest enterprises were racetracks, casinos, and bars.[4] The legend of Tijuana was forged out of this "sin city" image of permissiveness that attracted the thousands of visitors who crossed the border in search of what was illegal on the other side, especially alcohol and sex services.[5]

This asymmetry in the degree of permissiveness on alternate sides of the border prompted a torrent of visitors from north to south beginning early in the twentieth century. In later years this flow coincided, though in inverse direction, with the northbound movement of migrant workers driven by the economic and wage asymmetries between the two nations. Over the course of the twentieth century, Tijuana became a highly transited and visited city, a space where diverse human flows intersected with an uncommon degree of intensity.

At the opening of the twenty-first century, Tijuana was one of the most visited cities in the world (Bringas and Gaxiola 2010). In 2006, it received 22 million international visitors, most of them (80 percent) for short stays. In the same year, 29.4 million people crossed through Tijuana on their way to the United States. Thus there were more than 50 million border crossings at Tijuana in 2006. The high mobility reflected in these figures defines a city in constant commotion, with high-frequency but low-duration interactions in an environment that is highly conducive to the types of encounters associated with the sex trade.

Sex tourism is not limited to a demand for women's services; it also includes male and transsexual (transvestite and transgender) sex workers, as reported by Bringas and Gaxiola (2009). Each of these categories of workers pursues its trade in clearly differentiated spaces, delineating microcosms that divide the old city center into zones of diverse erotic entertainments: On one street, women dressed as schoolgirls; on another, transvestites and transgenders in accentuated female costumes; on other streets, women in scanty, skin-tight clothing; and on still others, as in Santa Cecilia Plaza and Teniente Guerrero Park toward evening, men and young boys awaiting their clientele.

Over the years, the influx of visitors coming from north to south and the flow of migrants from south to north have been conditioned by macroeconomic forces of national and even international scope. These have exerted a somewhat diluted impact on sex work in the city, opening or closing the sex frontier. In the last decade, the city has felt the impact of heightened national security following the events of September 2001 and, more recently, a decline in the number of visitors as potential tourists are dissuaded by the violence associated with narco-trafficking and by the ongoing economic crisis in the United States.

For the short term, at least, we are not likely to witness a return to the tourism levels seen from 1998 to 2000, when some eight thousand young people would arrive from the United States to Tijuana's nightclubs every weekend evening (Romano et al. 2004). In late 2008, Víctor Clark Alfaro reported a sharp decline in the number of sex workers and the closure of a large number of bars in the Zona Norte (Ibarra 2008), echoing newspaper reports about the impact of the worldwide economic crisis on sex capitals around the globe, such as Hamburg and Prague (El Universo 2008).

In the Heart of the Zona Norte

We walk among the bustling throngs on Tijuana's central avenues, negotiating our way around other pedestrians who have come for shopping, recreation, or entertainment. Close to the city's cathedral and the municipal market, and just yards from the international boundary line, lies the Zona Norte, the "tolerance zone," an area of five brightly colored city blocks teeming with bars, taverns, dance clubs, hotels, and restaurants. Hotels where polleros *(people smugglers) stash their migrant clients sit side by side with hotels used by female sex workers, with little to distinguish one from the other. Next to these are dance halls and the popular table dance clubs, which begin staging their shows early in the day, and the all-night restaurants and taco shops that cater to the local clientele, including the zone's male and female workers.*

It's morning, and the hustle and bustle of the preceding night is reflected in the people's faces. A man washes down the sidewalk before setting up his stand of Chinese imports. A woman lays newspapers out on the ground, where she will display the used clothing she's offering for sale. We walk until we reach First Street and then Coahuila Street, where we find the "line," a string of women leaning against the wall, waiting for customers. They look us straight in the eye, watching for any sign of interest. Some are young, others not so young. Some are barely children, disguising their youth under heavy applications of makeup. Others wear schoolgirl uniforms in hopes of looking younger than their years.

The Zona Norte never sleeps. Some of the women have gone home to rest after spending the entire night traipsing between the street and their hotel rooms, but by day others have arrived to take their places. In similar fashion, the night's clients give way to a wave of daytime customers. You can hear mariachi music coming from the Plaza Santa Cecilia, where Mixtec street vendors hawk Mexican handicrafts to an ever-dwindling number of tourists. There is music in these streets as well, but it is less vibrant, less festive. It filters out through the black and purple velvet curtains of the table dance clubs that languish in the light of day.

We reach a restaurant where we find Rosa and Martha drinking coffee. At the next table, a man talks to himself, yells, in fact, while he scratches his dirt-encrusted arms. The women seem unfazed by the surroundings and converse at ease. Their clothing bears no resemblance to the apparel of the working women standing on the sidewalk. After we finish our coffee, we go to a house in Colonia Libertad. The two women are friends and go everywhere together. Both appear more relaxed at home, and they lead the conversation.

Rosa sits down expectantly. Her trim figure is highlighted by tight-fitting black pants and high open-toed heels. She leans back and crosses her legs with professional sensuality. Light coming through the window illuminates her smile and is absorbed by her black hair, which falls in disorder around her face and neck. She answers enthusiastically, all the while moving her eyes and hands in harmony. The day is drawing to a close when she finds the right moment to begin to tell her story.

Growing Up in Texcoco and Traveling to Mexico City

Texcoco is full of flowers in springtime, but by autumn everything is dry; even the trees shed their leaves. My parents and grandparents were born in Texcoco, in the state of Mexico. I was born there too, in 1961. I was the fourth child in a family of nine—six boys and three girls.

Our town was very poor. The houses were adobe, with red tile roofs, and all around the town there were pine-covered hills. There was well water for the fields and the houses, so it wasn't a desert. My father was a peasant farmer; he planted corn, beans, and cabbage on a parcel watered only by rainfall. We all helped him in the field. He taught us how to plant corn and beans. I learned that you have to open up the soil so the crops can grow; otherwise the young shoots can be trapped within the earth and not sprout.

When I was a little girl, I walked six blocks to school every day, but I didn't like school at all. I found it boring, but my father forced me to go. I preferred working in the field or staying at home to help with the housework. The truth is that when you're little, you don't place much value on school. It's only when you're older that you realize how important school is for getting ahead.

I finished only elementary school; I didn't go any further. My parents were very unhappy when I quit school. They told me, "You should study and learn; otherwise you'll be mute, unable to speak. Look, we couldn't do any better for ourselves because we didn't make an effort to learn." But when you're a kid, you don't care. Besides, we were always short of money at home; there wasn't enough for me to continue my studies. It was better to go to the field to plant. So I stopped going to school when I was eleven. I worked in the field with my dad, and I started helping other people with chores around their houses: ironing, cooking, [doing] laundry. I liked working more than going to school.

So that's how I grew up, between work and the street, among my girlfriends and the boys. I took off like lightning, as they say, and I met a boy when I was thirteen. He was my boyfriend, even though he was older; he was twenty-two. We had sex and that created a real problem. He didn't force me, because I was willing, but my father accused him of raping me.

What happened was this. After I was with my boyfriend—after we had sex—I was afraid to go home. So I went to my aunt's house and asked her to let me stay with her. I told her what had happened, and she went to talk to my parents. My father was so angry! He went to file a formal complaint with the local authorities. The medical examiner checked me over to see if it was true that I'd had sexual relations, and found that I had. They went to arrest my boyfriend, but they didn't find him because he'd already left Texcoco. The last time I saw him he said he was coming back for me, but he never returned.

My father scolded me; he hit me. He said, "You're going to Mexico City to work with your sister," because my sister was there working in a house. He sent me there, and I stayed with her for about six months. But when a person is stubborn and they tell you, "Don't do that or that," you just get more pigheaded. I say this because while I was living in Mexico City I learned that my boyfriend had returned to Texcoco, so I called him. I got in touch with him, and he came to see me in Mexico City. The upshot was that I got pregnant. When my father found out, he really chewed me out.

Love and Abuse in Texcoco

I was fifteen when I got pregnant. Oh, boy! I had to leave the house where my sister was in Mexico City, and I went to my aunt's house again, in Texcoco. I got a job in a workshop making shoes and sandals until my first daughter was born. My baby died when she was three and a half months old. Her father never took responsibility for her. When he found out I was pregnant, he vanished from the scene. I said, "If he doesn't want me, why should I look for him?"

When my daughter died, my father was very angry and he disowned me. My mother came to visit me, though, even after my father threatened to hit her if she went to see her "such and such" daughter. My brothers were also supportive. Time went by, and I kept working in the workshop and living with my aunt.

After a while I hooked up with someone I'd known before, but I hadn't wanted to be with him earlier. We met up, and he persuaded me to be with him. My father forgave us when we went to tell him about our situation. We went to live at his mother's house. In the eight years we were together, I had two children—a son and a daughter—who are still living down south. We had a church wedding after we'd been living together for seven years. He went to church a lot, and the priest kept telling him, "You have to get married, you have to get married." He never wanted to get married in a civil ceremony.

Things went bad for me because he treated me really, really bad. He was mean, even though he didn't drink. I don't know what it was with him; I don't know if it was his nerves, but he would knock me around; he would attack me. He didn't drink, but any little thing would upset him. He'd throw things on the ground and at my face. He berated me for having had a daughter. But I told him, "I never misled you; you knew who I was." He also blamed me when I didn't get pregnant right away. We'd been together for three months, and nothing. His mother asked me, "What's the matter? What's he mad about?" I told tell her, and she said, "What a jerk! Does he think it's going to happen whenever he says?" She told her son, "Instead of abusing her, you should take care of her; she must have some female problem." And it was true; I did have some problem, because a woman gave me a treatment and I got pregnant a month later.

His mother worked every day tending a stall in the municipal market. So she didn't realize that her son was beating me—not until she saw the bruises. I didn't say anything because my husband had threatened me. He said, "If you tell my mother, I'll kill you." When his mother saw me all black and blue, she said, "What happened to you? Did that bastard beat you?" She yelled at him, hurled abuse at him. But then he blamed me: "You went and told my mother." But I hadn't told her anything. I didn't even tell my family.

I didn't want to trouble anybody with my problems, because I saw the same thing when I was growing up, with my father hitting my mother. I saw how he beat her. I said, "What's the point of complaining to my mother? I'm just going to worry her more." That's why I kept quiet. I didn't even dare tell my brothers. But it got to be too much. He hit me so much that I had to tell my aunt. She asked me, "Does that bastard hit you?" I finally told her, "Yes, he does, and I'm fed up. I think he's going to kill me!" But then I'd tell myself, "Why would he kill me? My life isn't his to take." But he was so aggressive; he'd hit me so hard. He even threatened me with a knife once, and another time with a razor.

And you never thought about reporting him?

No, I think I was afraid. That's why one day I decided to leave him. I told my aunt, "I'm going to leave." I planned to take my children, but he wouldn't let me. The boy was ten years old, the girl, five. He told me, "If you leave, I'm not going to let you take them." And I said, "But they're my children." I had to leave them. I went to a girlfriend's house, right there in Texcoco. She saw how he treated me, and she said, "Look, there's a girl in Tijuana who says there's work there and things are going pretty well for her. She could take us in." I didn't know what work she did, but I said, "I need to think about it. I can't see my children; their father won't let me see them." But I also thought that I could earn some money and pay for their care. Even if he wouldn't let me see them, I could send them money. So finally I decided to come to Tijuana.

Fleeing to Tijuana

When I was twenty-five, I took a bus to Tijuana with my friend. We were on the road for two days. That was in 1987; we went to the friend who lived here. She let us stay in the hotel where she lived, in the Zona Norte. The next day I asked her, "What's the deal here? Where can we work?" She told me, "Look, this is what I do." She told me more or less how she worked, providing sex. She said, "If you don't want to do this, there are the maquiladoras or all the shops." We chose the shops. We went looking for work in a store, but they wanted more schooling, more knowledge; they wanted people who had finished high school. In the maquiladoras, they didn't care so much about education, but they paid almost nothing. After struggling for days, the friend told us, "You can work like me if you want. Why don't you give it a try?" She explained sex services in detail. She said she had sex with men for money. She explained how to deal with customers. . . . Just sex! No kissing!

To tell the truth, the first time I felt really bad, because I had never worked performing sex services. It's ugly. The first time you think about this, about that. Of course you feel bad, because you're not brought up to have sex with lots of different people. I was unhappy. I wanted to return to my husband in Texcoco, but I said, "What is there to go back to if I left him because I couldn't stand the life he made for me, so much abuse—no, no more." It takes about a month to get used to this life. You think how you're going to get ahead, make some money to send south. I sent money to my mother so she could take it to the children.

I earned very little, but it was more than they paid in the maquiladoras. When I first arrived, it paid a bit more than the maquila. We charged about 50 pesos. I didn't work every day, but when I did work I performed four or five services a day.

Little by little I got used to it, and I went on working. In time I met another person here in Tijuana. He works in a taco shop near where I worked, on Coahuila Street. I met him when I was servicing him; he was a client. Time passed and he asked me out, and we started living together in a room in the Zona Norte. Did I care for him? Yes, I did. It was all sweetness in the beginning, but things changed; he drank a lot and chased women. He was single, but he was a real womanizer, and he began to hit me. I said to myself, "What's happening? What's happening to me? I've fallen into the same rut as before. It's not possible!" But I stayed with him. I don't know why. I hadn't had my daughters yet; I've got three daughters.

I got pregnant with my first daughter when I was twenty-six. Even pregnant, I kept on working. When my daughter was born, we were still together but we were having a lot of problems. I don't know why I didn't get up the nerve to leave him. I think I fell into the same trap. I was afraid again. I'd ask myself, "What is this that's happening to me again?" Because he hit me really hard; he drank a lot. Things went on like that, and about two years later I got pregnant again and had twin girls. I didn't want to get pregnant. It was pure carelessness. But I'm not sorry; I'm not sorry for having had my daughters. My daughters make me very happy.

Were you using condoms and birth control at that time?

Condoms? No, years back most people didn't use condoms. They started using them about fifteen years ago. I used them only when the customer asked for them. I did take birth control pills, though. But I wasn't taking them when I got pregnant with the twins. So I got pregnant and gave birth to my daughters. I stayed with him, but it was a hellish life. I would leave my daughters with a babysitter so I could go to work. When I finished work, I'd pick them up and go on with my life with that man. But, like I say, he was a real womanizer. He'd even take women to our house, and somebody would always tell me about it. I'd confront him, and he'd tell me it was nothing but lies. And, of course, he'd hit me.

My income was what supported the household, because he worked only when he wanted to, and if he didn't want to work, he wouldn't. I told myself, "This is not a life, this life I'm living with him . . . and on my own money." So I decided to leave him when my twins were four months old. I left, and though he came after me I never went back.

Work and Motherhood

I moved to another apartment with a girl from work. She'd seen how that guy beat me, and she let me stay with her until I found a place. I continued to work. I'd take my daughters to be cared for by someone I trusted, not just anybody. The woman took care of them at her house—just my girls. I don't like it when they take care of other children, because they can't give them as much attention. My old partner said he was going to take the girls away from me because he was their father. I said to him, "That's your right, but you've got to prove to me that you can support them." He knew he couldn't.

One day my older daughter got poisoned when the woman taking care of her gave her some bad medicine for her cold. I was working when they tried to notify me that she was sick. They couldn't locate me, so they called her father. He blamed me because the girl was in that state . . . all swollen. He said, "It's all because of your stubbornness. Come back home." I told him no. "She's my daughter. If she dies, it's nothing to you. I've never asked you for anything for the girls, right?"

At that time I was working every day from ten in the morning until seven in the evening. When I finished work, I'd go to pick up the girls and we'd go home. That's how it was throughout my girls' childhood. I never hooked up with anybody else. Now the girls are grown up; the twins are nineteen, and the older one is twenty-two. All three are registered with my maiden name; they don't use their father's name. It's as if they didn't have a father. That's because he wasn't a responsible parent. I'd tell him, "Let's go register the girls," and he'd say, "Later, later." When we left, I decided to register them. I baptized them too, all on my own.

I've sent them to school. I sent them first to kindergarten, then to elementary school, then junior high, and finally high school. My oldest daughter is at the university, the Autonomous University of Baja California. She'll be starting her second semester studying psychology. The other two will graduate from high school in June. They've already taken the university entrance exam. One wants to study psychology; the other one loves sports. She's studying at a karate school; she's a black belt.

I've got another partner now; he's a taxi driver. But we don't live together, because I've tried that twice before. I say, "What kind of life have I got? What am I going to teach my daughters? Let them see how men mistreat their mother?" Because I lived that life in my own home with my mother, and then I lived like that with my partners, and now my daughters would see the same thing. I've had sexual relationships, but always away from home.

I really care for my current partner. My daughters know him because he's come to my house during the six years we've been a couple. He doesn't live with me; he lives with his parents. He's divorced and has two children, also grown up. I tell him, "You can't ignore your children, because you're all they've got." So, for example, if one of them gets sick, he's got to deal with it. They—his kids—love their dad very much.

Do your daughters know what kind of work you do?

Yes. My daughters found out from their schoolmates in elementary school. One day my eldest came home from school crying. She's the quiet one. She was in third or fourth grade. She was just a kid. I asked her why she was crying. She told me, "Mama, my schoolmate says they saw you on Coahuila Street, that you were standing there where the hookers work." I told her, "He's crazy. Don't pay any attention. Tomorrow I'll go talk with the school principal."

By then the school principal knew all about me because he'd seen me there—on Coahuila Street—and every day when I'd take my daughter to school. So he knew perfectly well who I was. I went to the school and talked with him, and he told me, "Don't worry about it. Everybody has to find a way to survive. Don't worry; don't be embarrassed." I also went to talk with the teacher about the problem with the boys in the class. She told me, "They're just boys; don't pay any attention." But I told her, "Look, those boys don't have cause to say those things to my daughter; they should thank God they have both parents, a mother and a father. My daughter doesn't have a father. I pray that those boys never lose their fathers." The teacher, very friendly-like, talked to their parents, and they apologized to me. They said, "Look, it doesn't matter what work you do; everyone has to earn a living. We're not going to judge." They promised me that it wouldn't happen again.

That same day in the afternoon, we were eating supper at home. When we finished, I told my daughters that I'd spoken to the school principal and the teachers. I told them, "I did what I promised to do. I went to talk with them and I confronted them. Now you need to know all of it." I had to build up my courage to talk to them. It was hard to tell them. I cried; I couldn't help it. I told them, "You can judge me; you can reject me. That's your right. Go on; do it!" Soon the four of us were crying. I told them, "I don't do this because I like it; I do it so that you have whatever you need. Do you think I like this life? No, I don't like it." I was crying all the while I was talking to them, and I saw tears streaming down their faces. I left the table and went into the other room. My daughters came after me and hugged me; we cried together. They told me, "Mama, forgive us. We're not the ones to judge you. If you're doing this, it's so we can go to school, so we have food to eat. You mustn't feel bad, because you are not a bad person and we'll always support you. Don't be ashamed, because we're not ashamed."

Nothing else has happened since then. When they go downtown, they come to see me and say, "What are you doing, Mom? Let's get going, or she'll never get rich!" When they come by, they always say hello to my friends. They're never ashamed of me. Even now that they're grown and have boyfriends, they've never shunned me.

But what I do tell my daughters is this: "You need to study hard, because I'm doing all of this for you, so that you have what I never had. As long as I live, I never want to hear that you're messing around in this. As the saying goes, 'I might roll around in the mud, but not you.' So whatever you may think of me, you'd better steer clear of this. Because if I ever hear anything about you, you'll see what you get . . . because I'll hear about it; these things always come to light." Many of the women who work here [on Coahuila Street] bring their daughters to perform sex service. I don't want that for my daughters. They tell me, "Mom, now that we're in school we know what kind of life is open to us."

What about the children you left in Texcoco?

I lost contact with them for a long time, because he [their father] wouldn't let me see them. I managed to talk with my son about eight years ago. He's married now, with four children, and he understands what happened. Many people told him how his father mistreated me. I tried to contact him for years, but he didn't want to talk with me. But finally he agreed to hear me out. I asked him to forgive me for leaving them, but he told me, "You don't have to explain it to me; I know how my father treated you. I'm the one who should ask for forgiveness because I said bad things about you, but now I know the truth." My daughter still doesn't talk to me. She hasn't forgiven me. My son says to give her time, that now that she's married she'll see what it means to be a mother.

Twenty Years on the Street

Many people criticize us. They classify us as the lowest of the low. They think we've got an easy life, but that's a lie because it's not easy running these risks. What risks? Well, when you go to have sex with somebody, you don't know who you're dealing with. Because once you're in the room, many clients ask for services that weren't agreed on in the street. Or they're on drugs and go berserk. Or they ask for something you're not willing to do. They call us whores; they say we choose the easy life, and they ask us why we don't get a job. The citizens who criticize us should understand that this work is very dangerous. Our work is difficult. Those people who criticize us are worse than we are.

These days I start working at ten or eleven in the morning and end at seven in the evening. The crisis is hitting us hard. I charge 150 or 200 pesos for sex, and 100 more if I have to strip. There are fewer customers. Sometimes I wait all day . . . and nothing. When business is good, I'll turn three tricks a day. I've made as much as 800 pesos a week. Maybe the number of clients has dropped because of all the killings in the city. So many things have happened here in Tijuana.

What do you do to protect yourself at work?

We don't have any way to protect ourselves. All we can do is work during the day and not go into a hotel room with a client who's drunk or on drugs. There's nothing else! We don't drink. I don't drink or smoke. I enjoy a beer every once in a while, at a party or something like that.

Hotel security is very important. We find customers on the street and take them to hotels in the Zona Norte. We don't leave this area, because it could be dangerous. Sometimes a client brings somebody else along or maybe a group of friends. And that's dangerous. Yes. And condoms, absolutely! When the client says no to using a condom, I tell him, "Too bad; it's good for you and good for me." Sometimes they say, "Can't you see that I'm not infected?" But, really, how am I supposed to know?

Nobody can help us; we have to watch out for each other. If something happens, if somebody screams, the rest of us hear it and call the police. We work inside the tolerance zone, so nobody bothers us. We have our cards from the municipal health service, where the doctor records our checkups. We go to the doctor every month for a vaginal exam, and we're tested for HIV every four months. The police remove any girl who doesn't have her medical card handy, and they fine her.

There was a time when the police were hassling us a lot. This was about eighteen years ago. The police were hounding us. They didn't let us work. They demanded money. They put me in jail. Then in 1992 we founded an organization called María Magdalenas, and we held protest marches in the city. We talked with the *panistas*,[6] and things calmed down. Now we have a place to hold our meetings; we've had many presentations about HIV, about condoms, about self-esteem. I was president about eight years ago, and last year we held a press conference, because they'd raised the cost of our medical exams from 400 to 600 pesos. I had to talk to a bunch of journalists from the other side of the border. Only a few of us are organized; the rest say it's a waste of time. But when problems arise, they come to us for help!

When somebody wants to start working, what does she have to do?

She has to go to the health service, get checked out so that they'll give her a card. Then here on the street, she should keep some distance from the women who are already working, so that everybody's not all bunched up. She can get a room in the hotel, and that's it. The tolerance zone is really big, so there are many places to work. Just picture it! It goes from First Street to Coahuila Street! We don't give a cut to anybody, no pimps. We're independent. A customer comes, pays for the time in the hotel room and for the service, and that's it. Nobody else is involved, not even the police.

I've never worked out of a bar. I suppose that's organized differently. The women who work in the bars think they're different from us; they look down on us. But there's no reason why they should, since they strip without getting extra pay for it. Moreover, since they have to hang around in the bar waiting for customers, they smoke and drink a lot. But with us, we get paid extra to strip, in addition to the sex.

I've been working on the street for twenty-two years here in the Zona Norte. Yes, working every day. Sometimes I take a break, like when I'm menstruating. You can tell there's been a slowdown in sex work. There was more work five years ago, but now it's dropping. It's even worse this year; there's very little business.

The Profession of Listening: Clients in the Zona Norte

Our job is to provide sex services; it's like any other job. We simply provide a service to someone, to a client. We're like any other workers. The only difference is that we sell the use of our bodies. We're human beings like everybody else.

How you present yourself is very important in our work, because that's how you attract customers. We're not going to show up all messy, because the client will say, "I've already got messy at home. If I want messy, I might as well stay there," right? So the way that we dress and fix our hair and makeup is very important for bringing in customers, because the john will go with the one he likes best. Working all these years, I've learned that you have to make the best impression you can on the client. The client chooses the one he likes best, not the one who most wants to go with him.

What kind of people are your customers?

We get Mexicans and also people from the other side: emigrants, Anglos, Chinese. They can be accountants, construction workers, everything. Sometimes the guys coming from the other side think they can get services here that they can't get on the other side, but we don't do that. For example, if a client asks for oral or anal sex . . . well, no. And each service has a different price. I perform normal, vaginal sex. Some women may like other stuff, and that's why it's important to spell things out clearly in the street, so you don't have problems once you're in the hotel room. The Chinese can be a problem; they don't like to pay, and they want more service. Some Mexicans are nice, but others can be really aggressive and want other services. That's why you have to make it very clear what you're going to provide, because otherwise they can turn violent in the room. About five years ago, a client left a girl all bloodied up. He stabbed her four times. She was in the hospital a long time. But she survived! Another time, some john knifed a girl in the stomach. She didn't die either. Both girls recovered and then retired.

What are your customers looking for?

There's a bit of everything. For example, some want sex, but others— many others—come because they want to talk about problems at home. They vent, telling us their problems. We tell them to try to understand their wives, to build a good marriage, or to give their relationship another try because there might be a chance to rekindle the love they had with their partner, or

whatever. . . . I don't think they come so much for sex as for advice. They get
relief with us and they change. Imagine! There have been cases where they've
really changed. Many of these guys are alone here in the city. Their wives are
far away, and they have a right to seek relief. If we weren't here, what would
they do? Even with all of us working, women still get raped. Just imagine if
we weren't here! It wouldn't be good.

Of course, when they want to go to the room to talk, they still have to
pay. Thirty pesos for twenty minutes in the room. That's the rate. If they want
more time, they pay for another twenty minutes—for both things, of course,
for me and for the room. Because I also charge for my time. That's how it is.

Half a Life in Tijuana:
Between the Sword and the Wall

As a daughter, I'd like to return home to be with my mother, because she's
getting older and who knows how many years she has left. But I'm caught
between the sword and the wall, between my daughters and my mother. My
daughters don't want to leave here, so it would mean communicating with
them long distance. Now, as a mother, I want my daughters to have what I
didn't have. I want them to have the best of everything. That's why I tell them
to work hard at their studies. I'd like to see them have careers so they can
take care of themselves, because you never know what kind of people they'll
end up with. And if they separate from their partners, they'll be able to fend
for themselves. They'll have work skills, some way to support themselves.

I don't want to be doing this work in the future. That's exactly what my
daughters said to me, "Mama, you've got to see that you can't keep on doing this
work; you've got to find something else to do. Something that enables us to get
ahead but something so you don't have to do that work anymore." They think we
might be able to have a used clothing store or a little beauty salon. That's more
or less what I've been thinking. To stay here in Tijuana because, as I told you,
my daughters are growing up and have boyfriends here. It's not the same once
the children grow up, is it? I've been renting an apartment for the past twenty-
some years. My daughters have been working during summer vacations. Now
they say they're going to work even more so that I don't have to go to work. They
say, "Mama, we need to start looking for a lot to build a house."

I feel like a Tijuanan now, after all the years I've been here. Nearly half
my life! My daughters were born here, so they're Tijuanans, of course. But not
100 percent, because they've got blood from down south too. But they say,
"Mom, we're 100 percent Tijuanans."

Do you have papers to cross the border?

No, I don't have papers, and in truth at this point I'm not interested. I
would have been in the past. At one point, I got enthusiastic about it, but

you know that it's rough to be an immigrant over there. I've heard that some of the women went across the border to work on the other side. They keep pretty quiet about it; they don't tell us much, not even how it's going. I suspect it's not going well, because they come back soon. I know they work in the agricultural areas on the other side, with farmworkers. I think it's riskier there, because they say they have to service clients one right after the other. There are lines of men waiting for sex, and guards watch over the girls while they work. I think they're at a higher risk of infection over there, because if you have to service guys one after another, there's no chance to take proper care of yourself.

I wouldn't want to live there. Here in Tijuana a person is free to go wherever she wants, but not over there. That's why, when people from over there come to Tijuana, they seem to breathe more freely, and on Avenida Revolución they go around talking and drinking at ease, but not over there. You can tell that there's less freedom over there than here. Some of my clients are from over there, and they've told me how hard it is to live there.

Where would you like to live in the future?

At some point I'd like to move back home but, as I told you, I don't know what's going to happen with my daughters. I stay here for them, because they don't want to leave. And if they stay, it will be like before for me, with no way out, with nothing. I won't know what they're doing, what's happening. I hope I can persuade them to get married.

My father died six years ago. My mother is sick; she has diabetes and she's living in the state of Mexico with my brothers. They tell me, "Come over here. What are you doing over there by yourself?" My family is so far away, and here I have only my daughters. But I think it would be hard to return now because my daughters have their boyfriends. If I tell them, "Let's go over there," I think they'd like to go to visit, but not to stay. When I tell them, "I'm going south," they tell me, "No, Mom. How can you go? You've got to stay here with us. We're not going to let you go." I hope that someday I can get all my children together—those from there and those from here. That's my dream.

4

A Straight-Dealing Drug Trafficker

Narco-trafficking and the Border

In November 2008, the Mexican army, supported by the navy and federal police, took control of the streets of Tijuana, temporarily replacing the municipal police in tasks related to public safety. This operation marked another attempt to stem the city's uncontrolled violence. It followed on the effort of the previous year, in which military patrols had been assigned to the city's main traffic arteries in order to retake control of areas destabilized by gangs of narco-traffickers. These gangs moved about with impunity, not just in Tijuana but in all large cities on Mexico's northern border. In 2007, the Mexican government spent more than US$2.5 billion and deployed twelve thousand soldiers across the country in hopes of containing the violence tied to narco-trafficking, which was expanding at an unprecedented rate thanks to the drug cartel's infiltration of police forces (INCB 2009).

The year 2008 had been the bloodiest in the history of the war on and among Mexico's drug traffickers. There were 6,756 executions linked to organized crime, 880 of them in Tijuana (M. Martínez 2009). Yet despite these alarming statistics, 2009 would be even worse, with nearly 8,000 drug-related executions in the country. This extraordinary wave of violence appeared to reflect two interrelated factors. The first was the ratcheting up of pressure against the drug cartels: When Felipe Calderón assumed the presidency in 2006, he made the war on drugs the

Illustration: Tijuana-Ensenada Freeway. *(Photograph by Alfonso Caraveo Castro.)*

government's highest priority. And second, gangs of narco-traffickers were fighting among themselves for territorial control and distribution routes.

Ever since its origins early in the twentieth century, Tijuana has been associated with the demand for alcohol, drugs, and sex services that exists on the U.S.-Mexican border, and the U.S. market for illicit drugs is enormous. In the United States in 2007, for example, some 35.7 million people over the age of twelve used an illegal drug. This figure represents 14.4 percent of this U.S. demographic (INCB 2009). Though it is very difficult to determine the exact value that this market holds for Mexican drug traffickers, various estimates place it between US$6 billion (Chabat 2002) and $25 billion (González-Ruiz 2001) annually.

Traditionally, Mexico was a transit route for Colombian cocaine headed to the U.S. market, as well as an important area for the growing and distribution of marijuana. In the 1980s, Mexico was already a significant supplier of marijuana and heroin to the United States, but its involvement in the trafficking of cocaine was still marginal, other than providing a transit route. Toward the end of the 1980s, about 70 percent of the marijuana and 25 percent of the heroin entering the United States originated in Mexico, and about 60 percent of cocaine consumed in the United States passed over Mexican territory en route (Chabat 2002).

In the early 1990s, groups of narco-traffickers in Mexico began wresting control from the Colombian cartels. The takeover was facilitated by the success of the Colombian government's attacks on the drug cartels in its own country, efforts that were supported by the U.S. government. Since then, the Mexican mafias that had been delivering Colombian cocaine to the U.S. market began to demand half the shipments in payment for their services. This dramatically changed the balance of power with their Colombian partners and elevated the Mexican cartels to a dominant position (Brouwer et al. 2006). By the end of the 1990s, the Mexican cartels not only controlled the cocaine and marijuana markets but had also begun to play a leading role in satisfying the demand for methamphetamines (Finckenauer et al. 2001; Brouwer et al. 2006).

But the Mexican cartels did more than take control of methamphetamine trafficking; they also became producers. Among other effects, this shift sparked a rise in consumption within Mexico itself, especially the use of crystal meth. According to estimates by the U.S. Drug Enforcement Administration (DEA), drug traffickers in Mexico control between 70 and 90 percent of the production and distribution of methamphetamines consumed in the United States. The main production centers are in Baja California, Jalisco, Guerrero, and Michoacán (Finckenauer et al. 2001), and at least some of these locations have high-tech laboratories that are able to produce hundreds of pounds of product each week. In 2007, Mexican authorities dismantled twenty-six methamphetamine labs; nine of them were categorized as superlabs (INCB 2009).

Partly because of increased production in Mexican territory, but also because of the increasing difficulty of getting drugs into the United States, the cartels have sought to expand the local market, giving rise to a significant growth in drug consumption in Mexico. Evidence of this can be found in the notable decrease in cocaine shipments from Mexico beginning in 2007, leading to a shortage that pushed the U.S. price for a gram of pure cocaine to twice the previous level (INCB 2009).

According to a study conducted in 2008, the trend toward increased consumption of illegal drugs in Mexico has had three notable results: (1) There has been a significant increase in the use of marijuana, cocaine (especially crack), and methamphetamines. (2) The age at which people begin consuming drugs has dropped considerably. (3) The numbers gap between male and female drug users is narrowing (INCB 2009). It is no coincidence that the areas of heavy drug trafficking are also the areas of highest consumption. A previous study had found that 14.7 percent of the Tijuana population between the ages of twelve and sixty-five had used some illegal drug; this is three times the level for this age range in the national population (5.3 percent). Ciudad Juárez is second in level of drug consumption, at 9.2 percent (Brouwer et al. 2006).

As drug use rose along the border and gangs of drug traffickers battled one another for territory, the retail distribution of drugs in Mexico's northern border cities ceased being a small-scale undertaking. According to some observers, retail sales in Tijuana are now also under the control of the large cartels, with drug sellers paying the cartels for "protection." These networks base their operations on the social fabric of the city—in poor neighborhoods, under the protection of local gangs, and often with the complicity of the police (Garduño 2009). Despite some decisive blows by the army against the principal narco-trafficking gangs, despite patrols by the military and federal police throughout the city, and despite increased oversight of the local police, Tijuana still has some four thousand points of retail drug sales, which operate secretly and efficiently to supply an expanding local market.

Going to the Center of Operations: Grupo México

It's a hot July morning in Tijuana. We make our way through heavy traffic on Libramiento Sur, a broad roadway that traces an expansive triangle beginning near the Pacific Ocean, at the extreme western end of the international border, looping southward and then eastward and ultimately reaching the border again, now at an easterly point next to the Tijuana Airport. Constant road repairs and heavy trucks slow traffic to a crawl in the stifling summer heat.

Near the southernmost point of the Libramiento Sur triangle, just beyond the Pacífico Industrial Park, which houses some twenty maquiladoras, we exit onto a narrow road that leads into the Colonia Grupo México. The contrast between this neighborhood and the ultramodern industrial park is extreme. Shabby streets wind between hills and beside ravines; they are flanked by a patchwork assortment of dwellings. Some are just shacks built of boards and tarps; others are solid constructions of two or even three stories. All seem unfinished, all are discolored by a layer of dust, and most are unpainted. Some streets are paved with cement, which has clearly been laid down only recently. But most of the streets are barely passable dusty tracks.

Colonia Grupo México began as an irregular settlement founded by land invaders. In the 1980s, it was among the most rapidly—and chaotically—growing neighborhoods on Tijuana's southern rim. Thousands of homeless families flocked here to invade land on the hillsides and in the canyons, encouraged by social leaders who offered support but had no plan to guide the area's urbanization. The neighborhood now has electricity, running water most of the time, and some paved streets, but its improvised origins are visible everywhere.

At the highest point in the colonia, a traveling market obstructs traffic. People shop and converse in the middle of the street, unconcerned about the cars nosing this way and that, trying to find a way through. After negotiating a path around these small commotions, we follow a steep track to the patio of a large one-story house, seemingly abandoned. A lonely trailer sits in the middle of the patio, with the city visible beyond. We are atop one of Tijuana's highlands, surrounded by ravines filled with homes and garbage.

Our host is waiting for us in the trailer. Our guide remains outside, talking with another man who appears to occupy a higher rung on the ladder of the drug business. We sit down in the cramped space and say hello to a slim, dark man dressed in jeans, a T-shirt, and cowboy boots. In the light coming through the small windows, we see his angular, somewhat distrustful face. He's reserved, earnest, powerful. There are no welcoming smiles. He is a man of action, and he is not comfortable in situations like this. He asks for a cigarette and begins to smoke while he attempts to relax in order to tell his story.

Growing Marijuana: A Child on His Own in the Mountains of Nayarit

You can call me Juan. I'm forty-one years old, and I'm from Santiago Ixcuintla, Nayarit. My father's been a peasant farmer there all his life. That's where he was born, and that's where he stayed, in the village, growing beans . . . corn and beans.

Santiago Ixcuintla is a small settlement, with some five thousand residents, more or less. It's very green. There's lots of vegetation, plenty of water, rivers, forests, canals. They grow lots of fruit there too: mangos, papayas, bananas, plums. . . . If I try to list them all, I'll never finish! . . . Life is good there. And my father's plot is near the village; he's got some twelve hectares.

There were seven of us at home—my dad, my mom, and five children, two boys and three girls. I was the second child; I stayed at home until I was eighteen. What I remember from those days is that we left school at midday. I'd go home, eat, and then go help my father, who was waiting for me in the field. I'd help him cut hedges, repair fences, put in stakes.

I was always by myself. What happens is that I . . . how can I say this? When I was a kid, I didn't like to play; I didn't like sports. I went around by myself; I spent my time alone in the mountains. . . . The other boys in the village were different; they played marbles, spun tops. You know? Not me. I didn't like to do any of those things. What I'd do is just go my own way. . . . I had a 22 single-shot rifle. It was my dad's. I'd grab it and go into the mountains. Later on I still went into the mountains, but then it was to water my plants.

What kind of plants?

Marijuana. I started growing pot when I was still a kid. I'd plant the seeds, some here, some there. . . . That's why I had to go water them.

I knew about growing marijuana because you see it everywhere in those parts. If you go out with your rifle or whatever, if you go hunting, you come across plantings of marijuana everywhere. They're really well hidden. We're the only ones who know our way around there. Somebody who's not local would never find them.

Lots of people there were growing pot. Not everybody, but some. In the beginning it was people from the village growing it, but things changed over time and then people from outside came in and would pay the locals to grow marijuana for them.

Were you already using marijuana?

Yeah, I was using it. That's why I grew it. I started after I left elementary school; I was about thirteen. I finished only the sixth grade. After that I worked with my dad on his land until I was eighteen. I first tried marijuana about the time I finished elementary school, just to see what it did. . . . Sometimes people do things just out of curiosity. That's how you get started, right? Out of curiosity—to see what it feels like, what it does to you—and that's how I started. . . . That was when I harvested my crop, you know? And I put it out to dry and everything, and that's when I said to myself, "I'm going to try it; I'm going to see how good my harvest is." But there's nothing there in the mountains, no paper to roll a joint, so I used a corn husk, a really thin one. And since I didn't know what I was doing, I made it really big, like a cigar. I rolled it and lit it. That's how I got started. Can you believe it? That was the first time and I rolled a huge joint. . . . I lit it and smoked about half, and my face started to feel all swollen. I tried to stand up but I couldn't. I thought, "Yikes, now how am I going to get out of here?" There was a stream nearby; I'd planted my crop by the stream. So I ran to the stream to wash my face and get wet. . . . I spent the whole day there until it was almost dark, when the effect of the marijuana was finally wearing off, thanks to water and more water. I ate a lot of mangos too, because the pot made me very hungry.

The effects finally wore off, and I went home and said, "No, I'm not going to smoke again, no more marijuana." It happened like that because the marijuana was fresh and really potent. The resin glands were exploding when I pulled the plants out. I couldn't finish smoking it; I left it. That was all. But then the second time I said, "Okay," but that time I wasn't alone. I was with a friend, a guy older than me. I took him with me so he could see my plants and hook me up. . . . "I want you to sell it for me," I told him. "You know people, and that's how they'll get to know me."

He rolled a joint to test it, and there I am, so what am I going to do? I've got my friend with me, so no problem. But I told him, "You know what? I get really stoned, so watch out for me. Otherwise I'll fall in the stream." So, yeah, I took two puffs and felt good, not like the other time, when I was toasted. Not this time; I just took two, three puffs, and that was enough. . . . I said, "If I feel good with just a little, that's what I'll do." And that's how I got the knack of it—just a little so that you don't get really stupid and lose your balance.

The Narco-agriculture Business

I just planted a little in the beginning . . . just for my own use. Later I grew more. . . . I'd have some forty or fifty plants, and I'd harvest two or three small bags. It wasn't just for my own use then; I'd sell some too.

I still didn't know anything about selling, but there was always somebody . . . some way to sell it. So bit by bit I learned the "who, where, and how" of it. And that's how I figured it out. That's how I learned to be a grower, with some plants for myself and some to sell.

The thing is, I wanted to make money. If you like money, you've got to hustle, right? And that's where the idea came from. Sometimes when my friend's buyer arrived, he'd come and tell me, "Look, if you want to, you can sell there; you can sell at such and such a price." These guys came from Guadalajara, from Tepic, from big cities. They'd come to the village in their pickups, just like normal. . . . Like everything, there's a trick to it. They'd come in just like the people who came to buy beans. They're the ones who come to buy beans or corn, seeds, mangos, whatever. They're just regular buyers, but they're the same people doing the business, you know?

Did your dad know about this?

Yes! Everybody in the family knew. . . . Well, a bean crop isn't worth anything. The crop hardly pays anything at all; it barely covers the costs of the work in the field. That's why people stop planting those crops; they look for something better. I started looking around for something early on. That's why my father never said anything to me, because if his crop didn't pay, mine did. He always played it straight; he just planted his beans. He did it his way, I did it mine. Right?

What happens is that this pays better; you can earn a little more. Back then, when I'd sell ten or twelve bags I'd make about 15,000, even 20,000

pesos.[1] You can make that much every six months, two harvests a year. . . .
And I'd use that to help my dad, because I've always been responsible that
way, and my dad couldn't make it by himself. I helped him out; I still help
him. And I'd keep a bit for myself. . . . I even had a bunch of girlfriends then,
because I was never short of money.

So my harvest was a sure thing, assuming they didn't catch me. I had to
go alone, and I did everything by hand, with just a machete. The first time,
I put in fifty plants, right? And when I saw that everything was working
well, I planted more. I'd clear another little bit of land; you shouldn't clear it
all or it will be easy to spot. You just clear enough so the sun gets in, so the
sun reaches the plants. . . . So the second time around, I put in about two
hundred plants. And that's how I increased my crop, all hidden away. . . .

Over there, people don't bother you. People don't go around snooping
here, snooping there . . . The less people know about these dealings, the
better. . . . And if it's land that's owned by somebody, they never trespass.
And if they do, well, you fire off a few shots and they figure out the risks real
quick. That's why the people there respect boundaries. When people don't
have any business with you and they come up to your place, you shoot at
them, because they have no business snooping around there.

The plant is ready when the cola [the flower cluster at the end of the
grow tip] is really long. You pull out the whole plant, roots and all, and hang
it so the resin runs down the stem and over all the leaves. You have to cut
the plants when they're still very green. Then you hang them in the shade,
and they dry there in the shade so that the resin covers all the leaves, until
everything takes on a kind of sheen. Wow, that resin is really potent!

I learned all that when I was a kid. I spent my time going around, just
watching. I watched a guy from Jalisco, a fellow who was always by himself,
always alone. He wore camouflage, like a soldier . . . pants, jacket, even an
army hat. I liked to go see him, and we'd talk there in the mountain, and he
gave me lots of advice, see. And he told me about it. He taught me how to
plant, how to prune the plants so they produce more. . . . That guy taught me
everything. . . . He's dead now, may he rest in peace.

The Road to Tijuana: Trafficking
in Both Directions

I decided to leave my village because I met someone from over there, from
San Luis Río Colorado.[2] That was around 1985. He'd come to visit some
people in the village, some relatives, but I hadn't met him before. That's
where we met. We started talking, and we got along really well. He liked to
smoke pot too, so we hit it off. . . .

He's the one who invited me here. Since he really liked to smoke, I said,
"Let's go." He said, "Yeah, let's go." "Okay," I said. I had money, and I really

wanted to get out, to see new things . . . so we came here. I told everybody, "I'll be gone a couple of weeks or so." But I liked it, so I stayed in San Luis for about four months. What did I do there? Nothing, really. I had some money . . . and I had pot. . . . I brought it with me in a backpack, because it was easy to do that back then. My backpack was full of marijuana. Soldiers were patrolling everywhere, so I put the backpack up high in the bus; I wasn't worried at all. The trick is not to be afraid. . . . And that's how we got through, and we got here to San Luis with the backpack. There was enough marijuana for us to stay here for four months. . . . I still had enough left to get to Tijuana. . . . That's when I ran out of money.

I met other people, friends of my friend, in San Luis, and they persuaded me to come here. . . . When I was getting ready to come to Tijuana, I told my friend, "You know what? I'm going to Tijuana, with your friends from there." He said, "Well, do what you want. You'll always have a place here." "Yeah, I know. Thanks." And I came here and got to know people; I built up a network, and here I stayed.

The first time I came, we had a job; we had to pick up some cars. Those friends would take cars, stolen cars, down south. And that's how I got connected and began working. I worked with them for about a year, driving cars down south. . . . I remember one time I went to my house there and took my parents a pickup truck, a Silverado. I left it for them . . . and that's how I spent that year, coming and going.

All we did was deliver the cars. Other people would steal them. Those guys specialized in that. It didn't matter to them if a car had an alarm or an anti-theft club. Those guys are real experts, real professionals. They'd pay us for picking up the cars in Tijuana and delivering them in Nayarit or Jalisco. In those days they'd pay me US$1,500 for each car I delivered.

When I'd pick up a car, it would already have registration papers . . . because they'd make fake papers. When everything was in order, I'd take it to its destination. On the way back, we'd load up with other merchandise. I'd bring up to seventy or eighty kilos of marijuana. I'd fill one of those big green army bags. . . . I'd stuff it full and bring it with me on the bus. And that's how we started trafficking in both directions, coming and going.

Aren't there inspections along the way?

Yeah, sure. That's why you talk with the bus driver. Who knows where he stows the stuff, but you know it's there, safe. The driver puts the bag somewhere he knows they won't find it, and that's how he makes a bit of change. . . . Everybody gets something. If you don't do it like that, it just doesn't work.

So I spent about a year working with them. After that I started working for myself. I was always on the lookout for an opportunity, and I hooked up with some other people. I kept on doing the same thing I used to, delivering cars and bringing back merchandise. But now I was working for myself, and I found two or three guys to help me. By then we didn't just go to my ranch. We'd go to a lot of *ejidos* [communal land] and ranches there in the hills . . . because I'd already made a deal for the merchandise. So we'd arrive and say, "Okay, here's the pickup truck you wanted. Where's my merchandise?" You see?

Everything was done through contacts, right? If you're not connected, you can't do anything. It's a chain. You have to know somebody, and that somebody takes you to meet somebody else, and like that. You buy from me, you sell to him, and so on . . . and everybody in the chain has to make some profit. Because now, for example, you even have to pay a cut to the police. But when I'd go back to my ranch to bring my merchandise, we didn't pay the police, only our contacts. . . . You always have to have some ready cash so you can settle accounts. That's how the world turns; there are always accounts to be settled.

My goal is always to double my money. For example, if I buy a pickup for US$2,000, I take it down south and sell it for $4,000. I make $2,000, but from that I've got to cover my expenses and whatever I had to pay out along the way, so I end up with about $1,500. There's another accounting for the merchandise I take on the way back, because I need to pay transport, pay the bus driver . . . but that's separate, because that's on the way back.

This is how it works. The client tells me what car he needs—a black Silverado, a silver Ford F Series pickup. . . . Then I tell the guys who lift the cars what I need, and they go and get it. And when they come with the car, they say, "Here it is. Give me a couple thousand." But I tell them, "No, I'll give you $800, $1,000." You've got to bargain, because what did it cost them? Just a few dollars to get hold of it. But I've got to deliver it; I've got to get papers for it . . . because the car they deliver to me doesn't have any papers. I've got to arrange documents, false papers. I've got to deal with the people who produce the documents so that I can move the car without any problems.

That lasted until 2002. After that it got harder. We started having problems; it got more complicated. And then I also started with a problem.

An Ephemeral Conjugal Life: Between Crystal Meth and Love

When I was here in Tijuana I met the woman who would be my wife. This was in 1989. . . . I met her because she was the sister of a friend of mine. It turned out that we were neighbors back home, except she was from a different ranch. I'm from one ranch, and she's from one nearby.

It was Christmas. We were at her house. Her brother had invited me,

and that's where I met her. Well, we talked and got along really well. We'd
run into each other, and then we'd see each other someplace else, until finally
we hooked up.

This was in 1989, and our first daughter was born that same year. The
second one was born in 1991, and the last one in 1998. Those are my three
daughters, all with the same woman, with my wife.

We split up in 2002 because of problems I was having. . . . Work was
going fine, but since 1997 I've been using crystal meth, and I was having
lots of problems at home. A lot of people would come to the house, and that
caused problems.

That's when I decided to go to Nayarit. I spent two years there. Well, not
all that time, because I'd come and go, but I was there for most of that time.
What happened was that I went to plant marijuana. I wanted to do something
big, really big, and that's why I went to plant. Besides, things weren't going
well here, and I wanted to get away. I was away a long time. When I came
back, I found out she was with somebody else. I haven't hooked up with
anybody else since, but she has. She's with another guy. She's living with him
and has a little boy. I've got my two daughters here with me, the two oldest
ones, and I've got a grandson. They're my only reason for living, as they say.

How did your crop turn out?

It was good, really good. Those were good times. What happened was, I
had the problem with my wife, I was hurting. . . . I made a lot of money, but
I spent it all, I threw it all away on women, booze, drugs, everything you can
think of. I went through every penny I had, and I don't even know how I did
it. I spent money by the fistful. So I ran through all the money I'd managed to
put together.

That's why now all I do is sell—marijuana, crystal meth, coke. I just sell;
I buy and distribute. That's what I do; that's my life now. I started doing this
in 2002; that's when I linked up with some people, some real heavyweights.
They handled a lot of money, and I liked that. They trusted me, and I started
hanging out with them. I tried crystal meth with them. Before that I only
smoked pot. . . . Crystal meth is different; the experience is way more serious.
It's a chemical, and if you're not careful, things can go very bad. Crystal meth
is a powder that you smoke; you can smoke it or snort it. . . . You can get ice
too. It's like ice crystals, and it's really good. . . .

It's got a kick to it, so—how can I explain it?—it energizes you. . . . The
first time I tried it, I didn't even want to stop working. You don't want to sit
down or relax. It's the opposite. You're hyperactive, and time goes by really
fast, without you being aware of it. . . . When you look back, the day's already
over. It's eight o'clock at night; it's already dark!

So what I did then . . . if one thing speeded me up, I took something else to bring me down—marijuana. That's how I kept balanced, and I'm doing okay, not racing and not lazing around. I'm doing okay.

The problem with crystal meth is that it's addictive. The more you have, the more you want. And it has really awful effects. Some people die. . . . They dehydrate. . . . They don't want to eat, get cleaned up, nothing. You know what I mean? I'm not like that. I take care of myself. I keep busy. I eat well. Besides, there's a drugstore across the street. I go there and tell them, "You know, I need some vitamins." I take them and I get better right away. And I don't overdo it. Crystal meth comes in rocks, right? The most I use is two a day, two rocks, and one or two joints. That's all.

Is it a good business?

Well, the trick is to keep turning over your investment, because if you run through what you've invested, nobody's going to give you any merchandise, just like that. So you've got to have cash or something to offer. . . . For example, if my contact has merchandise and I don't have cash, I'd better have something else for him. He'll give me the merchandise if I've got something to offer him in return.

These days an ounce of crystal meth goes for about $500. That's what I have to invest, and I've got to double my money. I sell it at $10 a dose. I've got to get back $1,000 to recover the $500 I invested, and the rest is my profit. Lots of people are adding stuff, cutting the drug to increase the quantity. . . . They cut it with pills, vitamins for horses, with ephedrine.

Lately I've also been moving cocaine. It's the same deal. I get half, and we distribute based on orders. People call me and ask for some product. . . . Everything is done by phone. They call me and tell me what they need, and I go to wherever they are, a pool hall, a bar. I take what they need to wherever they are. These are people I already know. That's how they have my number. They're all people I know.

A Season in Hell

The danger is that somebody will talk too much, like, for example, we're talking here, and if I say something about somebody I know and he doesn't like what I say. There are people who'll sic somebody from the government on you, you know? Just like that, for something they don't like, something that offends them.

Has that happened to you?

Yeah. One time two cops came here to the house and took me away. That was in 2004. They came for me and they locked me up in the pen, in the penitentiary, for two years. . . . That was a tough experience; yeah, that was awful. They caught me red-handed; they came because they already knew. . . . I had a bag of marijuana and about a pound of crystal meth, and that's how they got me.

First they took me to the ministerial police, here in Tijuana. They kept me there for two days, interrogating me, asking me who I worked for. But they didn't break me. Ratting on somebody else isn't a smart move, not for me or for anybody else. Because if you name somebody else, if you involve your contacts, that's a really serious thing. Better to stay locked up and just bear it. And worse, if you don't play it straight, if you don't keep your mouth shut, they can kill you, even if you're in jail.

From there they took me to the La Mesa penitentiary.[3] I was there for two years before I got out. It's hell to be locked up all the time, like an animal. . . . It's ugly; it's sad—twenty-six prisoners in a cell that measures twelve by fifteen feet. Seven beds and one toilet, so people have to sleep under the beds, on the floor. If you want to use the toilet, there's not even any place to stand. And if you step on somebody by accident, they get really mad and start a fight. . . . There are fights at any hour of the day, for any reason.

The people there are very bitter, full of resentment. They spend their time thinking and thinking, all mashed together with no chance to get out. That's why any little shove, even by accident, turns into a fight. Most everybody has some kind of weapon for attack or defense: a shiv or something to use if there's a fight.

Prisoners spend the day waiting for mealtime; there's nothing else to do, you know? What they give you isn't much, so they're just waiting for something to eat. Not me, because I was lucky enough to have money to buy stuff, but there were some young guys who were always hungry, and they'd ask us to give them some food . . . crackers or a soda.

Breakfast came at six o'clock in the morning. They'd serve us in the cell, with everybody all on top of each other. They'd bring pots of food, and we'd put our bowls at an opening there in the bars, and that's how they'd feed everyone. Then again at midday, and again at six o'clock in the afternoon. All we'd get is oatmeal and bread. . . . You never get full; there's never enough food.

We'd get out of the cell only once a week, on yard day, for recreation. It lasted two hours; we'd go out to the yard and play basketball. One week they let us out twice, but then only once the following week. That's how it was, two days, then one day. But we'd be locked up all the other days, all crowded together.

In our building, Sunday was visiting day; each building had visitors a different day. My daughters would come to visit me sometimes. They brought me some money in the beginning, and then later I gave them money, from inside out. They helped me, so I gave them money.

Where did the money come from?

Well, everything's for sale in there; if you've got money, you can buy anything. You know what I mean? They'd pay the guards to bring in my merchandise, and I kept on selling inside. I paid off the guard at the entrance door, but I was on the third floor, so I also had to pay the guys guarding the doors on the floors below me. I paid all three. That way there was no problem; they even watched out for me.

What happened was this. When I arrived and they put me on the third floor, they had just moved a guy to the Islas,[4] so there wasn't anybody selling on the third floor. They'd taken away the guy who was distributing, and that's how I made my agreement with the cops, with the guards. So I started spreading the word, telling people what I had. . . . That's how it works inside.

I sold marijuana and crystal meth. There was some smack [heroin] around too, but I wasn't involved in that—just crystal meth and pot. Everything costs more inside, because you've got to spread the money around so they'll let you sell. You just make enough money so that your time inside isn't so bad. Besides, you can't bring in very much, because sometimes the federal police come from Mexico City to do an inspection, and if they find somebody who's high, or if they find lots of money, they go really hard on you.

One time the federal police came at two o'clock in the morning. We were all asleep, when suddenly: "Everybody up, hands behind your heads, on your knees!" They had us kneel down, and then they searched us one by one, just as we were. "Out with it; out with it! Come on!" That time they didn't find anything on me, because the guards always warned me. The guards themselves would take my stuff and put it somewhere that the federals wouldn't find it.

Those were two really bad years, but at least I got out. I wasn't in too long. Who knows what would have happened otherwise? You can't stand it for long. I got out because some people helped me get out early. It cost me. I had to sell some land in order to pay the lawyers and to get the charges reduced, to get rid of the charges of drug possession and drug sales. Once those were dropped, the rest was easier. I spent about US$15,000 on that, just to get them to drop the charges, in addition to what they paid so they'd let me out. I don't know how much the people who got me out paid for that; they never told me.

Back to Life: Keeping Quiet, Watching, and Getting Revenge

Did you know who turned you in?

Yes, I knew who'd fingered me. You know these things. I didn't do anything to him, because informers like him are better off disappearing. It was two years. That doesn't sound like much, right? But that's a lot of days to be locked up. You come out feeling bad, really angry, and whoever did this . . . he'd better get lost, for his own good.

People who do this know what's coming to them. They know that whatever bad stuff they do . . . it'll catch up with them, even if they're dead and buried. That's why, if they know what's what and they can't take the heat, better not get involved. Those of us who know what we're doing, we have to be able to stand the pressure. If something happens, we have to take it. Then everything stays okay.

Now that you're out of jail, are you still doing the same thing?

Yeah, I'm still doing that. But I only deliver; I just take stuff to where somebody's asked for it. Nobody comes around here. The less attention there is to this place, the better. That's how people get busted, when there's a lot of coming and going and people begin to notice.

Things are harder right now. There used to be more movement, more money coming in. What's happening is that people are fighting for position, and guys who have a good position don't want other people coming into their territory. If somebody wants to sell, well, you have to pay. That's how it works.

Another thing is that now there are lots of military police around. When I make my deliveries, I have to be careful that they don't grab me with something. If they stop me and search me, I'm better off paying them something and getting them off my back. But they always warn us, "Be careful; there's a patrol in such and such a place, and there's another one over there." They warn us and tell us, "Things are hot. Don't go out. Don't take anything out now." There's always somebody who gives us a heads-up.

Do your daughters know what you do?

Yes, they know. It's not a problem. They know, and they respect me. The two older ones are already married. In fact, they're coming to visit in a bit; they'll be here soon. They live nearby. The oldest one has a beauty salon, and the other one lives with her husband, by the church. Right now she just takes care of her little boy; her husband works in a metal business where they buy scrap metal and recycle aluminum, copper, bronze, stuff like that. He's the owner's son. And the youngest is still living with her mother; she's about nine years old.

Are your daughters in any danger because of what you do?

No, nobody's going to mess with them. If something were to happen, it would just be a matter of going and getting whoever did it, bringing him here, putting him in a room, and giving him some good "therapy." "Are you ever

going to do this again?" "No, never again." "Okay, go on then; that's it." That's
how it is; those are some pretty rough therapies.

Did you ever cross the border?

Yes, once, just to see what it was like. That was around 2000. I went with
a friend; we took some *pollos* [undocumented immigrants] to the other side.
We took them and crossed there to one side of El Hongo.[5] That time we took
eleven, all adults; there were some young women too . . . poor things. They
were terrified of the coyotes and the snakes!

We walked part of the day and part of the night. When we were coming
close to Highway 94, it was dawn. We walked about a day and a half in all,
more or less. The thing is that there aren't any roads there. It's just mountains,
hills, and ravines, so you need to know where you're going. I just followed my
friend Ramiro, may he rest in peace.

We'd agreed on a price of US$200 per person, and he was going to give
me half, or $100 for each one. But we didn't make it; we couldn't even collect,
because they caught us. The arrangement was that the people would pay us
once they reached their destination. But the *migra* [Border Patrol] caught
us. They put us in a panel truck and took us to the station, and from there
another panel truck brought us back to the line.

They let us go because nobody had said anything. We'd talked to the
migrants in advance, told them that if we got caught they shouldn't say
anything, that we were all the same [all migrants] and that our guide had left
us and that's why we were wandering around lost. . . .

When you mentioned your friend, you said, "May he rest in peace."

Yes. May he rest in peace, because he died. He talked too much, and they
don't forgive that around here. He was hanged, there in the little park by the
church. It was about four in the morning; it was an awful night. The fog was
so thick you couldn't even see fifteen feet in front of you. And that's where
they found him, hanging from a railing in the park.

Aren't you afraid?

No, because . . . it's all a matter of doing things right. You always have to
do your work right, not do anything improper, nothing that puts somebody
else at risk. Otherwise people complain, they protest, and not with words.
The complaints come in a different form.

You've got to play it straight. A person in this business has to be upright
and reliable, somebody others can count on, because if you let people
down, you're not going to make it. Around here you can't say you don't have
all the money or say they didn't bring you anything this time around. If

you disappoint people, then you're somebody who's letting the other guys down. . . . Like if you said, "Today" and then you come up with "Give me another chance . . . until tomorrow," well, maybe you'll give them another chance. But if things don't work out any better tomorrow, then you send in somebody to take care of things. And that's why stuff happens like it sometimes happens. In these dealings, you've got to be on time and you've got to deal straight.

5

An Indigenous Woman Street Vendor

Indigenous Migrants to Mexico's Northern Border

Northern Mexico—the ancestral home of the Tarahumara, Mayo, and Yaqui Indians—has experienced an increasingly visible presence of other indigenous peoples, such as the Mixtec, Zapotec, and Purépechas, from Mexican states as distant as Guerrero, Oaxaca, Tlaxcala, and Michoacán. Most of these indigenous migrants are agricultural day laborers, whose movements respond to the demand for labor in the vast agricultural corridor of northwestern Mexico and the southwestern United States. However, very early in the history of these flows, there began to appear another type of migrant—street vendors—who, in contrast to the day laborers, lived not in agricultural camps but rather in cities.

Beginning in the 1970s, the presence of indigenous migrants began to alter the urban image of the borderlands. By 2000, the indigenous population that had arrived from other Mexican states accounted for more than 95 percent of the total native population in Baja California and Coahuila and 78 percent in Tamaulipas. In the entire border region, indigenous migrants accounted for a little more than one-third of the overall native population. Baja California's indigenous population has swelled because of recent migrations, and it has now surpassed that of the northern states of Coahuila, Sinaloa, and Tamaulipas, which historically have had larger native populations.[1]

Most of these migrants live in urban municipalities along the border. An exception is Baja California's agricultural region in the central part of the state, an area

Illustration: Plaza Santa Cecilia, Tijuana. *(Photograph by Laura Velasco Ortiz.)*

where approximately 16 percent of the population speaks an indigenous language (COESPO-COLEF 2003b). The Mixtecs are the most numerous migrant group in the borderlands, numbering almost as many people as the Yaquis, a native ethnic group of Sonora; other groups that have settled in the region are the Purépechas, Mazahuas, Otomís, Mayas, Totonacs, and Triquis.

The various migrant ethnic groups have followed distinct routes in their journeys to the North. In the urban areas of Tijuana and Ensenada (Baja California) and Nogales (Sonora), Mixtecs are heavily represented and, to a lesser degree, Purépechas, Triquis, and Zapotecs. In contrast, in Ciudad Juárez, the Mazahuas are the most numerous group, and they are highly visible in street-vending commerce. In Matamoros, in the northern state of Tamaulipas, the Nahuas are the most numerous, alongside the Otomís, Mayas, and Totonacs. In Nuevo León since the 1990s, the census has recorded the presence of Mixtecs and Mazahuas. All these groups incorporate themselves into the commerce connected with border tourism and the informal economy, in addition to working as domestics. The labor participation of women particularly stands out in those activities (Clark 1988; Pérez 1990; INI 1993; Velasco 1995, 2000, 2010; Durin 2008).

According to Browning and Zenteno (1993), labor markets in northern border cities are characterized by the presence of modern industries, such as the manufacture of electronics, electrical appliances, and automobiles; the large number of women employed in industry, especially maquiladora export manufacturing; and broad segments of the population that are international commuters, people who work in one country and live in another. In the case of Tijuana, 14 percent of the economically active population (EAP) works in export maquiladoras, and of all border cities, Tijuana has the highest proportion of the EAP employed in commerce (21.5 percent). Similarly, it has the highest proportion of international commuters, since 8 percent of Tijuana's EAP work in the United States (Browning and Zenteno 1993; Alegría 1990). These data are indicative of a dynamic economy—one closely connected with Tijuana's circumstances as a border city—which has also driven the growth of an energetic and versatile sector of self-employed workers, also called "informal employees" (Contreras 2000). Tijuana was one of the first border cities that experienced the slow appropriation of its urban tourist center by the new indigenous businesses, primarily women vendors, who offered passersby all kinds of retail merchandise, from chewing gum to bracelets made of colored thread or glass-bead necklaces. With the passage of years, incipient street vending has transformed into a stable commercial practice, organized around consumption by tourists coming from the United States. Today the presence and participation of these indigenous merchants is inextricably woven into Tijuana's tourist scene.

Mixtec Women in Tijuana

Unlike the men of the same ethnicity, Mixtec women usually went directly to cities after leaving their rural hometowns, which was a generalized trend in Latin

American female migration during the 1970s (Velasco 1995). The experience that the Mixtec men had already had in the Bracero Program was the determining factor for the first women who migrated from central Mexico to the North.[2]

Of all of Mexico's northwestern cities, Tijuana was the first destination for Mixtec migrants, and it became a gateway for settlement in other border cities, such as Ensenada, Mexicali, and Nogales. The first Mixtec migrants still recall arriving in Tijuana in the 1970s, after sojourns in various places in northwestern Mexico's agricultural corridor. Some Mixtecs began migrating to Sinaloa, Sonora, and Baja California as early as the 1950s to work in export agriculture. There is evidence that growers in northern Mexico took advantage of the Bracero Program by attracting California-bound braceros to work for a while in fields in northern Mexico (Sánchez 1994, cited in Flores 2000, 50). The Mixtecs' relationship with agricultural areas on both sides of the border continues.

Tijuana urban settlement was characterized by its familial nature, in contrast to other places in the region, such as the San Quintín Valley, which were populated primarily by male, mostly single, agricultural workers, who only gradually brought their families to the North (Velasco 2000). Changes in U.S. migration policy during the 1980s facilitated family settlement in urban border areas. Particularly important was the 1986 Simpson-Rodino Law,[3] which made transborder mobility for workers with documents legal and enabled Mixtec family members, particularly wives and children, to settle on the Mexican side.

Arriving in the borderlands, these migrants organized their lives around the search for housing, work, and schools for their children, in that order of priority. The women made these needs the driving force for their daily activities. By the 1980s and 1990s, those needs had become the principal motive for their collective organizing. The presence of Mixtec women on the streets of Tijuana, as well as other border cities such as Nogales, Tecate, Ensenada, and Mexicali, goes back to the end of the 1970s.

Ofelia Santos was born in the Mixteca Baja (Mixtec lowlands) in Oaxaca. A native speaker of Mixtec, she learned Spanish as a second language during her adolescence. Through her story, we see the process that led to an indigenous presence on the downtown streets of Tijuana in the 1970s. As an indigenous leader, Santos has dedicated her life to the struggle over borderlands urban space, a place that is, above all, a source of livelihood for the Mixtec people. Santos is the founder of a street-vendor association representing those who work in Plaza Santa Cecilia, in the heart of the city's tourist district. Her words are testimony to the slow transformation of Avenida Revolución from the noisy, crowded, boisterous thoroughfare that formerly attracted thousands of tourists every weekend to the semideserted street that one sees today. In her story, this street plays a central role as a microcosm of the major changes in the borderlands, particularly the effects of U.S. anti-terrorism policies after September 11, 2001, and the violent war between Mexican drug cartels.

The daily struggles for urban space, the milling about of tourists, the monitoring by the police, and the candor of the people passing by all color the events in the lives *of these women and their families. In the course of the narrative about Ofelia's daily battle to continue as a street vendor, another struggle appears, one that turns on the household, the life of a married couple, and the relationships with her children. Her story comes primarily from an interview that took place in 1994; the final passages come from a later interview, done in 2005.*

To Be an Indigenous Resident on the Northern Border

I was born in 1942 in the town of San Francisco Higos, in the district of Silacayoapan in Oaxaca State. In the town, there were horses, burros, and many birds. I can hardly remember anymore. . . . I worked making hats from palm fibers or helping the townspeople who had a little bit more. They would give us two or three liters of corn or beans.[4] My mother was a widow; her husband had died. So we were very poor. That is how I grew up, until I met my husband—we only lived together—when we went off on our own.

I got married at fourteen, and a little later my husband went to the *otro lado* [other side], to the United States, while I stayed behind in my hometown. For several years, my husband came and went between the town and the United States, crossing the border with the *braceros*.[5] That is how we lived our lives. I was there in the town, and he was living in the otro lado, coming and going. During that time, our first two children, a girl and a boy, were born. I remember that in 1965, my husband returned from the other side, and for a time, he was farming the land in the town. Yes, that year, the Bracero Program ended, and in that same year, my third son was born, the tallest one. But things got hard in the town. We didn't have food, and we had to leave. . . . I was the first in my family to leave the town. Together with my husband, we left our native land because we wanted to give more to our children than what we had had. Now my brothers are here too, in the North, but I was able to help them, because I now knew how things were done.

The Battle for the Street

I first went to Tijuana during the Echeverría years[6] . . . in 1975. I arrived in a really bad state, with only my children and my husband. At that time, I had been working in Culiacán, Sinaloa, and before that I had been in Guamúchil and Hermosillo, working in the cotton harvest. A lot of people from San Francisco Higos worked in the fields. They had already been to Tijuana, and they said that there was a lot of work there. My father-in-law had also been in this city, and so he came to Culiacán, and he told us, "Go on up there. There's a lot of work!" So I got together a bit of money, and I grabbed my three kids, and I came to Tijuana. But when I arrived, things were very hard, because I didn't know anything, and no one knew me. . . . After arriving, I rented some rooms, and I went around begging, selling chewing gum. And I suffered a lot . . . but I got to thinking, "How am I going to manage when I have to pay the rent?"

I've worked all my life, always. In Sinaloa I worked in the fields, picking tomatoes. I also harvested squash and chilies, or we spun thread. I made money there selling oranges, watermelons, and other food to the workers. Later on, in Culiacán, when they would not give me work in the fields because of my children, I began selling food and candy.

Once I was living in Tijuana, I began thinking, "Why shouldn't I do the same thing I did in Culiacán?" So I bucked up and began selling . . . what else? My husband found work in a *yonque* [automobile junkyard]. I went to sell on the streets, taking the bunch of kids with me. But it was different. I got frightened because the police would pick you up. . . . They told us they didn't want us on Avenida Revolución. Since those days, the street has changed a lot. I remember when things were different, and I would sit in the center of the city and cry. And I asked myself, "Why did I come here? I should have stayed in my hometown!" . . . I felt desperate because the police would not let us sell.

Right now, he [Juvencio, her husband] is working in the otro lado . . . but he has also suffered a lot throughout his life, which is why I let him do as he pleases. He comes and goes every day. He leaves at four in the morning. Like many here in the Obrera,[7] the people share the cost of gasoline and give each other *raites* [rides]. Now he's got his papers. After a lot of paperwork, they came through. He works as a bricklayer; it's very heavy work. . . . Others, like Miguel, Juvencio's brother-in-law, work in the fields in the otro lado. He also got his papers in '86, under the Rodino Law, just like my husband did. Miguel works in a *nursería* [plant nursery]. He tells us that they pay him US$4.25 an hour, but he works ten hours a day, from 6 AM to 3 PM, and of course, they pay him for only eight hours, because until he collects one hundred extra hours in a month, they cannot pay him overtime. Miguel says it's a nursery where almost three hundred people work, all of them from Guerrero, Oaxaca, and Michoacán. It seems that this year [1994], the owners are taking on people without real documents; in other words, they can get you false papers. Workers go there and pay $100, and they give them a permit and a Social Security card, even with a photo! Right now, they are asking only that the newcomers be recommended by the people who are already working.

Organizing with Our Words

When did you begin organizing the other women?

During the years of Xico Leyva Mortera[8] . . . in 1977. We were isolated, abused by the inspectors and by the *fayuqueros* [people who bring U.S.

consumer goods into Mexico without paying duty], and even by the other vendors. They would say to us, "Hey, Indian woman, go back where you came from!" At that time, there was a leader in the neighborhood, Feliciano Guzmán. So we went to him, looking for a president, for support. He was first our adviser and later our president. He stood up for us. He understood, and he defended all the Mixtec women. That was the time when Víctor Clark arrived.[9] A lot of *licenciados* [lawyers] began to arrive, many people from the otro lado, gringos,[10] I think, since they were light skinned. That's all there was to it: The war was on, and the people defended the Mixtec women. Yes, Feliciano ended up leading more than three hundred Mixtecs, almost all women. There were many widows and mothers who did not have husbands.

I took advantage of this. I learned a lot of words in Spanish and that took away the fear, because then we were able to talk and defend ourselves. Before, if they jailed you and accused you of something, you could not say, "That's not true!" How? With what words?

That was the beginning. Then the professors arrived.[11] They got involved, but problems started—fighting and envy—and the group fell apart. That was when Licenciado Arón Juárez, with Filemón López, got involved. Finally, Feliciano turned the group over to Arón . . . and until now, they continue asking for union dues.

When Filemón came in, they invited me to meetings, but I didn't last long because I went to the CROC.[12] This is a union for everyone: workers, campesinos, street vendors. They take everybody. Yes, I remember that one day while I was chatting, a man arrived, and he said to me, "Listen, *mija*,[13] why don't you go over to the CROC so that you can fight for your permits, so they won't walk all over you." That was Elías Nilsen, a poor man who also helped us.

I was in the CROC for eight years. The first year, I talked with Federico Valdez,[14] the municipal president, and he told me, "Look, mija, come tomorrow, and we will talk there at the Municipal Palace. I'm going to help you in good faith and with good words." So I went, accompanied by Elías Nilsen, who is a good person but the CROC doesn't know how to make use of him. I needed help because I didn't have much confidence going alone, and I was just learning how to handle the struggle. At the palace, Federico told me, "Mija, we're going to give you permits, and we're going to continue working together." At that moment, I understood what the permits were. Because the truth was, I had not understood what these permits were all about. I had been thinking that one went to the street to sell and that was all, that nobody would have a reason to bother you, steal from you, or abuse you. Well, I said to myself, this is the deal: The government has to give me a permit, on a piece of paper, and with that, everything is taken care of.

Finally, with my own eyes and my own work, I knew that on all sides, it was the same thing, nothing but fights. I wasn't finding opportunities for anything anymore. . . . Then I understood that it is better to work personally, with our own words, and with our own friends who will not trick us. Then I spoke up, and I said, "You know, don Elías, I can't be here working with all of you much longer. I'm going to leave. I want to work by myself. I no longer get along with you because you look for fights with the government. You want to be the opposition, and I don't like being in opposition to the government. Twice they jailed me; twice I was fighting on Revolución. And did you come to get me out? My people got me out, my friends." And that's because that's the way it was. I'm not making it up. We would go into the street, and because we didn't understand, because we were closed, ignorant, well, we went out there to fight with—who else?—. . . with the *carabineros*,[15] other street vendors! They were scolding us because they had their permits, but we did not. And well, how were we supposed to know? Then we got into a brawl; one man hit me, and so I hit him right back. And there we were, going at it in *chingadazos* [big blows] on Avenida Revolución. We really fell to it. We grabbed each other, and then we were in the revolution for sure! Of course, they were men who knew more than we women did, since they didn't get arrested. They knew how to defend themselves. So we had to learn to let our fists do the talking, in order to defend our livelihood.

Now they have permits, and I also have a permit. We women also have permits. So I learned how to deal with the permits. Then I left the CROC, because they were on the take, just for themselves. Those who understand more, the *chingones* [big shots] of the CTM,[16] all those people get permits, land—and all of it for themselves! On the other hand, those who are behind them [their supporters]—who guides them? The leaders don't say anything. The [federal] government is not to blame. It's always trying to help. In Baja California, they are just puppets who are installed here. Those are the ones who don't guide the people.

> *How did you women organize in order to remain on the street, independent of the unions?*

This was how: One day it popped into my head, just like a little bee. Little by little, it got into my head, and like the seeds of a little tree, it began to take root and to grow, and as far as it has come as of today, it still hasn't withered. When I left the CROC, I said to my *compañeras* [women co-workers], whoever wants to come with me, fine; those who don't, let them stay behind; that's not a problem. I went with some three or four women. But the rest cried for me. Of course! I got some 350 permits. The first year, they cost 12,000 old pesos;[17] the second, 27,000; and after that, they rose to 32,000; and now we are paying 300,000 for each permit.[18] They continued asking for my help. . . . Then I suffered a lot, because I didn't know very clearly what to do, and I thought it might be better if I told them to go see Elías or Filemón. But no, they continued asking my opinion. And what was I going to do? I didn't need them, but they needed me. And I had to be responsive.

Then I began to talk with the government whose administration was ending and with the one that was coming in. We reached an arrangement: "Look, mija, I'm going to give you the permits, but you're going to have to organize them— each woman on a corner, selling a little of each thing, and no one standing right on Avenida Revolución. They have to be clean, and no children can come along, because we do not want the streets to be dirty or else the gringos will stop coming." And they took all the women off Avenida Revolución, those of Filemón and those of the CROC. "Go on and get out of here!"

Plaza Santa Cecilia: A New Place to Work

How did you manage to get set up in Plaza Santa Cecilia?

That was how we were, until those *panistas* arrived.[19] They called on me, and we talked: "You know, mija, you're going to go to Plaza Santa Cecilia, and you're going to simmer down." It went on like that for years, offering us the plaza. But we, being so stupid, didn't want to take it, because the people wanted to be only on Avenida Revolución. That's because they thought that the tourists wouldn't come to the plaza.

And you've got to understand, when we went to see the plaza, it was a mess, full of trash, drunks lying around, withered plants. . . . Well, who was going to go *there* to shop? Then we formed the Carlos Salinas de Gortari Association of Street Vendors. We named it that so that the president of Mexico at that time would help us. I started as the president, with ninety women. Most of them were Mixtecs, but there were a few Mazahuas and mestizas. I got to thinking, why shouldn't we improve that plaza? And with a lot of hard work, we managed to do just that. We washed the pavement. We sent out to get the fountain fixed—that cost 2 million old pesos. Each one of us chipped in, and I gave each woman her receipt. We planted plants. Even the restaurant owners—who at first didn't want us there—later defended us when the issue of the permits came up again. Because, as it is each year, each year is a problem. We are never safe. Each government makes a different promise. Of course, they're not going to be able to throw us out, but one has to be talking and *conviviendo* (coexisting) with the government.

We took over the plaza three years ago, and now everything is different. Every day, early in the morning, we wash it down and water the flowers. Now the gringos come to shop, but we achieved it with our own efforts. I told the women, "Look, you're not going to beg. You're going to leave your children in the daycare, and be sure you're clean when you come here." But it took a lot of work because the women didn't want to leave their children behind. And here they would come, with the kids in tow. They were leaving the youngest ones behind, but the ones that were a little older, they brought them along—they still bring them. . . . I understand. It's hard to leave them; one wants to be able to see them because in the neighborhood, what are they doing? They get together with the *cholos* [bad kids], and they start to get into trouble. It's better here, where they can learn to sell.

Right now, I have a lot of responsibility, both for my own work as well as for that of my *compañeras*. . . . How am I going to leave them, knowing what I suffered? What they are going to suffer? For that reason, I talk with them, and they take care of me. They ask my advice: "Look, my husband hits me," and I go and I talk with him. I tell him, "No, look, you're not going to behave like that around her, because she is your wife and you have children." Then he listens. But if he doesn't listen, I call the law, because that's why we have governments, and the government also has to understand that. The women, they are like little girls, waiting, because they don't know. . . . Sometimes they go to Filemón, then with Elías. So we're like little animals. When they throw a handful of rice, the women hop about here or they hop about there, like little doves. When the others do a bad turn to the women, then they come back to me. I saw that happen with the plaza. They went with Filemón and with Elías, because the women thought that the government [i.e., government officials] was not going to throw them off Avenida Revolución, and when they saw the plaza, they thought that it would be difficult to sell anything there. But the government did throw them out. And then they came to me, asking that I make a little space for them, and what was I supposed to do? They are my *raza* [race, people]. I told them, "No fights with the government. I'm going to introduce you to the government, and let's see what they're going to do with you. We are citizens of Baja California, and we want to work with the government, and we want it to guide us. We no longer want somebody else to guide us. We want to speak for ourselves [without any union or party representative as an intermediary] in order to know what the government says."

In 1992, Solidaridad[20] gave us 60 million pesos to buy some little carts. I went to talk to the municipal government, and I told them, "Look, we women want to have some tables, something pretty, so that they won't see us sitting there on the ground. Because when you're selling on the ground, when it's windy out, you're eating dirt." Then the government said, "Okay, we'll give you some money, and you put in half, and we'll put in the other half." And that's how we did it. We knew a man who had already made some carts for other street vendors here in downtown. They were very pretty, made out of wood. Well, we asked him if instead of tables, he would make us some carts. We ordered forty little carts, but he delivered only twenty. And that *cabrón* [son of a bitch] ran off with the rest of the money. "Yes, yes, I'm going to make them. Come back tomorrow. Come back day after tomorrow." And nothing, and one day, he just disappeared.

Now I'm talking with the municipal government's lawyer, and well, what are we going to do? We already gave him all the checks, and now we can't find him. It's that we're women. Look at the juice vendor. The cart maker tried to do the same thing to him, but the vendor went and told him that he'd screw him good if he didn't deliver the cart. And there he is, selling juices from his little cart. But us, we cannot even speak Spanish well. So the cart maker comes up with, "Look, mija, I'm really down on my luck!" They stole his tools. . . . What are we going to do? . . . He already screwed us over by taking our money. And now I have to answer to my *compañeras*. They paid their money and look where the carts are! That's why I went to the government, to ask them for guidance. . . .

A Day on the Street

Would you tell us what your day is like selling on the street?

Our day begins at five in the morning, when my husband goes to the otro lado. Next I wash the clothes, because I still have four little children: one twelve, one nine, one eight, and the youngest, six. I still have to dress and feed them. When my daughters were here, they would help me with the household chores. But now they're married, and the only one who is still single went to the otro lado to work. So when the sun is barely up, the clothes and food are ready.

Life on the street is very hard. Every day one has to get the carts out of their parking place and unload the merchandise. For that, I send my son and my daughter-in-law first, so that they can drag the two carts from the Partido Revolucionario Institucional (PRI [Institutional Revolutionary Party]) parking place to the plaza. You wouldn't believe how much they weigh! Before, we were paying the *locatarios* [business store owners around the perimeter of the plaza] as much as $10 a week for each cart that they were guarding. But that just doesn't work out. There are days that I don't sell anything, and it's not good business. That's why I went to talk to the people at the PRI, and I told them about our problem. They told me, "All right, mija, we're going to help you! Bring your carts here, store them at night, and take them back out not any later than eight or nine in the morning, before the party militants arrive." Yes, they are good people, but one has to talk to them, to make them understand. And of course, one sometimes has to give them something, any little thing, some food or a gift, because we have to show our gratitude. That's what I tell my people!

So by nine or ten in the morning, we are like little ants running around the plaza. Everybody is sweeping and washing, because we have to take care of it, so that it will be pretty. We have to see to it that the fountain is clean and that the plants don't wither. For that, we organize, and we chip in each week to buy some soap. The water has always been a problem. For a while, we asked the business owners, but now they don't want to give it to us. They are *chingones* [abusive people or people who take advantage of others]. They complain that we are dirty Indians. But as I told doña Elodia at the municipality, "You ought to go to Oaxaca. There the streets are clean! I suppose you want us all to come and pick up the trash that the municipality ought to be cleaning up!" I go every third day to the municipality, so that they will send us a *pipa* [water truck]. And they do give it to us, even if they are *panistas* [PAN party members], because they also help when we make them understand. That's why I tell them, "Look, mijo, you are the government, I am the people. You help; then I help. And that's how we go raising ourselves up, and so we go. You leave us alone about the votes, and we will work hard. That's also what I say to the PRI."

The days for selling are Friday, Saturday, and Sunday. The streets are filled with gringos all the way from the *línea* [the international border] to Revolución. They're good; they treat us well. Only they want to buy everything very cheaply. I say to them [*speaking English*], "What do you want, lady?" and she says, "This." I tell her $20, but she says $10. Well, it just can't be done. Sometimes I forget the numbers in English. Then I tell the person, well, whatever I can remember. There are some days that I sell everything cheaply and others when the only thing that comes out is [*again in English*] "forty" or "seventy." We need to know English. That's why I want my children to learn to speak it. Here each person has her own system for selling. I don't raise the price on the goods much, so that when they barter, it isn't lowered much either. Because the gringos also barter! Oh, you bet! They are really *cabrones* [smart alecks]! But Gloria, for example, she doubles the price of everything, and so when they ask for a discount, she doesn't feel like she's losing so much. Here there are a lot of *pochos*[21] who speak only English. They really like things from the South, the silver and the masks. How those things catch their eye!

Our little carts and tables are like confetti—so colorful. We sell things from many places. We have little old men made of papier-mâché, onyx birds, clay masks, little plaster crosses, and dolphins, fish, ducks, and eagles all made of Sonoran ironwood. We have a lot of *alpacca* [nickel silver], earrings, bracelets, chains, necklaces, and silver from Taxco, palm baskets, little woven things, coin purses, and knapsacks from Guatemala.

We buy from many people who come here almost daily, toting their cases containing jewelry or little pigs or leather wallets. They come from many places, from here in Tijuana, and from Michoacán, Guerrero, Chiapas, and even Guatemala. They almost always give us credit, and we pay them back weekly. That's how it's done. Sometimes the sales don't happen, and then we tell them, "Well, there's no money. Come back next week." Well, they come back, the poor little things. What else can they do? It seems that now there's war there in the South, because those people from Chiapas returned home very quickly. They say that they have to go to be with their families, because the army is crawling all over the towns.[22] Yes, the fight is everywhere. We're all *jodidos* [screwed]— some of us are here with the gringos, others are there with the army. Poor little things. Well, what can they do? Imagine walking everywhere trying to sell your little things.

Some days, the tourists come only to look. They pick up one thing; they pick up something else; then they don't buy anything. They only walk around looking. What we earn here, we spend each day on food or the children's clothes or school supplies. There is nothing left for anything else. But it's okay, because when there is more money, whether it's because my husband is earning or my sons send me something, I save it in order to buy livestock or to do something for the house.

Have things changed in Plaza Santa Cecilia?

Yes, they've changed a lot. When we came to Tijuana, we had a really hard time. Now [June 2005] we're doing pretty well, even though the people who come here are creating havoc by stealing or using drugs. We had a rough time when we arrived in Tijuana, but we're people who stand up for themselves and we'll talk to those in the government. Now we're seeing how Tijuana has grown and how Avenida Revolución and Plaza Santa Cecilia are mostly empty of people.

Things are different, because when we came here they'd haul us off to jail for selling stuff on the street. It's different now. A while ago I went to the licensing office and they told me, "If there are more people from where you came from, tell them to come over here." They want more vendors, more activity on Avenida Revolución, more vitality, because there aren't any tourists. . . . The street is dead.

To Be a Mother and Wife for All

Tell us how you manage things with your home, your children, and your husband. What do they think of your work?

I never leave my children alone. They could get burned or something could happen to them. They always were here with me even when they were small. I would put them in a little box, just as if they were puppies or kittens. That's how I had them. I now have ten. Seven were born here in Tijuana, and I also took them to work with me. They were here with me selling all over the place, and when they jailed me, they jailed the kids. . . . It was very hard. When the government told us that they didn't want children on the street, [I said,] "Look! What are we going to do?" We told them, "How can we leave them alone at home?" That's when Carlos Salinas came here to the Obrera. I talked with him, and I told him about the problem: "We want a nursery for our children so we don't have to be on the street with them." And that was how the Indigenous Nursery was built. When my children were small, that's where I left them. But now the mestizas have taken over the nursery, and the Mixtec street vendors have no place to leave their children. This has to be fixed because that's why we asked for it—so that we wouldn't have to be

on the street with our children. Many of us now have our children attend
a school near the plaza, so that when the school day ends, the children can
come here to the vendor stalls. Here we can see that they eat and do their
school work.

Oh my, the house is another battle! My husband sometimes scolds me:
"Mija, you're always walking everywhere; you're always talking! Leave it be
already!" But all he does is work all the time, with his pickax and his shovel,
in the fields on the otro lado, in the United States. But with politics and with
the words themselves that I have learned, I understand and I'm calm. I tell
him, "Look, cool down, mijo." It's not that I run around everywhere without
reason. I'm in a struggle because I want to *comprender*[23] more, and I want to
give more to our children. I tell him, "You have to understand and calm down,
mijo. Let's stop arguing."

And, of course, he's right! There are problems in our life, in our marriage.
Sometimes the wife isn't home, and the husband wants to be waited on. He
wants her to give him his things so he can change when he gets home . . .
but he has to understand that I am *comprendiendo* [learning] more, not
the life of everyone else, but rather *comprendiendo* the life of our children.
Sometimes he gets jealous, and I tell him, "Stop being jealous because we're
old people. When one is young, that's when one can be demanding. Nothing
of 'you want to go your way, and I'll go mine!' No, old man, stop thinking
these things. Right now, it's a matter of trying to get ahead." And he'll come
out with, "No, I want to get married [to someone else]," and I tell him, "Well,
go ahead and get married!" That's the idea that we Mexicans have: "Go on;
get married. What can I do about it?" . . . Thank goodness that I'm now able
to earn money. I have my friends, and if I don't have money, I go here or I go
there with them. I tell him, I have one, two, three ideas: "I no longer want to
live as I did before, when we were all so poor. Now I get dressed up, so you
have to give me money." He turns over his entire check to me, and that's how
we are getting ahead. As I tell him, "Don't think that if you get married, you
can forget your children. No, they're still yours! So, don't begin with that stuff
about you knowing how to defend yourself! You better shut up, mijo!"

He has always treated me well; he's always been at my side. Sometimes,
when there were problems, he'd knock me around some, but all men are like
that. Some men even forget about their wives. Thanks be to God that I was
never needing anything. Everything that he earned, he gave to me, and that's
how we got ahead. Just like I'm telling you, my work, it's no longer for us now,
it's for our children. Someday we're going to die, and what's going to be left
behind? Well, the children! You don't take anything with you, and you don't
eat in the hole [the grave]. I tell him, "We're working for the children, and the
children are working for their children, and that's how things are supposed to
be!" . . . And so he gets to thinking, "Ah, mija, that's how you are! You talk too
much, and you never get sick!"

My children are now grown. All of them want to bring me this or that.

They are always giving me things. But it's not right that I take from my children if they are trying to make their own lives. They need those things for their own children, for their wives, don't you think?

To the contrary, I think about helping them even more, because there are mothers who feel very emotional about their children, and there are mothers who don't.[24] I get very emotional about them. Yesterday I was talking with my son: "Look, mijo, if I see that any of you are misbehaving, I have to speak up, because I'm your mother. I never abandoned any of you. I kept you here in my house, and now there's no need for you to be here and there, abandoning your own children." They understand, because they say to me, "*Mamacita,* look how you love us, how you've brought us up. . . ." And they begin to understand. I had ten children. The older ones are now on their own, with their wives. Four of them are on the otro lado. Two married couples live here, and four are still my responsibility. These are the ones that still need to be raised. I tell the older ones, you've already come out ahead; now I want to help the little ones. That's why I have to work. I'm not waiting for either my children or my husband to give me money. To the contrary, I ought to give it to them.

My concern really is education because I didn't have any schooling. . . . All it is, then, is just thinking. I don't know how to write or read, but I have come to understand my own life through my thinking. But my children don't want to study. . . . So far, they've all left school after completing the sixth grade. All my life, I was in charge of educating my *señor* [husband]. We've already formed a family, a home. So now I continue with the life of my children because I, who am a *mujer cerrada, cerrada* [a closed-minded or ignorant woman], my sons go here and go there. They leave their wives, and they leave their children penniless. I start to think, "How can I manage this situation?" But I have people, friends, who talk with me, and they tell me, "Look, Ofelia, this is how it is." Then I understand.

There have been problems, while I was going daily to sell on the street, while I was struggling with work, at home, things were lacking. I didn't notice what was happening with my children. It's sad, because afterward, when I found these problems, I said to myself, "And now who's going to fix it? Who's going to stop them? Who's going to get involved here? . . . The neighbors? No, all they do is watch. . . . They could even cause more problems, but they're not going to calm things down." . . . "No," I told myself, "the person who's going to fix this has to come from your own home." And well, who else? My husband gets up at five in the morning, and he goes to work on the otro lado, and he doesn't come home until seven at night. What's to be done? It was a burden, it hurt me a lot, and I had only my God and my politics. That was all I had to set the life of my children straight.

I spoke with all my children, and I had to calm them down, put some order in my household. I told them, "You want rules. Well, here are your parents' rules, and if you don't like it, get out and forget about your father;

forget about your mother! I no longer want anything. I don't care if you are my daughters-in-law or my sons." Here all my daughters-in-law are mestizas; they are not Mixtecs. But I don't treat them badly. I have my daughters, and if they want to eat, they can eat; if they want to sleep, they can sleep. The only thing that I don't want is for them to be running around. Because that was the problem: the street. My children were in the street! And I told them, "So why shouldn't your wife go out, if you are out running around? Your wives also get together with their girlfriends, but if you behave properly, your woman is going to behave properly." At one point, my girl wanted to get divorced, and I told her, "No, mija, look, don't, because I didn't divorce your father." I married my husband at twenty-five years of age because we hadn't gotten married before. We were just living together. Then I began making my life, and now they have to make their lives.

I strongly believe in the law: It's what we've got; it's what I had in my own house. "If you don't believe in your father and you don't believe in your mother, then [at least understand that] I've got the law on my side. I can apply it, but I am your mother. So, first, I am going to call your attention to this, both the women as well as the men. If the woman wants to marry, then get married and live together. I no longer want people living in my house, so go get your own house. And now the man who got married, he has his house, and he has to live with his wife. He has to leave his friends and start working to support his children."

Don't get the wrong idea; sometimes I am sorry when I think about the children, about my husband, about my house. I don't know. There are a lot of things that one has to be responsible for . . . so many things. Sometimes I start to think, "Why did I get involved in politics?" But, as I told my *viejo* [old man], "Well, I got involved, and now what?" Yes, sometimes I tell him, "Leave me be, mijo. Let's make our own lives," because it is very difficult.

The pain that a woman feels is greater than what a man feels; that's what I think, because we women have more responsibilities. We are more responsible in work and concerning the children. Everything, everything falls to the woman, that's what I think.

Did you teach your children to speak Mixtec?

No, the older ones learned a little . . . but no, I did not teach them. . . . Why use our words? What do we get from doing that? Nothing, I think—only that everybody will call us Indians, that we're from Oaxaca, or from who knows where. I don't want them to talk like that to my children, and for that reason, I don't want my sons and daughters to speak our language. I don't want them to feel the pain that I felt.

All my children live on the otro lado now [June 2005]. What am I going to do? I tell them, when you want to come to see me—here in Tijuana—well, go ahead, come visit me. And if they don't want to come, well, let them stay on the otro lado. As one of my sons said, "Thanks to my mother, thanks to my father, I grew up in Tijuana; then we came here, and we grew up on this side of the border. Here is where we are going to stay, because, thanks to my parents, we're no longer in Oaxaca, we're no longer in Tijuana."[25]

El Otro Lado: The Other Side of the Border

Your husband has documents to work in the United States. What is the situation for you and your children? Do you also have documents?

Look, my husband arranged papers for all of us, for his children and for me. He's worn out. He's been working [in California] for the same boss for many years. It's been hard, since he's always had trouble at work. I tell him, "Defend yourself, mijo." But since he doesn't speak any English . . . well, he can't defend himself. But sometimes I tell him, "It doesn't matter, mijo, we can look for a lawyer to defend you even though it may cost us the little bit of money that we have, because those bosses should not be allowed to do whatever they want." At work, they treat the workers badly. They shout at them. That boss shouts at them, saying whatever he wants. I tell my husband, "They're not going to shout at me, because I really like running my business. Why should they shout at me if I work willingly, with my money? If I make money, fine; if I don't, well, I don't make any money, and so be it. This is my work, even if perhaps I earn only a little. It's still my earnings." That's why I tell him, "Look, *viejo,* think about how they're going to treat you, however they want! How they're going to be shouting at you. It doesn't matter whether or not they pay you, but keep a cool head." . . . Yes, it's really hard to have to go to the otro lado with those damned gringos. But what's one to do? That's the struggle of our race—some of us here in Tijuana, and others on the otro lado.

How has your life changed during these thirty years?

I'm no longer a leader anymore [June 2005]. Now I'm a coordinator. I like being a coordinator, coordinating the people from my work, with their own work. I no longer support myself from the people; I support myself with my own work. Because a leader is a person who earns their money from the people. I mean, they pay them so the leaders will run around doing everything. . . . It's work because it's very difficult to be going here and there. . . .

I also have my documents, just like my children, but I didn't like going to the otro lado very much. The regulatory inspector [in Plaza Santa Cecilia] asks me why I don't go to the otro lado given that I've got papers. And I tell him, "Don't go around giving me advice about what I ought to do because you came from Spain"—because this regulations boy came from Spain, or who knows where—"I don't ask you where you came from or where you're going. You are doing your service for the community, you come here to provide us a service, and I don't ask you where you came from. So don't go around telling me what to do, because if I want, I'll go to the otro lado. But I don't want to, because I am Mexican." I have a passport, but, no, I don't like it there.

6

A Caregiver Commuter

The Commuter Dynamic on the Tijuana–San Diego Border

Daily life on the border between Mexico and the United States is linked to the dynamic of the international border gates that connect paired cities on opposite sides of the border. Tijuana has more drivers and pedestrians passing through its two border ports than any other city on the U.S.-Mexican border.[1] Every morning the principal media outlets in Tijuana and other urban centers on the border report border-crossing wait times. On July 28, 2008, a radio announcement at eight o'clock in the morning reported the following situation at the San Ysidro border gate: 250 cars in left-hand lanes, 350 in right-hand lanes, and 700 pedestrians waiting to cross. There was a similar crush of people waiting at the Otay gate, on Tijuana's eastern edge. The relevance of these reports for residents of Tijuana becomes clear when considered against the backdrop of the intense interactions that reach across this border. Border-area residents have many reasons for crossing the border: family ties, school, tourism, shopping, and work.

The shape of the interactions that take place between border residents in their daily lives is defined by the asymmetry that characterizes overall relations between Mexico and the United States. The particular interaction that seems most clearly to embody this unequal relationship is cross-border employment. This transborder linkage is personified by cross-border commuters, individuals who reside in Mexico and cross the border on a regular schedule to work in the United States. As Tito Alegría notes (2002, 39), cross-border commuters are an expression of the

Illustration: San Ysidro Port of Entry, Tijuana. *(Photograph by Alfonso Caraveo Castro.)*

relationship between two adjacent labor markets, each with its own conditions of labor, productivity, relative prices, and labor laws. The key factor that explains the existence and behavior of this group of workers is the wage differential between the two countries.[2] Following this logic, the presence of a cohort of cross-border workers derives from the way in which labor markets are defined on both sides of the border within the context of national politics and economics.

In Tijuana, this segment of the labor force has increased in absolute numbers, though throughout the 1990s it remained constant as a share of the city's workforce. From 1988 to 2000, cross-border commuters accounted for 8.6 percent of Tijuana's workers, higher than the corresponding percentages in Ciudad Juárez and Matamoros (Coubés 2003, 53). This proportion takes on more significance, however, when we consider the contribution of cross-border workers to the Tijuana economy, which is estimated at 20 percent of the combined income of the city's economically active population (Alegría 2002).

Living on one side of the border and working on the other generates consequences in the daily lives of cross-border commuters—both because of their access to differential resources on either side of the border and because of the challenge implied in crossing the border on a daily basis within the context of current border control policies. The conditions that govern their movement shape their lives and are a source of worry to these workers and their families. Most border crossers enter the United States legally, yet only about half of cross-border commuters have documents permitting them to work in the United States (Alegría 2002, 42). Not all Tijuana commuters work in San Diego; some have an employment circuit that stretches to encompass Los Angeles and Orange counties (Anguiano 2005, 128).

The events of September 11, 2001, altered the temporal aspect of transborder commuting, especially for those entering the United States on tourist visas. Because of closer inspection of immigration documents and longer wait times at the border, these workers tend to remain in California for longer periods than before. According to Anguiano (2005, 127), after 2001 the number of SENTRI passes[3] allocated to regular crossers was increased, along with the number of SENTRI lanes open to pass holders. Additionally, there was discussion about extending the SENTRI program to pedestrian crossers. In their interviews with cross-border commuters, Luis Escala Rabadán and Germán Vega Briones (2005) found that these workers often make carpooling arrangements for getting to and from work to minimize their travel costs.[4]

The structural conditions that frame the existence of cross-border workers are shared along the full span of the border. Yet the impacts are not uniform among all border cities or across all border-area residents. In Tijuana, the overwhelming majority of cross-border commuters are men (Alegría 2002; Escala Rabadán and Vega Briones 2005), in contrast to the pattern found in cities on the eastern portion of the border (Coubés 2003).

The data collected by Escala Rabadán and Vega Briones (2005, 155–161) allow us to draw a profile of a cross-border commuter. These workers hold low-skill jobs in construction, retail, personal services, gardening, domestic service, and janito-

rial services. Men are more likely to be found in construction jobs, while women are concentrated in retail or personal services, often working as housecleaners, nannies, and caregivers to the ill and elderly. Further, often they are in the United States on tourist visas. Most cross-border commuters are natives of Baja California or U.S.-born individuals now residing in Mexico. The women, especially, tend to have relatively higher education levels than is typical of workers employed south of the border. Finally, these workers share the perception that speaking English and being born in the United States guarantee a bright future, a future that is not possible on the Mexican side of the border. Cross-border commuters thus inhabit a transborder social universe, even though they owe their existence to two distinct national labor markets[5] and to national allegiances that are nuanced by the perceived contrast between employment and consumption opportunities on the U.S. side of the border and flexibility and freedom on the Mexican side.[6]

Crossing the Line Every Day

It's five o'clock in the morning. The sun is just rising, turning the sky to marine blue. The line of cars at the international border snakes all the way back to Second Street in downtown Tijuana. Drivers jockey for a place in the fastest line. "Get in the left lane! It's the fastest!" This is the advice offered by all the commuters who cross the frontier every day on the way to their jobs in the United States.

A second queue has formed at the same time, as a multitude of people press forward to reach the pedestrian line, which extends down the sidewalk for nearly a kilometer. Sleepy faces search for the man who sells coffee from a large thermos on his back. Border wait times vary depending on the time of day and the humor of the immigration agents. "If you get a Mexican American agent, you're screwed because he'll do a more thorough inspection," some people say. Street vendors offer to exchange dollars at a good rate, some sell places in the line at $5.00 each, and others hawk breakfast sandwiches. Finally the turnstile comes in view, flanked by two immigration agents, who check documents and give a careful visual once-over to each crosser. The United States is just beyond the fence. Everyone in the line watches the movements of the crossers and the inspectors with impatience.

The line is shorter this early on a weekend morning. The avalanche of shoppers heading across the border won't start until later.

As afternoon fades to evening, a long string of cars brings the workers back home, but this border crossing is quick. No one asks for documents when you enter Mexico. We find Eloísa at the taxi stand on the Mexican side, back from her day of work in the United States. She has gotten off the bus and passed through the turnstile with a firm step. She smiles at us from a distance. Her dark eyes are enormous, and they shine with the luster of a warrior triumphant in battle. Behind us dozens of stands selling tacos and tourist souvenirs flank the corridor that leads to Avenida Revolución.

We head to a quiet place to talk. Eloísa is used to the tape recorder, and today she is impatient to begin our interview. Her hair is tied loosely behind her and falls softly down her back; strands sometimes break free at her nape. At her waist her claret-colored blouse meets light-colored jeans. A simple outfit complete with flats to rush between her lives as a student, as a research assistant on scholarship in Tijuana, and as a caregiver in California. Eloísa looks us in the eye and begins her story.

The Souvenir Shops of Rosarito and the Founding of a Family

My name is Eloísa. I'm twenty-six years old, and I was born in Anaheim, California. My father came from Mexico City, and my mother is a native of Rosarito, Baja California.

My father came to Rosarito when he was sixteen. He came with his entire family, looking for a place at sea level where my grandfather could recuperate from an embolism. They chose Rosarito because my grandmother lived there.

According to the family history, my great-grandfather worked on the railroad and died in an accident. My great-grandmother came for his body and decided to stay in Rosarito. A bit later she met a man named Croswhite, Alejandro Croswhite, I think it was. They married and settled in Rosarito. That marked the beginning of the second part of the family, because my great-grandmother already had several children.

My mother was born in Rosarito. Her parents are from Guadalajara; I don't know why they came to Rosarito. My grandparents bought a ranch, and like many others in Rosarito, they opened a shop selling novelty items to tourists.

My father's family also had a souvenir shop, and my father worked there. But then the business began to decline, and he went to the other side. At the time, my parents were sweethearts, and my dad would come back to Rosarito to visit my mother. But a time came when my father told my mother, "You know, I can't keep doing this; either you marry me or we're finished." So they got married and went to live in Anaheim, California. My sister was born a year later, and I was born sixteen months after that, in 1981. Then the elevator company my father worked for went bankrupt, so my father decided to return to Rosarito, to the souvenir business, with help from the family. My dad opened a new store, patterned on the family business, and it lasted for about twelve years, until 1995.[7] That's when my other two sisters were born, Mariela in 1984 and the littlest one in 1985.

Growing Up in the Care of a Father and Grandmothers

A year after my youngest sister was born, my parents divorced. I was about five or six years old. We stayed with my father, and my maternal grandmother took care of us. My father kept working in the souvenir shop, so my paternal grandmother would take care of us during the school year, and in summer we'd go to my maternal grandmother's ranch.

What were your first years in school like?

Some of my uncles on my mother's side went to live in the United States when they were very young. I remember that when I was kindergarten age, I visited my cousin for two or three weeks, and they sent me to school with her in the United States. That's when we started to speak English, because many of our cousins didn't speak Spanish or they spoke a kind of "Spanglish." So they started speaking Spanish, and we started speaking English. And then we got more practice in the souvenir shop. From first to third grade I was at a Catholic school and everything was wonderful. But when my third sister started school, my dad couldn't afford private school any longer, so he transferred us to a public school. I liked the public school even better because the nuns at the private school were really strict. I think my public school years were the best, but I got hepatitis and they took me out of school for three or four months. When I went back, my eyebrows were almost gone and my hair was falling out. The doctor attributed it to nerves.

How did you do in junior high?

Junior high was a radical change. I was twelve years old. What I remember are the skirts, because in elementary school my grandmother, who was very Catholic, sewed our skirts for us and made them long, below the knee. In junior high, my grandma stopped making our uniforms. I remember that she sent us to a seamstress who'd make our skirts super short! Furthermore, they shifted me to the afternoon school schedule, and it was hard to adapt. The students were pretty aggressive. I remember walking down the halls and hearing, "Hey, do you want to fight her?" All I could answer was, "But I don't even know her." Those girls thought they were in control of everybody. They said they belonged to HEM [Hecho in México (Made in Mexico), a Tijuana gang]. They'd tag the walls, and they had cholo boyfriends. Well, I told myself that I had to do something, so I started hanging out with girls who claimed to be cholas too. That way, if somebody hassled me, I could rush to them for help. I became more aggressive, because the day came when I had to defend myself. I spent a year in the afternoon shift at school, and then they switched me to the morning shift the next year, and things returned to a normal, calm routine.

When I finished junior high, around 1997, I entered COBACH[8] high school in Rosarito. It was a whirl of parties and boyfriends. But I never had as many boyfriends as my older sister. She was always crying and moping, and I said, "I'd rather not ever have a boyfriend than be so unhappy." I did have lots of friends, though. I went to more parties than any of my sisters, but I didn't have a lot of boyfriends. My dad was always very lenient with us. He'd tell us, "Don't ask me for permission. Just tell me where you're going to be or if you won't be coming home to sleep; that's okay. But call me and tell me where you'll be. But you'd better be where you say you'll be. I'm not going to check up on you, but if I can't sleep some night and I decide to look for you, you'd better be there." My dad always gave us tons of freedom. I spent my days between school, the beach, and my house. I didn't go to the ranch after junior high; it had lost its attraction. We had surfer friends. We'd get up early, and while they surfed we'd gather seashells and then paint them and decorate them.

I was in the clouds all through high school, because people in Rosarito tend to be very sheltered. I see many of my friends who never left Rosarito, and they're stuck in a time warp, in the same life we had during high school. I think my life changed when I moved to Tijuana.

How did you get along with your sisters?

It's funny, really, because in school we were like two people who hardly knew each other. The moment we went through the school door, it was as if we didn't know each other, but outside school I always followed my older sister around even though she would push me aside. She'd say, "No, you're still too little." My relationship with her was pretty good. The one I didn't get along with was my littlest sister. They couldn't even leave us alone together, because we wanted to kill each other. We were always fighting. I was always short-tempered, and she drove me crazy. Now that we're adults, we get along fine.

The Dynamic of Souvenir Shops and Family Life

What I most remember about Rosarito is the two-lane highway, one lane going one direction and one the other. The streets weren't paved. There were souvenir shops for tourists everywhere, plus taco shops and drugstores. Then there's a time when my memory is blank, and the next thing I recall is the main boulevard in Rosarito when it was under construction, and there were deep ditches there. My grandparents' shop was on the main avenue, so we played a lot in those ditches.

I remember the gringos too. That was always our clientele. The whole market for souvenir trinkets revolved around tourists from abroad. Lots of people came from the interior of Mexico, but most of the clients were gringos. Many of them had businesses in the United States, and they came to Rosarito to buy merchandise to sell over there. In those days, we sold mostly fireworks and seashell wind chimes, more than pottery and furniture.

My dad started painting flowerpots and large pitchers, and he made wooden furniture. He also sold handicraft items, plates, little dolls, indigenous clothing, all that stuff. Blankets and serapes weren't as common then as they are today.

Lots of U.S. tourists would come during spring break, and my grandmother and father would have us keep watch to make sure no one was stealing anything. . . . My grandmother, like everybody from Mexico City, was always suspicious and on the lookout because in Mexico City they'd had shoe stores. They'd tell us, "You stay in the corners and watch to make sure they're not stealing." Or maybe they did that so we wouldn't just hang around the store and be bored.

What happened to the souvenir shops?

Well, tourism dried up and my dad had four daughters to support. He couldn't make ends meet, and he didn't have a fixed salary in the shop, because you earn only if you sell. So the day arrived when my dad needed a salary, a steady income. The shop wasn't providing it, so they decided to close it. My grandmother kept her store open longer but eventually closed it too. She was getting on in years or too tired to manage the store all by herself.

After my dad closed the shop, he went to work for the Rosarito municipal government; this was around 1987. He stayed there four years, and then he went to work for the Tijuana municipal government. At some point he decided he wanted out of that job. He worked in licensing, and sometimes people would try to bribe him to expedite their business permits. My dad didn't like that dynamic at all. He wasn't so easy to corrupt. He was determined not to take bribes; he said, "Here everybody gets the same treatment." So after working for ten years in the two municipal governments, he took a job as a salesman in Circuit City, on the other side of the border. He didn't have a set schedule. He could go to work at one o'clock in the afternoon or at seven in the morning. He didn't have any set days off during the week either. The only requirement was that he had to work weekends. After he was there seven years, electronics sales began to drop, and he left Circuit City for a job at Home Depot. He's still working there and hopes to stay in that job until he can retire.

After 9/11, the wait times to cross the border became impossible, so my dad had to get a SENTRI pass. Otherwise he'd have to leave four hours earlier to get across the line. For example, if he had to start work at eight in the morning, he'd have to leave Rosarito at four o'clock.

A Visa to Another Life:
A Mother's Flight and Imprisonment

After my mother divorced my father, she remarried and came to live in Playas de Tijuana. I remember we weren't on very good terms with her then because she'd married a judicial policeman who was a bit crazy. He was very authoritarian, and he got angry whenever we wanted to go to our father's house. He thought we should ask him for permission, and we'd say, "Since when do we need to ask you for permission, if we don't even ask permission from our own father?" Then he and my mom would start fighting like cats and dogs. My mother didn't have any children with him, because she'd had problems when my youngest sister was born and she'd had a hysterectomy. My mother finally left him. Better said, she escaped from him and went to the United States.

Why did she escape?

Because that guy was strange, and he would threaten her: "If you leave me, I'm going to kill your daughters and then the rest of your family." When my mom left Tijuana and fled to California, she was terrified of that guy. She was afraid he'd find her because she'd tried to get away several times before, and he beat her. My mother was in a very tense situation. She was very young, and she believed he'd carry out his threats. The last time she left him, the guy beat her and kept her sedated until she begged him to take her to see a doctor. He finally agreed, and when the doctor saw her—he was a friend—he said, "Luz, you've got to leave him. Every time he beats you up, it gets worse. He could kill you one day." He told her, "Look, here's what we're going to do: I'll say you've got an appointment with me, and I'll talk to my friend, who's a psychologist, so she can meet with you." My mom started sessions with the psychologist, who counseled her to leave, but to tell the guy that she forgave him for everything and that she would never, ever leave him, that she loved him. And as soon as he left her alone, she should grab her things and go. And that's what she did, because after the last beating, the guy wouldn't leave her alone a minute, not even to go to the bathroom, because he was afraid she'd escape. He'd already taken all her documents away, her passport and her birth certificate. But my mother had sewn her U.S. visa inside the lining of her purse. It was well hidden, so when he checked her purse he didn't find it. With that visa she was able to enter the United States. She was about twenty-nine years old. She was very young; she'd married my dad when she was sixteen. By the time she was eighteen she had my sister and me, and at twenty-two she had four daughters.

Eventually she went to Montclair, California, where she went to work as a secretary in her brother's business. But soon there was trouble. One of my uncles had a business making prefabricated houses. One of his partners worked for the FBI, and that guy was stealing confiscated drugs. I don't know if my uncle was mixed up in that, but when the FBI discovered this guy was stealing drugs, they went after my uncles and my mother to deflect blame and avoid making their own agent's involvement public. When the FBI arrived, they arrested everybody for the theft of over two tons of cocaine. They included my mother in the arrest because she'd spoken with the guilty agent on the phone. They carted everyone off to jail, but because they couldn't prove the case against them, they offered a deal. They couldn't let them all go scot-free, because they needed a scapegoat, but they'd give them light sentences. The first guy got five years, the next got eight years, and the third got eleven years. They gave my mom five years, but three years had already gone by before they sentenced her; she'd spent three years in jail in Los Angeles. Once she'd been sentenced, they transferred her to a high-security prison in Dublin, California. My uncles were imprisoned longer. I was just finishing sixth grade, and I'd go with my sisters to visit her in jail.

What was your life like then?

Even though they told us our mother was in jail, all we saw was a detention facility. What I remember most are the hearings. There were six or seven hearings before she was sentenced. In those days our English wasn't very good, and we understood only a few words here and there. We'd hear "cocaine," and we asked our mother why the judge said that word. Before entering the courtroom, my mom would ask the guards to remove the chains so that we wouldn't see her like that. We knew something odd was going on, but we didn't know why we could see her only every three or six months.

My dad kept his distance from my mother for a long time, because they divorced on pretty bad terms. But when my mom had these problems, they started talking again. Maybe for our benefit.

Life as a Student in Tijuana

I came to Tijuana to get my undergraduate degree in communications at the UABC.[9] For the first four semesters, I commuted every day from Rosarito. Over time the daily commute got harder and harder. Besides, I wanted more space, my own space. I talked to my dad and told him, "I'm sorry, but I'm going to move to Tijuana." He didn't like the idea very much. Since he never remarried, he's very protective, and he said, "Don't go. If you want, I'll build you a room of your own; I'll buy you a computer." But I told him that it wasn't just that. It was a personal thing, that I had to learn how to survive on my own, without depending on him. That's when I came to Tijuana, in 2002. I moved in with my boyfriend. That worried my dad too, but I explained to him, "We're going to live together, but like students. It's not like a little married couple. Nothing like that! We're going to finish university, and we'll go on from there." My dad was worried that I wouldn't finish college. He told

me, "Promise me that you're going to finish university. I don't have millions
to give you, but it's important that you study, unlike some of your friends.
You can repay me with your university degrees." I've almost paid him back; I
owe him 25 percent of my degree—I have finished the university but haven't
gotten the degree yet, as I promised.

When I first entered the UABC, I had a really hard time. I was lucky,
though, because a cousin of mine, the same age I am, entered the university
at the same time, so we hung out together. At that time, we didn't know
Tijuana very well; we only knew the way to the movies, nothing else.

The Lives of Others: Working as a Caregiver in California

In 2002, I moved to Tijuana, and that's also when I started working as a
caregiver in Point Loma, California, during summer vacations. My aunts work
as caregivers, and my mother too, since she got out of jail.

After my mother got out of jail, she married again; she married a gringo.
Since she'd been convicted of a felony, she forfeited her right to ever reenter
the United States, so for a long time her husband would come and go between
Rosarito and the United States. A little while before September 11, 2001, my
mother and her husband were like cats and dogs, because they'd see each
other only once a week, and then all their accumulated stress would just
erupt.

It all happened like a prank. My mom went to Tijuana to take one of my
aunts to the line. And my aunt, joking, said, "Hey, Luz, I dare you to cross."
And my mom said, "I'll bet you that I will." Before 9/11, it was pretty easy
to cross without papers; you just had to say you were a U.S. citizen. That's
how my mother crossed the border, and since then she's lived there with her
husband, as an illegal, of course.

Ever since, she's been working in Point Loma, taking care of an elderly
woman. After a bit, she invited my older sister to take care of the woman on
weekends. Usually it takes at least two or three people to care for someone,
because it's too much for a single person to manage for the whole week. So
my sister started working weekends in the United States. Three months later,
my mom got a chance to take care of another elderly woman, who lived in
Anaheim, much closer to my mom's house. I was on vacation then, so my
mom asked me if I could take her job from Monday through Friday.

I earned between $600 and $700 during that vacation, because they paid
me $10 an hour. When I went back to school, I kept the job, just working
weekends. It was a good job because it didn't cut into my school schedule and
the pay was good. On a single weekend I earned what I now earn for a whole
month of work as a research assistant. And once I had a steady job, I knew I
wouldn't have to go back to my father's house in Rosarito.

What does work as a caregiver involve?

We take care of elderly people in their final years. For example, the husband of the first woman I cared for was bedridden after he'd had an embolism. We cared for them in their home. We didn't work for one of the companies that send caregivers to houses because those companies generally send you to take care of several people at once. We worked for ourselves, which is better for the families because they don't have to pay taxes on us.

I'd leave Tijuana at six in the morning. I'd cross the border and take the trolley to Old Town [San Diego]. That took about an hour. Then I rode a bus that left me about ten minutes from the house. I'd arrive at ten o'clock, because at ten-thirty we had to get the woman out of bed. She's diabetic, and she's been on insulin so long that her brain has atrophied. She can't remember things. Everything you tell her goes in one ear and out the other. I remember when I first arrived I found it hard because she'd ask me, "What's your name?" Two minutes later she'd ask me the same thing. It was like hitting the replay button on a tape recorder. Every day there'd be a fight about something. There's an illness called Sundown Syndrome that affects older people in the late afternoon and early evening. They become confused and say, "I want to go home." It was the same thing every afternoon; she'd yell, "This isn't my house; I want to leave!" When we needed to give her medications or an injection—because she'd broken her hip and was in a lot of pain—she'd fight us and say we were trying to kill her. And she'd start to yell, "Help, help!" Luckily, all the neighbors understood that it was only because they were elderly.

The work is hard, and the workdays are long. I started at ten in the morning and finished around nine at night, when the woman went to bed. I stayed there to sleep, but I didn't take care of her at night. Her son took over at night, when the woman was tied to her bed. She'd wake up suddenly and say, "I'm going to be late for school." She'd held on to her childhood memories. She'd say, "The plane's going to leave without me; I've got to get up." In the middle of the night, she'd start to scream that she wanted to be untied. That was really hard for me. I'd have to fight with her every day, and every day she'd try to chase me away. It was a daily battle to get her to take her medicine. Besides, her son didn't help out enough. When he was young he wanted to be a doctor, but when he was in the eighth semester of medical school he was in an accident and needed brain surgery. Under California law, if you've had brain surgery you can't practice medicine, so he wasn't able to complete his studies. Later he decided to go to Chicago to study, but then his father had an embolism and three months later his mother started to lose her memory. So the son looked for work in California and stayed with his parents. His father had saved enough money for them to live comfortably.

Work as a caregiver presupposes some nursing training. Did you have that kind of preparation?

Sort of, because a week before beginning the job, you go to Secure.[10] You're there two or three days while they teach you the basics: the medications schedule, what to do in case of a spike in blood sugar. They give you tips. If a sugar reading is low, you give injection number 1. If the sugar is high, you give shot number 2. You've got glucose tablets. They taught us how to give injections, how to take a pulse, and to call 911 in case of an emergency.

If there were a health emergency, would you have legal problems in the United States?

No, not if I call 911. Whether she's dead or alive, you have to call 911. If you don't, you can be charged with negligence. I have U.S. citizenship because I was born in Anaheim. I can say that I don't work there, that I was just volunteering, just helping out. All my sisters have U.S. citizenship. The first three were born in the United States, and my dad arranged papers for my youngest sister. My dad arranged her citizenship papers when she was still very young, because it used to be easy to do that.

What happened after you left the job in Point Loma?

I worked in Point Loma for four years. When I left, the woman was ninety-two years old and her husband had died. My younger sister stayed to care for her. She quit after a while because they wouldn't increase her pay. When you're caring for an elderly person, the time comes that no matter how good the salary might be in comparison to salaries in Mexico, it's not enough because the work is so hard. For example, she asked for $15 an hour so she could earn at least $120 on a weekend. But they wouldn't agree. The gringo, the son, said, "You should be happy because you earn a relatively high salary here." That's true, but the work merits more pay. "If you don't think so," she told him, "contact somebody from an agency to see how much that would cost you." In the end, he wouldn't agree, so my sister left.

What's your job in Anaheim?

I'm a caregiver. The elderly woman in Anaheim is named Rosy, and she's related to us somehow through marriage because her sister was the grandmother of one of my first cousins. Rosy is ninety-four and has Alzheimer's. She's 100 percent gringa.

I went to work for her on my mother's recommendation. Rosy needs care around the clock. She has a daughter who lives there, but she doesn't take care of her mother. The daughter has some kind of socially recognized drug addiction. She claims she has intense back pain and spends the day swallowing every pill she can find. But after knowing her for four years, I've come to realize there's nothing wrong with her. It's all in her head.

When I started working with Rosy, she could still talk but she wasn't able to walk very well. You had to help her. Her legs wouldn't support her, so my job was to make sure she kept her balance. At first, it was hard for me because she was not kind. For example, the first time I prepared her breakfast, she asked me, "Who taught you to cook? The food doesn't taste like anything." It was hard to endure that kind of treatment. She's one of those women who spit out meat that's well done. She liked her meat almost raw. I had to be more patient with her about things like that because she was different from the woman in San Diego. I could argue and fight with her, because she'd soon forget all about it. But Rosy never forgot anything, and she'd constantly remind you about it. After a year she got the early symptoms of Alzheimer's. Now she's like a baby. She doesn't talk. We have to feed her, change her, bathe her. We have to do everything for her.

Do they pay you the same wage?

No, for Rosy they pay us a fixed salary of $160 per day. If I work the weekend, I earn $320. But it's all day, twenty-four hours. You can sleep, but it's not the deep sleep you get when you're at home. We sleep with monitors nearby so we can check her breathing. It's a very light sleep. Rosy wakes up at night, and since she can't talk anymore she just yells. She complains every night, so you've got to be on alert for everything.

She doesn't recognize anyone anymore; at most you'll get a smile. There's no interaction at all between her and her daughter. I wonder how much her daughter cares about her mother, because the daughter's adopted. Rosy had only one child of her own. She wanted lots of children but wasn't able to, so she adopted—first a boy, and then she became pregnant and had another boy, and later she adopted a girl, the one I'm talking about. But this daughter was like the prodigal child. She got pregnant at sixteen and gave her newborn daughter up. Rosy said she didn't want any more children in her house, much less a bastard. It seems that Rosy always pushed her daughter to the side because her behavior wasn't acceptable in good society.

Rosy was married twice, and both husbands died. She made a lot of money in real estate. She owned a large house in Washington that they sold for about $3 million. With the money from that sale, she bought the house we're in in California. She gave her natural son about half a million dollars as inheritance, and she held on to the rest for her future care.

Her son manages her money. He pays our salaries, and he provides money every two weeks to cover household expenses and purchases.

So you don't just take care of Rosy? You also manage the house and
purchase provisions for the household?

My mother takes care of that because she has a car. I come from Tijuana.
I leave at five o'clock in the morning to cross the line and take a van that
charges $28 to take you to Anaheim and from there back to the line.

My mother used to take Rosy to the hospital to see her doctor. But
not anymore, because the U.S. government takes care of expenses for the
elderly who are sick: medicines, diapers, equipment, bed, wheelchair—the
government pays for it all. My mother used to handle everything because you
can't count on the daughter, because she's very unpredictable. She works in
jewelry stores and she gets hurt mysteriously every two or three months. Then
she collects disability and just hangs around at home, doing nothing. During
the time we've been there, she's worked in three different jewelry stores. And
she's always in bed, taking pills to help her sleep.

I've worked as a caregiver for seven years, ever since I entered the
university, with no breaks. Basically I just work weekends. During vacations,
I sometimes worked all week when my mother had to go to dog shows. My
mother has show dogs, and she has to travel to take them to competitions.

Far from the Chameleon:
Life Is on the Other Side

Now that you've finished university, how are you combining your work
in Tijuana with your work as a caregiver?

Well, they're very different. One of my professors said to me, "Why didn't
you study nursing?" There's no connection between communications and
caregiving. But I took a job as a caregiver because it's a good job, with good
pay. I can't survive on what I earn from my work in Tijuana. Besides, when we
started working with Rosy, she was still pretty lucid and she made us promise
that we wouldn't leave her until the day she died. So, besides the fact that we
need the money, more than anything it's for Rosy, because we determined we
were not going to leave her alone. She told us, "Don't leave me alone with my
daughter, whatever you do. I know that one day I won't remember you, that
one day I'm not going to recognize you, and perhaps I'll say things that make
you feel bad, but please don't leave me." So we're with Rosy until she passes. I
don't think the day is far off.

Rosy will be my last patient, because the work is just too hard. The elderly
take too much out of you. It's really stressful; when I get home on Mondays, I
end up sleeping the whole day. It's physically exhausting because if the elderly
person gets depressed, you get depressed too. Then, for example, with mental
illnesses like Rosy's there comes a time when they're always hurling insults at

you. In these last stages, Rosy has become very aggressive and troublesome. She pulls your hair, she bites and hits, she spits her food in your face. And she's becoming racist. She asked me, "Where are you from? You look like you're Mexican, and that means trouble." She was never a racist before, and I resent comments like that.

A moment ago you said you can't survive on your research scholarship. What do you plan to do if you quit your caregiver job?

My work as a research assistant is just a first step. I want to get a master's degree. When Rosy dies, I'll go back to being a starving student and find a scholarship.

I'm not sure I'll study here in Mexico. At first I thought about going to the ITESO[11] to study communications and culture, but since I also like the visual arts, maybe I'll go to Spain.

My partner and I are making lots of videos. We've collaborated on short films. For example, we made one about the fire breathers here in Tijuana. We film life stories. Most are migrants, and almost all are youths. They tell how they came to Tijuana, why they migrated, what they plan to do. We're interested in the codes they create at the intersections and how they mark their territory. What we've seen is that it's a fleeting career, because one day they're fire breathers and the next day they're washing cars. We've had the opportunity to get to know the fire breathers over a six-month period, and we've documented the changes in their lives. Many of them now have formal jobs, like working in a restaurant, for example. Others have gone back to school. Others now have a wife and kids.

Why did you decide to accept a research scholarship?

I was finishing my degree in communications when they sent an e-mail to the Humanities School saying they needed a research assistant at the Center. I responded right away, and about a week later they told me I'd been accepted. When I finished my degree program I was very interested in research, and I said, what better place than to be here among researchers.

I've been here three years, and I think being in this work environment has given me a lot. I've learned nearly twice as much . . . as I learned at the university. When I started work here, I had a tremendous deficit. Every little while, they'd ask me, "Have you read this? Have you read that?" And I'd just say, "Well, it wasn't in the program." Here's where they encouraged me to get a master's degree. They'd say, "So what's the deal? When are you starting a master's program? You can't stay here forever on a scholarship."

I don't want to go to graduate school in the United States. Many of my friends say, "Eloísa, why look anywhere else when the United States is right here?" If I went to school in the interior of Mexico, I'd have a hard time finding a camera of good quality or at a reasonable price. Here I can cross the border and buy a good camera and a good computer at a very reasonable price compared to what they cost in the interior of Mexico. So for me what the United States offers is access to technology.

What does the border mean to you?

For me the border is very complex. The first thing that comes to mind is the image of a line of overlapping metal plates, one after the other, all along the border, and I envision it as a giant chameleon with a broad array of colors that represent the enormous diversity among the people who come here. Until recently, it made me mad when people compared Tijuana with Mexico City, but I have to admit that if somebody calls for a protest in Mexico City, there'll be a huge turnout of demonstrators. In contrast, in Tijuana it's hard to get ten people together because everybody's from a different place. There's no homogeneity, no shared identity that can support a protest. That's why I see Tijuana as a giant chameleon, with many colors, each shade different from all the others. There's not even any unity of color.

When they say, "You're from Tijuana," I say, "No, I'm from Rosarito," because I grew up in Rosarito. But the two are very much alike. They're practically the same because they're so close together. But the dynamic in Rosarito is very different from that in Tijuana, where everything is rush, rush, rush or get run over from behind. Life in Tijuana is very fast-paced.

I don't like the United States very much. It stresses me out. When I was about to enter the university, my dad told me, "You can go study in the United States. Why not go to the United States?" Because besides my being a U.S. citizen, my dad was working at Circuit City and he could have found me a scholarship through his work. And when I was working in Point Loma, the doctor who cared for the elderly woman told me, "Eloísa, why don't you want to study here? Given that you're half Mexican and half American, I think you'd have good opportunities here, because many schools are trying to build diversity in their student bodies." I don't know why, but I don't like the United States. It seems cold to me, without flavor. On weekends I don't even want to cross to go shopping. Here in Tijuana, everything is a disaster, a mess, and then you get to the United States and everything is so orderly. I don't know. . . . I just don't like it.

7

A Border Acrobat

Undocumented Migrants

*A*t the close of the nineteenth century, the U.S.-Mexican frontier was characterized more by the fluid nature of cross-border movement than by
obstacles to immigration. Images of migration flows from that period hold
no hint of today's border control infrastructure, with its imposing walls and fences,
security cameras, and movement sensors. But even before the fences went up,
one actor emerged as a central protagonist in the crossing stories of thousands of
clandestine migrants. Known among migrants as la migra, the U.S. Border Patrol
was created in 1924 as an agency within the U.S. Immigration and Naturalization Service (INS). Following the terrorist attacks of September 11, 2001, it was
incorporated into the new Department of Homeland Security.[1]

The clandestine entry of Mexicans into the United States is not a recent phenomenon. It appeared with the beginning of the Bracero Program, a bilateral guest
worker program established in 1942, and it intensified when that program ended
in 1964.[2] Forty years later, the logic of U.S. border control efforts shifted; border
enforcement no longer was viewed primarily as an expression of U.S. immigration
policy but rather was seen as a response to national security concerns over the rise
in cross-border trafficking of arms and illegal drugs and the possibility of terrorist
attacks.

Today's undocumented migration differs markedly from what it was in the
second half of the twentieth century, not only because the confluence of immigra-

Illustration: Watching the border, Tijuana. *(Photograph by Alfonso Caraveo Castro.)*

tion and national security policies has caused a thickening of institutional density pertaining to border control issues but also because increases in the quantity and regional diversity of Mexican migrants have resulted in the widening and set-tling out of migrant networks in the United States. Between 1970 and 2003, the Mexican-origin population residing in the United States rose by 5.4 million, to a total of 26.7 million. Of this population, 9.9 million were born in Mexico; the remaining 16.8 million are second- and third-generation descendants of immi-grants (Zúñiga, Leite, and Nava 2005). Among these various generations, several million are residing in the United States without documents giving them legal residency rights. According to one highly credible estimate, the number of undoc-umented Mexicans in the United States in 2005 was 6.2 million, or 56 percent of all undocumented persons in the United States at that time (Passel 2006).

Today undocumented Mexican migrants' places of origin, final destinations, and transit routes are more varied than at the end of the twentieth century. Data on migrants deported by the Border Patrol reveal that 42.5 percent of all deportees in 1993 had entered the United States via Tijuana, but by 2003 this figure had dropped to 18.4 percent. Because of enhanced border enforcement near Tijua-na, migrants redefined their preferred clandestine crossing points, shifting them eastward. During this period, Mexicali, Baja California, and Nogales, Sonora—two semidesert areas with extreme climatic conditions—emerged as important migrant crossing areas (EMIF 1993–2003).

The heavy flow of undocumented migrants converted these border cities into stations where migrants could wait and prepare for a border-crossing opportunity, with all the social and urban consequences that their presence implied. These cities also became places of refuge for the thousands of people arriving with little or no money, often without Mexican identity papers, many without local kinship or friendship ties, and sometimes sick or injured.

The majority of migrants returned to Mexico by the Border Patrol in 2003 were men (83 percent), with an average age of 27.6 years and a mean education of 7.1 years. That year, the majority (93 percent) of undocumented migrants crossed in search of work, and most (73 percent) had no previous border-crossing experi-ence, reflecting the fact that they were coming from new regions of out-migration with less-developed social networks. Between 1993 and 2003, the fraction of the migrant flow coming from Mexico's southern and southwestern regions rose from 13.7 percent to 29.7 percent (EMIF 2002–2003).

Over approximately the same ten-year period, the United States invested mil-lions of dollars in enhanced border control infrastructure. In contrast, except for the creation in 1990 of Grupo Beta, an unarmed police force aimed at protecting migrants along the border, Mexico's infrastructure for assisting refugees, the nearly half-million people deported to Mexico's border cities each year, continues to rely almost entirely on donations to programs run by social or religious organizations with minimal support from the Mexican government. In the case of Tijuana, the cause of meeting migrants' needs has been taken up by a network of migrant shel-ters; notable among them are the Casa del Migrante (Migrant House), the Salvation Army shelter, the Madre Asunta House (for women), and the YMCA house (for young people).

Tijuana's Casa del Migrante was founded in 1987. It was the first of several shelters established by Scalabrinian missionaries, who have since extended their outreach to other cities on Mexico's northern frontier, including Ciudad Juárez, Chihuahua, and Agua Prieta, Sonora, and to cities on Mexico's border with Guatemala, such as Tapachula, Chiapas, and Tecún Umán and Guatemala City, Guatemala. In Tijuana, the Casa offers accommodation to all migrants, regardless of nationality. Some are deportees; others are simply waiting for a chance to cross the border. The Casa provides temporary lodging, food, spiritual support and guidance, and basic medical services for up to fifteen days, alongside its continuing mission to defend and promote migrants' rights.

"I Was a Stranger and You Welcomed Me": The Casa del Migrante

The metal bars of the creaking turnstile never cease revolving as a steady stream of returned migrants flows back into Mexico through the San Ysidro border gate in Tijuana. With faces drawn in exhaustion, eyes heavy from lack of sleep, and bodies battered, hundreds of people arrive day after day at the Mexican immigration post. Every year the U.S. Border Patrol returns nearly half a million migrants to Mexico via cities on the U.S.-Mexican border. Nearly a fifth of them are returned to Tijuana, where they form an army of windshield washers, fugitives from the municipal police, and homeless people in search of shelter or a handout that would enable them to return to their places of origin.

Amid this human suffering and Tijuana's pervasive indifference, the Casa del Migrante is an oasis where people can heal their wounds, rebuild their strength, and then resume their journey, whether it leads them south and home or north across the border once again. The Casa is in Colonia Postal, one of Tijuana's oldest neighborhoods. It is six o'clock in the afternoon; at the entrance to the Casa, a group of men gather around a door above which is written, "I was a stranger, and you welcomed me," a verse from the Gospel of Matthew. It is a plain three-story building with a central patio where guests gather after a day of bustling around the city in search of work, information, or aid. Father Luiz Kendzierski welcomes us with a smile and leads us to an office where a social worker interviews each arriving migrant. Their stories all have a disturbing similarity: Most of the new arrivals have been returned to Mexico by the Border Patrol and have no idea what to do next, a smaller number of them are waiting to make their first entry into the United States, and a few have already chalked up several failed crossing attempts. Daylight is slowly fading, transforming these human shapes into doleful shadows waiting for something as yet undefined. The air is heavy with the stress of waiting.

All the people on the patio are men; women are housed in a separate building.

We gather some chairs together in a corner of the patio and begin conversing with all the guests in turn. They welcome the opportunity to be interviewed, possibly because it lightens the tedium of waiting. The men around the patio look at us and seem to ask, "When is it my turn? I also have a story to tell." Porfirio, who is called "Maromas" (the Acrobat), leans silently against the wall. He has waited for hours, watching from a distance. Darkness surrounds us when he finally approaches, sits, and says, "I'm next." He's been at the Casa del Migrante a couple of days. He is slender, smiling, and a fast talker.

Heading toward Mexico City

I was born on October 22, 1969, in Santa María Moyotzingo, in the municipality of San Martín Texmelucan in Puebla State. It's a lush, green place, where they grow a lot of fruits and vegetables. My parents were peasant farmers; they grew corn, beans, and lentils, and they raised small livestock. My mother was a seamstress too.

There were fourteen of us, eight sisters and six brothers. I was the seventh child. I didn't like country life or farm animals. I liked having nice things, money and clothes, but because there were so many of us my father couldn't afford those things. I'd see everybody leaving my town for Mexico City and then returning with money, unlike the people who never left the village. So when I finished third grade, I left for Mexico City.

I was twelve years old when I left Santa María Moyotzingo. None of my brothers had left before me. I was the worst of them all, but now I'm the best.

I left home with only a bag of clothes and came to the city. Just the sight of all the people everywhere and the enormous cars scared me. I went around asking people where the market was, because my godfather from my First Communion had a stall in the market, La Merced market. I managed to make my way to the market and find my godfather. He gave me a job, and I stayed working there for about three years. My godfather took care of my earnings, and he would give me money each time I went back to the village. A hundred pesos was a lot of money in those days. I'd give a little to my father, a little to my mother, and I'd spend the rest.

I lived at my godfather's house, but I wasn't comfortable there because he just had daughters, so it was all women, no men. His daughters had professions, they had careers: a doctor, an engineer, a teacher, and another one, but I don't know what she did. My godfather was a merchant.

There were four girls, and it was really uncomfortable because they were free on weekends, when I wanted to go out on my own, but they wouldn't let me. I was just a kid, and the girls would take me to the movies with them; they treated me like a little brother. My godmother would scold me too; she wouldn't let me go out. They let me go out for only a couple of hours. That's why I left and headed north.

The United States: Sweeping Up the Dollars

They told me you could earn a lot up north, so I came to Tijuana. It was 1986.
I was in my village, and lots of people were arriving from up north and telling
us what it was like. They said you could sweep money up with a broom! Dollars!
I was seventeen. I grabbed a bag of clothes and came to Tijuana. I didn't know
anybody here, because my plan was to head straight across the border, but
I ended up working here. They didn't pay much; I worked for only a week and
then—I remember—I gave away all my clothes. I just kept a shirt and a pair of
pants and headed for the *bordo*.[3] I remember back then there was just chicken
wire along the border, no metal plates, and it was easy to cross. I was young;
I had long hair and my skin was lighter, and the migra didn't bother me at all.
I got as far as Escondido [California], and I went to work. I didn't do heavy work
because I was too young and they wouldn't give me those jobs. I'd do things like
delivering stuff, running errands. I wanted to work in construction, but they
wouldn't hire me. So I started collecting aluminum cans, just to get by, and
when I got older I could get better jobs. I did that for five years.

How did you manage to find work in Escondido?

When I was crossing the border I met a friend who was going across by
himself, and then we met up again in San Diego. I remember that he was
standing there in downtown San Diego when I ran into him again. He asked
me, "Where are you headed?" "I don't know," I said. I knew only that I was
going up [north of San Diego], and he said, "Come with me. I'll take you to
a place I know, and then tomorrow we'll see what work you can do there."
That's what happened; he took me to an abandoned house in Escondido
where there was a bunch of people.

The next day we got up and went to the spot where his boss was going to
pick him up, and I stayed there where people wait for work.[4] But nobody hired
me because I was too young, and in those days there was a lot of immigration
enforcement. The migra patrolled day and night, but I was pretty young so
they didn't pay much attention to me and they let me hang around there.
They never stopped me. Time went by, and they finally started giving me
construction jobs.

Around that time, I went to ask for a job in a Mexican restaurant. The
owner thought I was too young and he asked me, "What are you doing here?
You should be in school. You want a job?" I said yes, and he let me work
in his store; he had a store too. My job was cutting up chickens, bagging
merchandise, and arranging the shelves. The owner would send me to the
bank to make deposits. Then the secretaries and bank tellers would come
to eat at the restaurant, and they'd hire me to do odd jobs at their houses. I
cleaned chimneys, kitchens, and bathrooms. And they'd recommend me for
other jobs. I worked a bit in the morning, and then I would do other jobs in

the afternoon. I had a truck and my tools, so I could get from place to place real quick.

One day a gringo came from Atlanta, Georgia, looking for people. He wanted us to go to Georgia to plant trees. He had five airplane tickets, and he said, "I don't care whether you've got papers; I'll hire you regardless." The shopkeeper [Porfirio's godfather] told me, "Here's your chance; you'll earn more over there."

But everything the gringo said was a lie! He sang a different tune once we got there. They did hire us; we got on the plane and went. They had said they would pay us $6.00 an hour, but once we arrived they paid us only $3.00. They'd also said they wouldn't charge us rent, but they did. This was how it was, they said, because in the mountains of Georgia things were different than in California. The upshot is that we worked for two or three months, then quit. From there we went to a place called Dalton, Georgia.

We were walking down the highway when we met a fellow countrywoman, a woman from Chiapas. She saw us walking down the road and stopped, happy to see us, and she said, "Oh, Mexicans!" because you didn't see many Mexicans around there, near Tennessee. The woman stopped her car and asked us, "Where are you headed?" And we said, "Well, we're lost." Then she said, "I know a town where there are a few Mexicans and there's lots of work." She took us to her home, fed us, let us bathe, gave us clothing, and then took us to the entrance to the town. That woman helped us so much.

We went to buy some food at the Seven Eleven and were sitting behind the store eating when some very *gabacho*-looking people[5] came and spoke to us in Spanish. We were glad to see them. They took us to a church where there was a mission; that's what they call them there. They charged $5.00 a week, $1.00 a night. The people at the mission sent us to find work at a factory called Conagra, a turkey- and chicken-processing plant where they package poultry for sale in the stores. I didn't have any papers, neither bona fide nor fake, none at all.

The people coming from the mission all wanted to go in together, but I said, "No, not all at once. Let's look for work two at a time."

I went in with a friend. A young woman from Los Angeles met with us and asked for our papers. We said, "We don't have any." And she said, "How do you plan to work without papers? Don't you at least have fakes [faked visas]?" "No, nothing," we answered. She was really nice because she told us, "If you don't have anything, I'll take care of it." She had relatives in Los Angeles. She asked us for our photos and an address and then sent us to get work permits. Once the documents were ready, I took a job working nights. I gutted chickens. I worked in that factory for several years, three years. But then I thought, "I'm not going to keep working just anyplace they'll hire me. I've got to learn a trade." So I got a book and started learning how to lay marble and pour cement.

And that's how I learned, by reading and working on jobs. I remembered how I'd helped my brothers when I was a kid, so I had some idea. Thanks to God I got a job working in marble and granite in Georgia, but it was tedious, so I went to North Carolina, where I worked in construction.

Tijuana and Destiny

Later I went to Los Angeles, but I didn't like it at all. It was like being in Tijuana. Everything was lively, lots of activity, Latino music, Latino people, Mexican businesses. Nobody messes with the gabachos there in Hollywood. Los Angeles was not the place for me. . . . They were all crooks. I stayed only a week and then I told myself, "I'd better go to Tijuana." I hadn't been to Mexico for years, and I said, "I'm going home."

Thanks to God I met my brother in Tijuana and I stayed. It was destiny. God hears me, because I was working at a stoplight near the cathedral in downtown Tijuana, and my brother was returning from there, from the other side. Suddenly we saw each other and even after twelve or thirteen years apart, we recognized each other. We just stared at each other. Me here, him over there. We just kept looking at each other and that's how we found each other.

I worked with my brother in Tijuana for a long time. We installed a lot of marble on the towers on Aguacaliente Boulevard, on those big hotels. My brother and I also installed all the marble for the three dance floors in the Las Pulgas disco bar.

Did you have some savings to help you get settled in Tijuana?

Oh, yeah, because I had come from Georgia, from far away. You know that money's the only thing that counts here on the border; money is everything . . . because if you want to pee in a bathroom here, they won't let you in unless you have money. Or the police stop you in the street and want money . . . or if you're thirsty and ask for a glass of water in a restaurant, they won't give it to you. It's not like other places where it's "Sure, come on in," and they give you something to eat and even some extra food to take with you. That's how people are where I come from, because lots of people come through there who are coming across other borders. I remember when I was a little kid, people would come and knock on our door and say, "Please, can you give me a glass of water, maybe a taco? I've come a long way." My mother would even give them a taco for the road and tell them, "May God go with you." Not here. Here if you approach somebody to ask for a bit of change, right away they grab their purse and hide it. Maybe they think you're going to hurt them, but it's also because of the stuff that happens here in Tijuana. That's why people are like that. But there are good people too. I've met people who come up and say, "What's the matter? Do you want something to eat?"

"I'm Illegal; She's a Gringa": Marrying without Papers

My brother already went back south, but we worked together for quite a while. We were here in Tijuana for a year, and then we went across to the other side. That's when I got myself a gringa. I haven't told you yet that I married a gringa.

I'll tell you how I met her. In the late 1990s, I was in Escondido and I went to do a job at her mother's house. They let me work there, but I was still young. . . . I was about twenty-nine or thirty. I would always talk with her, and one day I asked her to a dance in San Diego, where the Tigres del Norte were playing. And from there, well, you know, and then the baby girl arrived. Her mother said we should get married, but her brothers didn't think so. Well, two of them were okay with it, but one wasn't. He didn't like me because I'm Mexican and she's a gringa. Me an illegal, her a gringa.

We wanted to buy a house in Escondido, but I didn't have papers, so we had to get married. I didn't want to get married because I didn't have any kind of identification. I decided to leave, and I came to Tijuana to get some identification, but they couldn't give me any because I didn't have my birth certificate. In order to get married on the other side they needed an original Mexican government identity document; I'd given them a fake one and they wouldn't accept it. So they wouldn't let me get married. I had to go all the way to Puebla for my birth certificate. Then I came back, jumped the fence again, and got married.

After two or three months, my wife's mother told me, "Get your papers." Then my wife took me to the immigration office in San Diego. I remember that there was a huge line of people waiting, and she told me, "Take this blanket and get in line. I'll bring you something to eat in a little while." I stayed there all night, talking with people in the line. They asked me, "Do you want to spend your whole life with a *güera*?[6] Because güeras are okay for a little while, and then good-bye. Otherwise, sooner or later you'll have to give her everything you've got. If you don't, she'll just take everything." And I started thinking about it. "Well, if I can come and go as I please, what do I need papers for? For work?" Thank God I taught myself a trade. I'd just arrange things directly with my bosses because I knew how much to charge. Working on my own, being self-employed, was better. I started work at the time I wanted, I stopped when I wanted, and nobody said anything. I got paid every week. A licensed tiler gets $6 or $7 for each piece of marble laid, but because I didn't have papers, I changed between $2 and $2.50 per piece. So I sat down with the gringa and I told her, "You know what? I'm not going to apply for papers." She was mad, but then she took me to an office where they told me how much it would cost to get a fake work permit.

That's what we were doing when a month later the World Trade Center towers came down in New York City, and I said, "What do I want papers for? Why should we throw away four or five thousand dollars on a fake work permit? We'd be better off going south [to Mexico] and setting up a business." She said yes to everything, and she even taught herself some Spanish. And when we got there [Moyotzingo] she liked everything and she taught herself to be like a Mexican. What happens is that she's jealous, really jealous, and there in Puebla I couldn't go out because she'd get jealous. And she'd had a profession on the other side; she was a teacher. And when she'd get out of work, she'd help me; she was with me all the time. But things were different in Puebla. If I wanted to go out with the guys, she'd want to come along, and it's different there [in Puebla]. It's not like the United States . . . no way. And then she was determined to get a voter ID card, but I told her, "You can't; you're from over there," but that really bothered her. She wanted us to get married again in Mexico, but I didn't want to because I was already suspecting what I now know is true. She was a güera, and that was the root of the problem.

Then the problems started with our little girl. In school they were determined that she become a Mexican citizen. They let her enroll for a year, but then they demanded U.S. government permission for her to be in Puebla. And let me tell you, the gabacho government was upset too, because I took her out of the country without papers. When my wife went back to Escondido, they wanted to take the girl away from her because we'd taken her without getting permission. We were supposed to get her a visa; you can't travel without papers.

All this is the reason my wife said, "Let's go back to my country." She went. She crossed over the border, but I couldn't cross, so I stayed working here [in Tijuana]. I thought I had a woman, but it wasn't so. Better for each of us to go our own way. It was over. She said, "Take care of everything you've got there in Puebla," because we had taken $67,000 with us—all my savings plus what we got from selling our house on the other side. We used that money to build the house in Puebla.

I'm feeling a little better now. I was depressed for a while and was drunk a lot of the time, but then I asked myself, "What good is this doing me?" I didn't want to separate, but they tell me that's how gringas are. What can you do? . . . There are lots of cases like that on the other side. Living with them is only for the short term. Life's different there. Women are very liberated, and a man can't tell them anything. What's more, if a woman says, "I'm going dancing and I'll be home later," she goes, just because. It's like that here too, but here you can talk about it, and over there the neighbors call the police and they arrest you just for yelling.

Did the police ever arrest you for that reason?

Yes . . . and then they wanted to deport me because I didn't have papers. . . . They deported me, but she followed me, because I didn't have any clothes, no money. . . . But that's over now. . . . It's better like this. God

wanted things like this. She made the decision . . . because we came here
from there together, and she crossed back to the other side and I stayed
here, suffering, unable to cross. When I finally crossed, things had changed,
because it had taken me some time . . . a month! I crossed and got a taxi.
When I arrived, I could feel that things were different. She didn't act the
same as when we were together. She had a new partner. She'd met someone
else, and it's really rough when they tell you that.

Living in the United States is good in some ways. A man earns good
money, but everything can change in an instant. Suddenly everything falls
apart, everything collapses, and you end up here [in the Casa del Migrante],
like me, and it feels awful.

"El Maromas" on the Border

This time the migra repatriated me, but in the beginning I'd choose to come
here every week or two. But ever since the Twin Towers fell, there hasn't been
any work. You can really see the difference. I remember that before the Twin
Towers collapsed there were lots of dollars in Tijuana. People would help you
out. Not anymore; you can see how things have deteriorated. There were a
lot of good-paying jobs. They [people smugglers] didn't charge much to cross
the border then. They charged US$300 dollars to take you from Tijuana to
Los Angeles, and I got involved in that too. In those days I'd get $100 or $150
to get people across. . . . Now the ride, just the ride, costs $300 a person. It's
$2,000 to get somebody across the border. One time I crossed a guy and I
told him, "Pay me whatever you think is fair," and he gave me $1,000. I didn't
charge, but people could charge $2,000 or $1,800.

Now they charge depending on where you're going. If you want to cross
through an official border gate, it's $4,000. The problem is that when you get
there, there's no work. Many people have to work for years to pay for their
coyote.[7]

I've been here now for two years. I always jump the fence, and I take
people across for free. Thank God, luck has been on my side for two years.
I'm not one to walk over the mountains. I cross just before reaching the
beach, and I come out at the trolley station. I take the trolley into San Diego,
and there I catch the Number 20 bus, pay $4.00, and go to Escondido. All
you need is determination and faith, because without them it's a real struggle.
When I'm about to cross, I go to church and make the sign of the cross, grab
a sweater, some money, and I'm on my way. You can't hang around there,
though, because the migra will see that you want to jump. No, you just get
out of the car and hide, quick. As soon as the sun sets, I start walking along
the shore. I always go alone. Even now, I still go alone. Sometimes I take
people with me who are having a hard time because they don't have money to
pay [a coyote], but I don't charge them. I crossed my brothers twice, but they
didn't like it over there. They just got into trouble. The police detained them

because they were selling drugs and stealing. They don't like to work. That's why, now that I'm here, when they ask me to take them I won't, because they've made a bad reputation for themselves.

I've got a friend with a ranch just there, in San Ysidro. I was working with him, so I took my brothers across to the other side. But I caught them planning to steal his stereo. I threw them out of my room and told them, "You know what? People come here to work, not to steal." Now they're here in Tijuana, but I don't go see them. They're younger than me, but they don't like to work.

I don't want to cross the border anymore because it's really awful. You have to stay awake all night, you get hungry. Thieves come and take what little you have, and if you don't have anything, they kick you around. That happened to me. Eight of us were walking and we sat down to rest near the crest of a hill when some thugs came up disguised as migrants; they were carrying packs and water bottles and they sat down to drink. When they finished, one of them took a pistol out of his pack and told us, "Don't move; you know what we're after. We just want your money; we're not going to hurt you." They searched us and stripped us naked—pardon my language—to make sure we weren't hiding anything. Then they made fun of us while they ate our sandwiches. . . . And they said, "Be careful what you say." What can you do? Nothing. Just keep walking and hoping the migra finds us. In that freezing cold, they took our jackets, our sweaters. It was horrible.

That's why I looked for my own routes. Nobody crosses where I do. I don't have any trouble, because in two hours I'm in San Diego. That's why around here they called me "Maromas" [the Acrobat], because one minute I'm here and the next minute I pop up over there. They say, "Here comes Maromas; you should take aim for him over there." But not now, not anymore. And they say, "Who are you going to cross for free now?" because the people who can pay are the ones who have family in the South. They have people who can help them, but there are lots of people who don't have relatives, who don't have anyone. I've known a lot of people who've asked for help to pay their way back south, because it's hard staying here if you don't know anybody. I know all of Tijuana and Rosarito now, but I used to be just like them. I've been really tired, really thirsty. But if you ask for water, they don't give you any. If you ask for something to eat, they won't give you any food. You walk by the taco stands, and you're so hungry that your stomach is growling. When you're sick, you want to be home. You think, "How I'd like to be in my native land, to be able to kill a turkey." That's how it is back home. Whenever you want you can grab a turkey, a rabbit, a sheep, or some pigeons and cook up some rice with pigeons. There in the country I can take a horse and go collect cauliflower, spinach. Everything's fresh: cilantro, onions, fruit.

I remember that the güera had to buy only oil and tortillas, because we had turkeys, chickens, rabbits. What I want is to go back, to go home. As my father says, "You've got a home here. What are you doing suffering over there? Come home; you're sure to find a woman." And I tell him, "At my age, I'm already too old for that." I promised God that if he allowed it, I'd return home when I turned forty, because I've suffered enough. Why should I go on suffering? I don't think my daughter will want to return to the house here in Mexico when she grows up. She may want to sell it. So why should I keep fighting? What's done is done. The truth is that I want to go home, work there, eat delicious food, because there's good food everywhere there. I'm just waiting for some friends to send me money. I know a lot of people in Ensenada, in Marina de la Misión, just beyond Rosarito. I worked there a long time ago, laying marble. They know me. I just want to put some money together and go to Puebla, because I left my house there empty. Why do I want to go and suffer on the other side? What's past is past. The güera's decided to make her life on the other side, and the girl's already growing up.

No Papers Here, No Papers There

I remember good times in the United States, when I had a lot of money. You could get legal documents, but I couldn't because I didn't have any identification, not even my birth certificate. My father and mother mislaid all my papers. Everything was mislaid; that's why I could never get papers in the United States.

Just five days ago I was installing some yellow stone in a swimming pool. I'm going to tell you how it was. A few weeks ago a longtime client of mine went to El Tigre market, and I crossed the street to see him, carrying my bags of groceries. Then a police car went by and they saw me. The minute I put my foot on the curb, I heard a noise—vroom, vroom! It was the policeman; he told me, "Stay there." I sat down on the curb and he told me, "It's against the law to cross in the middle of the block. I'm going to give you a ticket." He gave me a ticket that was due by April 16th. But five days before then, agents from ICE [Immigration and Customs Enforcement] and the migra came to my house. You know ICE is part of the migra, right? ICE is a group of judicial agents who round up people who don't have documents. Migra agents wear green, and ICE agents dress in black because they're police.

They got me, and I couldn't go to court because they returned me here to Tijuana. The police here grabbed me and tore up my papers and the traffic ticket, because here in Tijuana they detain you whenever they want. They already stopped me twice this morning and wanted to run me in on the pretext that I didn't have any identification. All I've got are some papers from the other side. At one point I had my Mexican papers, but once when I was here in Tijuana somebody stole my wallet and took my voter ID card. What I've got now are the papers from the U.S. immigration people and a deportation order for another twenty years. You know, sometimes those guys just play mind games with you. They've already given me three papers saying that I can't return. Their story is that if I enter the country again, they'll put me in jail for twenty years. But that's just their psychology; it doesn't really work like that! They want us to keep going back across so that they have a job. If what they say was true, they'd have locked me up who knows how many years ago [*laughter*].

This last time that I left they gave me another paper for twenty years, and that's why I'm really careful with the Tijuana police. Otherwise they detain you, lock you up, beat you; you don't get anything to eat, nothing to drink, they cart you from one place to another. . . . That's why, as soon as I get some money, I'm heading to Rosarito. I've got lots of friends there, and I'll get work there so that I can stay in Mexico. What's more, when I'm over there, my woman has me at her beck and call. She's probably already got somebody else. I lie awake. I can't sleep. And really, it's better to sleep [*laughter*].

That's why I didn't want a church wedding. Maybe I had an inkling that things were going to happen just like they did. That was always at the back of my mind, that this would happen someday. And it did happen, and now she's over there, on the other side. I talked with her a little while ago, when the migra returned me here. She got mad and told me, "You see? I told you that you needed papers, and look at you now!" Just so she'd leave me in peace, I told her, "You know what? Just forget me." She said I needed papers in order to work, but I told her, "I know how to work, and I can find a job anywhere. And I don't need papers, because if I want to go [to the United States], I just cross, and I do it without papers." After all the years I've spent here, I speak a little English. In Ensenada, my bosses are all gabachos from the other side. They live in mansions next to the beach.

Everything Changed When the Towers Fell

Tijuana and the people of Tijuana are wonderful. But what I don't like at all are the blasted police, excuse my language. I see that it's come out that they're involved in robberies and kidnappings. There are shootings every couple days; the streets are like a firing range. You hear boom! boom! on my ranch too, but there it's only hunters.

I like everything here; there are so many women [*laughter*]. The only thing missing in this society is a better police force. That's the only drawback, because there's plenty of work. The city is really pretty. I remember when I arrived in Tijuana, the city was so small. The hills were covered with little houses, one above the other. They were just starting to build Playas de Tijuana. Now it's like coming into San Diego. But then the Towers fell, and the whole world felt the loss.

The problem is that the governments themselves are bad. They stick their noses in where they don't belong. The United States subjugated the blacks, the slaves, and now they want to go after the Mexicans; they want to come in and govern us. I think the United States is behaving badly, and down the road they're going to reap the consequences, because the country has people from all nations in the world. Bush doesn't need to invade other countries when there's plenty of crime at home. Remember that Mexico used to stretch all the way to Los Angeles, San Francisco, all that. And now they don't want the people there. Not even the ones who are born there. I think that Arizona passed a law so that even people born there won't be citizens. They'll continue to be undocumented. You don't hear any of that in California, but you do in Arizona.

Would you like to become a U.S. citizen?

No, I know about all the people they sent to the war and how many of them died. A Mexican who died in the war was from Escondido. I knew his dad. What did they give the father? Not even enough for his son's funeral. I think they just send people to be targets.

I'd rather be 100 percent Mexican until I die [*laughter*]. Just look; these days if you cross to the other side, there aren't any jobs. People live crowded together in apartments, or they live on the street because they don't have money for rent, or a bunch of them live in a single room. It's really sad to see things like that; that's why it's better to be at the ranch. Like the saying goes, "Better to have nothing but beans to eat, as long as they're tasty and you're content." Nobody can put me on the street. Here you're always watching out for the cops and the killers.

How many times have you been returned from the United States?

I was there twenty-two years, so let's figure this out. . . . At the very least, they'd deport me three times a year. No, wait, more than three times. . . . Okay, let's say sixty times, including this last one . . . maybe a bit more. They've got a whole book on me in San Diego. They've added up all those times, and they told me that if I enter the country again they'll put me in federal prison. I've seen people who didn't comply, and they locked them up in federal prison for three, four years, because they'd already told them several times not to jump the fence. The government is getting tougher, so if I cross again they'll easily give me three years for breaking the law, because they've already warned me. And why should I go waste time in jail? Better to spend that time working here. If I do the math, the work I do there and the work I do here come out the same. The only difference is how you live on the other side. Over there you go out and you've got the whole sidewalk to yourself, the whole street to yourself. It's not like here, where there's more pressure. Sometimes you can hardly breathe. The work is about the same, because a lot goes for rent over there. You have to work a whole week just to pay rent, and then there's food, the phone bill, your share of the maintenance. If you're living in an apartment, that's not a problem, but if you're sharing a house you have to pitch in for everything. It's money here, money there, but, yes, it's more tranquil there. I think that if you want to eat well, you have to work. You may wish for it, but shopkeepers are not going to give you stuff for free. . . . This is my situation now . . . but I used to have a good cell phone, a nice watch, and now I don't have anything.

I'm not going to cross again because I didn't get to go to court. And since I always go to the same place, they know where I live. They have the information, and the judge can say, "Bring that guy to me," and you go straight to jail. It's not like here, where you can bribe them. No, you can't do that there. My wife doesn't want anything to do with me, and I don't want anything to do with her. It would be really dumb for me to go after her. Sometimes my heart aches, but I say no, better to resist, to forget. It's not the same anymore. And I can't go back. I'm better off thinking about work, about my parents, because they're getting older. I want to share whatever years they have left, because I've seen lots of people who don't get the chance to see their parents. That's why I'm working here, to save a little money and return to my village.

One of my brothers passed away a few months ago here in Tijuana. He fell off the roof of his house. I went to see him and he was in pretty bad shape. I crossed the border and when I came back I talked with my father in the South. He told me that my brother had died and just been buried. He'd hit his head really hard. They operated on him several times, but he didn't get better. Now I just have three brothers here in Tijuana; the others are in the South.

I'm the only one who's lived over there, on the other side. I'm the youngest, and I was my parents' nightmare, the one who contributed the least. Now I'm the only one who sends them money for food and medicines. I think about them and phone them often. The others who are here don't call them; that's why I want to go back. I'm tired of being here these twenty-some years. Thank God I'm still alive, because I stared death in the face many times when I was crossing through the mountains and jumping over the border. When you jump, you're on the edge between good and bad, and sometimes the bad gets you.

What if somebody had shot me or I'd fallen into a canyon? Or one of those times, what if I couldn't get out? Because I've fallen down, I've broken my ribs, seen eagles flying overhead. They say faith in God will carry you through, because, really, we're nothing without God. He breathed life into us and he takes life away. I say that because I've seen death close up, and thank God, I'm still here. I'm just resting up here; I'm resigned to staying in Mexico. And here, yes, I'm with my people. There [across the border] it's just going from home to work. You're cooped up all the time, just waiting for your turn to cook and then eat all by yourself. You have to line up to take a bath. You have to fight to watch the television, because somebody wants to watch the soaps, somebody else want to see a movie. Basically, you're alone, all alone.

But everybody wants dollars. Those bills are really pretty [laughter]. It was great to go to the currency exchange and change the little money you had and then go shopping and bring your purchases back here. What I want to do now is work here in Tijuana to put a little money together and go back to Puebla and buy some animals. I just want to work with animals; I've tried it and what I liked best were the sheep. I want to buy some lambs at some 300 or 400 pesos apiece; after three months I could sell them for 1,500 or 2,000 pesos. I've got two small parcels where I can pasture them. I want to work in Mexico now, because I've already spent nearly all my life on the other side.

8

The Mexicali Panther

The "Hot" Border

Over the course of the final decade of the twentieth century, the U.S. government launched a series of operations aimed at controlling the entry of undocumented people coming from Mexico.[1] One of them, Operation Gatekeeper, implemented in 1994, involved a major investment in infrastructure, high-tech surveillance, and enhanced enforcement aimed at intercepting undocumented migrants coming into Southern California.[2] This investment reflected the area's rising importance in recent years; in 1994, Tijuana alone accounted for 50 percent of all undocumented migrant crossings into the United States via the country's southern border. Operation Gatekeeper marked a watershed in border control, not only because it formed part of a migration policy tied to national security concerns but also because of its consequences. It shifted migrant flows, precipitated organizational changes in people-smuggling procedures, and drove up the risks for undocumented migrants.[3]

The immediate consequence was to move undocumented migrants' preferred crossing points from the western end of the border zone to more easterly points. The new clandestine border crossings, typically located in unpopulated areas to the east, required migrants to undertake longer and much more dangerous treks. This trend intensified after September 2001, as the terrorist acts of that month led U.S. policymakers to focus increasingly on national security. The Encuesta de Migración Internacional en la Frontera Norte (EMIF; International Migration

Illustration: Border Patrol, Tijuana. *(Photograph by Alfonso Caraveo Castro.)*

Survey of Mexico's Northern Border)[4] registered several changes in migrant routes between 1998 and 2006: (1) the emergence and rise of El Sásabe as a crossing point on the Sonora-Arizona border, which by 2006 accounted for 19.9 percent of all undocumented crossings; (2) Mexicali's growing importance as a crossing zone between 1999 and 2002 and its declining prominence after 2003; (3) the multiplication of "other" routes—crossing points in unpopulated areas that were used by small fractions of migrants—between 1999 and 2001; and (4) a new significant increase in crossings via Tijuana. After being the crossing point for almost half of undocumented migrants until 1995, Tijuana declined as a crossing zone, holding a fairly constant 17 percent between 1999 and 2005. Then, in 2006, the figure rose to 21 percent.

As border control intensified, the routes that "guides," or polleros (smugglers of undocumented migrants), had used in the past became, as the smugglers themselves said, "too hot." That is, these routes, which were now monitored by both the Border Patrol and the Highway Patrol (and which more recently have been commandeered by drug traffickers), were no longer usable. As increased border control forced migrants into more dangerous crossing areas, there was a related rise after 1995 in the number of undocumented migrants who died trying to cross the border (Bustamante 2001; Nevins 2003, 171). Among the various causes of death were drowning, hypothermia, sunstroke/heatstroke, vehicular accidents (either as passengers or as pedestrians), and gun violence (Alonso Meneses 2007, 174).

As the crossing became more dangerous, migrants turned increasingly to people smugglers. In 1993, only 12.3 percent of deportees from the United States had used a smuggler to enter the country; by 2006, the number had risen to 46 percent.[5] The increased difficulty of an undocumented crossing demanded better organization and greater knowledge of the terrain than was to be found among traditional or—as José Moreno Mena[6] (2008) identifies them—"community-based" people smugglers.

Before 1994, there was already a clear division of labor among people smugglers. According to Judith Adler Hellman (1994, 172), a clandestine crossing through Tijuana in 1993 involved a number of people with distinct tasks and positioned at various points on both sides of the border. And yet, Hellman notes (171–184), the interaction between smuggler and migrant client was still based on trust, something not generally in evidence in 2008. According to Moreno Mena (2008), Operation Gatekeeper spurred a process of differentiation between "community-based" and "professional" people smugglers. The former generally are natives of traditional areas of out-migration, such as the Mexican states of Guanajuato, Michoacán, and Zacatecas. With this group, as in Hellman's (1994) case of Pedro P.,[7] "business" relies on migrants' confidence in the smuggler's reputation, which migrants feel offers the best chance for a successful crossing. In contrast, professional people smugglers represent a new generation, young people between eighteen and twenty-five years old, many of them university educated, who are members of well-organized teams. Each team is led by an invisible leader who directs twenty or thirty young people, and they, in turn, recruit their own work teams. These smugglers tend to be based on the border, though not all are bilingual, and they usually live in low-income neighborhoods in cities such as Mexicali and Tijuana.

According to Miró and Curtis (2003, 21), migrant trafficking is second only to drug trafficking among the leading illegal activities in Mexico, and it functions in a less hierarchical and more flexible manner than other criminal activities. These same authors describe eleven organizations that smuggle migrants into the United States; six of them operate in Tijuana. These groups work with local operatives, using a sophisticated system of communication via cell phones. They concentrate their activities principally in the Tijuana/San Diego/El Centro and Tijuana/San Diego/Los Angeles corridors, at clandestine crossing points near the towns of El Hongo (between Tijuana and La Rumorosa) and Hechicera (between Tecate and Mexicali), or on the buses that cross the border at Mexicali-Calexico.

The increasingly complex operations of these organizations imply a constant upward spiral in costs. At the beginning of the 1990s, Pedro P. noted that smugglers were charging between $250 and $350 to take someone across the border, and for Central Americans the fee could rise as high as $600 or $800 (Hellman 1994, 180).[8] By 2002, as reported by Miró and Curtis (2003, 28), the fee was set at $2,500. The Border Patrol views the rise in smugglers' fees as evidence of the success of border control strategies such as Operation Gatekeeper (U.S. Border Patrol 1994, in Nevins 2003, 174). Given enhanced border enforcement, crossing a migrant now requires more people, more effort, and a greater investment in high technology and payoffs to corrupt authorities.

On the basis of interviews with activists and people smugglers in Mexicali, we were able to identify some of the roles in the division of labor within people-smuggling networks. Among them are the taloneros (recruiters), who procure migrants at bus terminals, parks, and hotels; the guías (guides), who cross the migrants; and the levantadores (the contacts in the United States), who collect migrants from drop-off points, take them to their final destination in the United States, and collect the fee for the smuggling service. This chain of operations also involves cuidadores, often relatives of the smugglers, who house and feed the migrants or who collect the rents for safe houses on both sides of the border.

The top links in these chains are the buyers (compradores), who "purchase" groups of migrants and then "sell" them to individual guides. These buyers have contacts throughout the extensive smuggling network and also at high levels of the judicial and immigration systems, enabling them to carry out their operations on both sides of the border. Miró and Curtis (2003, 21) found that some groups of migrant smugglers have also been active in drug trafficking. This accords with Moreno Mena's assertion (2008) that drug cartels have taken control of routes developed by people smugglers and sometimes charge them for the use of their own routes, either in cash payments or by requiring migrants to transport packages of illegal drugs. Furthermore, some crossing points are now controlled by groups of police, who also charge a toll to anyone going across.

The Mexicali Panther

One hot day in May, we drive down the Rumorosa highway amid ochre shadows, with a view of the Mexicali Valley down below. Once we arrive we meet up with Raúl in downtown Mexicali. He tells us he has to make a phone call, and we watch him place the call on his cell phone. "Everything's ready; let's go pick up the Panther."

We drive through streets crowded with Chinese shops and restaurants, all very near the international border that separates Mexicali from Calexico, until we enter a street so narrow that our car can barely pass through. Dilapidated buildings, bypassed by this border city's modernization, rise up on either side. A tall, dark man, smiling, waits for us at the door of a vecindad, *a residential building with an open-air patio surrounded by individually rented rooms. He wears jeans, a T-shirt, and white sneakers, and he's surrounded by several curious children. The inner patio is strewn with the remains of broken-down TVs, car parts, and what was once a washing machine.*

Our guest gets in the car, and we take a tour of the areas where the action is. These are neighborhoods with unpaved streets and houses all painted a uniform color by the desert dust. The Panther doesn't live here, but everybody knows that the Baja California and Flores Magón colonias are the best places to find a people smuggler in Mexicali.

People smuggling is a common economic activity, as another informant tells us, generally led by the household head or the young sons. The entire family participates in the business, which is dangerous but can also be lucrative if conducted properly. It is in these colonias that would-be migrants are housed before crossing. The mother in the family may take responsibility for preparing food for them, and the brothers entertain, accompany, and advise them. Here, in these colonias, the Panther recruits his team members—the taloneros, cuidadores, guías, *and* levantadores—*a human clockwork with the migrant at the center, keeping the mechanism ticking.*

We arrive at a secure location for the interview and sit down on the grass under a shady tree. The Panther is relaxed when we begin to talk, and the world becomes transformed in his enthusiastic words as he speaks, all the while looking toward the tape recorder.

Growing Up on the Border: Initiation as a People Smuggler

My grandparents moved to Tijuana in the 1940s; they came from Torreón, Coahuila. My parents were born in Tijuana, and I was born in Colonia Libertad, in Tijuana, in 1975, thirty-three years ago. A lot goes on in that colonia; everybody knows about it. I don't have to tell you that. Ever since I was little, I would see the people walking over the mountain. . . . Watching them, I learned, and I began to like the idea of smuggling people. It looked like an easy way to make money.

In 1982, my parents went to work in San Ysidro [California]. They had papers, and they took us all with them. There are five of us, three sisters and two brothers. I'm the youngest. I was seven years old when I crossed to the other side, and I went to school in San Ysidro until eleventh grade . . . almost finished high school.

Ever since I was a little kid, my dad worked at a car dealership, selling cars in the United States. While I was going to school in San Ysidro, I worked with my dad at the Chevrolet dealership on Fridays and Saturdays. I've received eight recruitment letters from the navy, so if I do one more year at an open high school in the United States, I can join up. I never missed school because my dad took me. But if he hadn't taken me, I probably would have skipped classes. I was always one of the first to arrive. When I would get to school the janitors would ask me, "Are you here to do the sweeping?" Everybody joked with me about it.

I liked the school in San Ysidro because that's where everybody from the colonia in Tijuana got together. My dad wouldn't let me go to Tijuana, but I met all my friends at school. That's why I liked going to school. I remember that there used to be "dead chickens" in the school parking lot. . . . Every day there'd be some dead guys. . . . We'd get to school in the morning, and the forensic teams were already at the school checking out the bodies. The women had been raped and shot dead. . . . I don't know; maybe it was the guys who attack the *pollos,* the undocumented migrants, when they're trying to cross the border. We would see them assaulting the migrants. . . . They'd take their sneakers and their clothing, all because they thought the migrants had money hidden in their clothes. So we saw a lot of stuff. Really criminal stuff.

I left school when I was seventeen because I got married, and two years later we had a son. . . . Then we got divorced. In those days I liked having money and running around, buying cars with powerful sound systems. Buying jewelry was a thrill. That was my style. I liked the jewelry just because I had the money to buy it . . . a heavy chain of fifty, eighty grams [of gold], medals engraved with a marijuana plant or some clowns, I really liked them.

Crossing through Colonia Libertad

At that time [at age seventeen] I started crossing people over the border. The first time I crossed somebody was around 1985. I went with my brother and a friend. I went via Colonia Libertad, crossing through the canyons at night. We went up a mountain and it was all canyons, every which way. After walking for a half hour, we came to San Ysidro; it was six o'clock in the morning. That time we crossed with ten or fifteen people. In those days we would charge $800 a person, from Tijuana to Los Angeles. . . . It was cheap.

After that, we would buy people at a little diner, where guys would sell them for about $100 each. They'd phone my brother or a friend, and we'd go pick up the people. Then we'd take them to the house, give them something to eat, and explain what the crossing was like. Then at night we'd cross to the United States. We had to tell them how to prepare, so that they wouldn't overload themselves, so we could travel light and arrive okay.

In San Ysidro, a driver would pick us up and take us to San Diego. There they would pay us our half and then take over, delivering the people to their destination "up north" and then collect what was owed. . . . Each one got his share. We'd always go 50–50. If they charged $1,000, we'd get $500 and the other $500 would go to the guys in the United States.

By then we had a safe house on the other side. It's a chain. It's like—we'd outwit the migra [agents of the U.S. Border Patrol] by Tijuana, and those guys would then buy our people and get them past the migra in San Clemente. And then we'd turn around and go back for more people. To cross through Colonia Libertad you had to know all the pathways. You get to know other people, because you're always on the move. That's how the chain starts to come together . . . getting to know lots of people. You might tell someone, "I need to work something on this side," and they'd tell you, "Come and work at Soler, at Playas, or Cañón del Muerto, behind Colonia Libertad, or by the airport." I know all the routes because I was always getting a lot of people through. Lots of people have accidents or get killed in the rush of traffic. . . . That never happened to us because we always get people across without any problem, and they arrive safely to their destination.

I know all the tricks. We were passing people through the parking lot of Voz de la Frontera [a local radio station]. I'd give $100 to the guard, "Chino Ley," so he'd let me through and I'd climb the building's tower. Up there on the roof, where they put the Christmas tree, I'd use my infrared goggles to see where the migra was. . . . And as soon as they moved, vroom! I'd climb down and call my people. I'd tell the guard, "Hey, get them moving fast." We kept the people hidden in a car in the parking lot, and we'd cross. . . . We did that for three or four years.

Running along the Beach

In the early 1990s, it was getting harder to cross through Libertad, because there was more border enforcement, and they built the fence. So then we started to cross at Playas de Tijuana, on the coast. We'd go there at night in a taxi and we'd wait there by the fence, where they erected some metal plates down the beach. We'd get in the water and follow the shoreline until we reached a tiny concealed airport. . . . We had to cross a stream, a canal, in our underwear—no clothes. Sometimes the water reached to our waists, sometimes up to our necks. You had to pay attention where you were going in order to avoid the undertow. Many people didn't know about it, and they'd walk straight into it. Even though they were traveling with guides, there was a lot of mist and they couldn't see the markers showing them where to get out of the water. I kept watch for people who were drowning, and I managed to save a lot of folks that way. . . . I'd get out by the little hidden airport, guided by the lights. . . . It's the kind of place where they keep crop dusters. They use them to watch for people who are smuggling drugs and stuff like that.

I'd get out of the water there, and I had a car waiting for me. They'd leave me a panel truck with the keys in the ignition, and I'd load up the people and cross the Coronado Bay Bridge to the "H" Hotel or the Palomar. The people could bathe there in the hotel, get something to eat, get some rest. . . . I'd start back [across the line] about ten o'clock at night, and by three in the morning we were back on the other side. We didn't have to walk far, but we'd stop every once in a while, waiting for the change in the migra's work shifts. . . . I followed the migra's trail, keeping track of their schedules. We've always worked like that. We know when the migra arrives and when they leave. I know all the schedules, and that's why I've never had any problems. I've been doing this my whole life. Five years ago I eased up a bit but I'm still working, just going across the fence. Why should I pretend to you that I don't!

Crossing through the Hills by Tecate

When did you stop working in Tijuana? Why did you change routes?

Because I began to see more migra around Tijuana. The agents began to patrol closer to the fence and into the mountains. . . . We came to Tecate in 1995 or thereabouts.

We'd go to a boulevard near the central bus station, under a bridge that's no longer there, because now they're modern, now they put in an underpass. We'd wait for the bus, along with some thirty or forty people, on the benches outside Calimax [a supermarket]. Lots of groups were going to the United States through Tecate. Two or three buses would go to Tecate every night at about ten o'clock. I'd give everybody money for the bus ticket, and off we'd go!

Just before we reached the first Tecate toll booth . . . we'd get off the bus and start walking along the foot of the hills. We'd hide the people in the scrub. We'd tell them, "Wait here a bit." We'd leave them and go to play pool in the colonia across the road until eleven or twelve at night. We'd meet our guides in the pool hall. We all came from the same colonia; that's how we knew them. We'd always meet up there in the pool hall. At midnight, everybody rounded up his group. The first group is always the bait . . . so that the migra apprehends them and the others can get through. It's all planned out. It's always been like that [*he laughs*]. Whoever goes first is the bait.

The first time they showed me how to cross people, they didn't pay me anything; they just let me watch. The second time around, my brother-in-law sent me out with twenty people. . . . I had to make new paths because I couldn't remember the route. I ended up with my face all scratched because it was nighttime and I couldn't see anything. I just guessed which way to go, making a path and worrying. "I'm not going to get there," I told myself, really worried. At daybreak I realized that the crossing point was right next to where I'd cut the new path. . . . That's how we gain experience, right?

I finally made it and came out on Highway 98,[9] where there's a checkpoint across from Tecate. It's all mountains, with Dulzura [California] down below. You have to wait there some three or four hours for a shift change in the Border Patrol. How long you have to wait depends on when you came out of the mountain, because the migra leaves at around six or seven o'clock in the morning. From there you cross the freeway, walk about fifteen or twenty minutes along the mountain, and then hide in the undergrowth, careful not to leave any footprints. We'd hide there until dark. In the meantime, we'd bathe in the water coming off the mountain. I'd brought some shorts . . . because I already knew, so I came prepared. It's like a waterfall, really cool! There was a kind of pool of clean water, and we got in.

We ate there and waited for dark. I had a bag of food; everybody had backpacks with food. We've always taken good care of the people, because they're the ones we work for.

How long did it take you to cross via Tecate, and how did you organize it?

We'd walk a long way because we'd come out there, by Potrero, by Dulzura, around there. We'd go down to Highway 98 and then cut around the checkpoint. It would take nearly two full days to get to San Diego . . . three nights, because we'd walk from nightfall until dawn, so we had to stay up all night. . . . From Tijuana to San Diego, it was three full days. During all those years, I'd go to the United States every third day.

We never had an accident. We saw guys attack people who were crossing with other guides. Once in Tecate, about six years ago, I'd been walking for several hours with some thirty people when I heard a young women cry out. . . . It was dawn. . . . We were going slowly. I was guiding a lot of people because I was working with my sister-in-law[10] in Tijuana and we were crossing toward that side of Tecate. That's when we heard the girl scream. She was in a group that was ahead of us with their guide, a young guy who was drunk, on drugs— something like that—and he was threatening the girl with a knife and was going to rape her. Our group was behind them, and we could hear them. Three of my friends from the Los Alamos colonia in Tijuana had come with me so I wouldn't have to go alone. Together the four of us were leading thirty people. Our people stayed a little behind, and we moved up closer when we heard the screams. And we saw that the guy wanted to rape the girl. Two of my friends, two guides, grabbed the guy and gave him a good beating—pow, pow—and we saved the girl. . . . We'd started across the border around midnight; that's when all the groups take off because it's when the migra shifts change.

People don't know who they're dealing with when they hire a guide, and a lot of bad stuff happens. . . . In those days [toward the end of the 1990s] I was earning $1,000 a week, sometimes even $2,000 or $3,000, depending on the size of the groups I crossed. I'd go to the United States every third day. I'd charge $100 or $150 for each person I crossed through Tecate. My sister-in-law was responsible for getting them north out of San Diego. That's when we started selling people for about $700. I'd get my $150, and the rest went to my sister-in-law.

I was a guide; what I did was to guide people across. I worked for my sister-in-law, and I settled accounts with her. I'd go as far as San Diego, and from there somebody from another organization would buy them, whoever we brought across. Those guys are there in San Diego to buy people; now they're buying them for around $500.

If I want to cross, how do I know how much to pay and who I'm supposed to pay it to? Do I pay it a little at a time?

No, you don't pay bit by bit. You don't pay anything out of pocket until you reach your destination. We arrange everything among ourselves. . . . Somebody just tells you that it will be $1,500 or $2,000. Whoever is responsible for taking you to your final destination, to the place you're headed, that's the one who's going to collect the full payment. So basically, each of us invests in turn; we each make our own investment along the way.

And what happens if I don't pay when I reach my destination?

Well, that's never happened to us. Honestly, I never had a case like that because I deal only with people who are recommended to me. We always check to make sure there's someone to vouch for them. We'd buy people who came recommended from the South. That's why our business grew.

Did you have to give a share of your cut to anyone else?

No, we didn't have to pay off any officials because we lived with the federal police, in the same house. That's where we'd hide people; a federal policeman lived there. . . . You can see the level of corruption in Tijuana. That's how we worked, just like I'm telling you. That's how we worked. Just think, we had about three or four federal police living in the house with us. I liked to hang around with them all the time, with my sister-in-law. . . . Sometimes when the bus from Tijuana to Tecate dropped us off, if it was arriving late . . . well, the federal police would pick us up in their own trucks. . . . They would help us move our people.

So are you saying that everyone involved in the business lived in the same house?

No, the guides and the people to be crossed were in one house, and we lived in another one . . . apart, with the family. . . . I wasn't married then. . . . I got divorced in the United States. . . . My wife and my son, who's now fourteen, live on the other side. I got married again in Tijuana and got divorced again. We had three kids: One boy is ten, another is nine, and the girl is seven. . . . My wife was always telling me to get out of this business; that's why we got divorced, because she was always telling me to get out of all this.

Toward Mexicali: The Arellanos' Ultralights and the Asparagus Field

When did you decide to come to Mexicali?

After 2001, when things got too hot around Tecate. See, you couldn't work around there anymore . . . too many migra . . . and the Arellano cartel began flying their ultralight planes through there in broad daylight. Yeah, the big ultralights that fly low along the mountainside—have you seen them? Like gliders. . . . Every day they'd launch three or four ultralights from high on the mountain. I started to notice that they were crossing drugs in large duffel bags. A truck would collect them down below and head for the freeway. Once on the freeway, they'd switch the bags to another car and take off.

After a while the area just got too hot and we couldn't cross people there. They'd already caught several of them . . . because they'd be carrying a lot more drugs each time, not just a single bag but a bunch of them . . . carrying up to six bags with each hand. They'd pass four people at a time; the one in front would have a submachine gun or a pistol. We had to find other paths . . . because otherwise you'd find yourself on the same path with the guys who flew the ultralights. Once they even gave us some hamburgers and sandwiches. They told me, "It's okay for you to come through here, but don't leave any trash because they could track us." They said the wind could blow the potato chip bags around, and the migra would see them. They told us to bury everything, cover everything up with dirt. They [the migra] come by in the morning and see the footprints, so they know that people came through in the night and are up ahead, so they can round them up. They know how long it takes to get from this point to that one. They know where they'll come out during the day or at night. They also know the crossing points and the distances between them; they know how long the trek takes, and they catch them. . . .

How do you learn to be a guide?

You can't really teach it, because everybody has his own routes. . . . Everyone makes his own routes. He has his routes; I have mine. I know his routes, and I can't take anyone through on his routes. If I want to work over there, I tell him and he lets me know if it's okay or not. I've asked sometimes . . . and he's said, "No . . . not now, because the situation is too hot." Nowadays nobody is going to give away routes or pickup points, none of that. Nobody's going to give away his network—nobody . . . because, you know, it's $1,000 for each one. When I want to move people through there, I tell them, "Hey, I've got five people. Can we take them through?" And he'll tell me, "Not now, you can't," or something like that. Because if their routes are really paying off, they're very protective of them. . . . Each person has his own route, and everybody knows it. You can't just follow any path at random, because you can bring trouble. . . . The routes don't last long. They get hot really fast because the migra discovers them . . . and you have to go looking for other trails.

A People Smuggler's Code of Ethics

Did you ever have problems with someone who got sick and couldn't keep going?

No, I never left anyone behind. I never liked to leave people stranded. If somebody hurt his ankle, we'd slow down. I'd walk at his pace, even though we shouldn't slow down because of the risk that we'd all get busted . . . but I didn't look at it that way. If you're thinking only about the money, like the guys who think only about the cash, you'd just leave them behind! I've found migrants abandoned on the trail. The guys who left them cared only about safeguarding their money; it's just greed. I'm not like that. What always matters to me is the people. . . . I guess that's why I never landed in jail, thank God. Neither here nor in the United States.

How much are they charging these days for crossing at Mexicali?

They're charging $3,000. For example, if I'm buying people, I go to her [his sister-in-law's] restaurant . . . and I give my phone number to people there so that they bring me people to cross. . . . I tell them, "Here's my number; call me and I'll buy your people. I'll pay you $200 each. I'll pay you top price so that you bring them straight to me." I can give my number to several people, and they'll call me. So I'll put together a group of ten or fifteen people, whatever turns up that day. Then I talk to my guides and the pickup guys, and we make our plan—who's going to cross them, who's going to pick them up in the United States. Because somebody's got to go in and take them to Calexico or to El Centro, California. You drop them off there and come back to Mexicali. That's where you collect for the people you handled. If you took eight people, they pay you for eight. If you took fifteen, then fifteen. However many you had, the risks you ran, they're paid for. They pay $200 for each person. The pickup person has to go only as far as El Centro. Then somebody else takes over and moves the crossers north to their destination.

How do you cross them?

They run through by the checkpoint when there aren't any migras in the canal. There's a canal with two floodgates that runs under the bridge, and that's where we go. . . . There's like a hole in the top section. . . . And there we tell the people, "Go to the fence that's up ahead, and then turn right and go until you reach a gas station." They have to run about five blocks. They go there by themselves and meet up with the pickup person, who's waiting there for them. He knows who he's supposed to pick up, because we all came together in one car. When we get out of the car so the people can go across, the pickup person drives across the border in the car and waits on the other side. There are five people—"Hurry up! Get in!"—and then they go to the place in El Centro. That's how it always works. One person's always in charge of getting the people across, another person picks them up, another one takes them to El Centro, and there's got to be one more person to take them farther north. When you deliver the people to their destination, that's where you collect. That's the way it works; it's like a chain.

Is there a boss who controls the entire chain?

There are two bosses . . . you see, the boss that gives you the people and makes you responsible for crossing them, [and then] I construct my own chain, getting the guides and the pickup guy. That's how I worked with my sister-in-law. She'd give me the people, but I never have her meet my guides. Because, you know, I'm working with people; I've got my guides, my team . . . and she doesn't have a team. She's just got a way to get the people and get the money. She gives me people, and I pass them to my guides, to my pickup people, and they take charge of transporting them farther along.

I never introduce my guides to my sister-in-law because she can cut me out and work directly with them. That happened to me. I was working last year when the AFI[11] caught me with eight people. The guides phoned me, saying, "Bring the people." So there I go in a taxi, and just before I arrive I get a call: "Hey, come back, because things are getting really hot. The migra's on the move." It wasn't true. I came back home, and the AFI apprehended me. It was the week before Christmas.

They took us to the Attorney General's Office (PGR).[12] They took mug shots of us, took our fingerprints. We were in the newspaper; they called us people smugglers. Lies! All lies! Well, that's how it is for the folks who don't have the money to get out of a jam like that. There we were, me and four other guys who worked in the business, and a woman from Tecate, who was caught in a house with four people; she was the one who prepared their food.

I thought my sister-in-law had abandoned me because she turned off her cell phone; they all turned off their phones. . . . But she hadn't turned her back on us; she called a commander with the federal police in Tijuana, and they let us all go. My sister-in-law is a big-time people smuggler, and she's married to a lieutenant colonel in the Attorney General's Office (I call her my sister-in-law because I'm with her sister). The guys from the AFI wanted to sell the people who were with me, but they didn't know that some had already paid $1,500. They said they could sell these people to some smugglers in the Attorney General's Office. There's just no end to the corruption.

Why do you think the entire chain is working?

Thanks to corruption, that's how, because if they caught me and nobody bribed me out and they locked me away, well then, that would be the end of all this. . . . But no, the municipal police grab people without cause with total impunity. They've grabbed me in public; once I was looking for a pharmacy and they took me to jail with my prescription and the money for the medicine. They take lots of people to jail just to get some money out of them. It's all bribery. If they catch somebody stealing a car and he's got money, they let him go. That's why it never ends. . . .

They lock up people smugglers who don't have any money. . . . You know, any smuggler who appears in the newspaper, it's because he didn't have any money; he couldn't make a deal with them. They always want a bribe. I don't think the corruption will ever end. A people smuggler who lands in jail . . . is one who doesn't have any money to pay. . . . And then they demand excessive amounts, $5,000 or more. I've been lucky because I've always had the backing of somebody in the federal or the state police. I've got lots of friends in the police.

What about the agents on the other side?

They're taken care of too. But it's a different deal because they operate differently. You know, I've got a friend here in the Calexico airport. . . . He's a security guard at the airport. He'd tell me, "At lunchtime, I'll give you a half hour so you can get your people to the airport." He'd buy tickets for a small plane that would take us to Los Angeles. These are small planes, for five passengers. The last time, he paid for our hotel and his brother brought us food. He would phone and say, "Get ready," and we'd bathe and change clothes. Then when everybody was ready, we'd go and hand in our tickets and get on the plane, and at that moment there wouldn't be anybody in security. . . . Corruption is never going to stop. . . . It's the same here and in the United States.

Would you like the corruption to stop?

Yes. Yes, I would. In fact, I would, because they're getting worse. There's every kind of corruption; some officials are just thieves. That's not even seen as corruption anymore. If they see somebody, they'll take his money and lock him up anyway. That's how they are; that's how the local police are. They think they're being smart. Lots of people in the colonia have bruises on their backs from being beaten with police nightsticks. Yeah, they'll grab anybody, beat him up, take his money, and lock him up. They'll plant marijuana on you, whatever they want. . . . That's why corruption will never stop; that's why.

From People Smuggling to Drug Trafficking

Did anybody ever ask you to smuggle drugs?

Yeah, they offered me that kind of work all the time. Here in Mexicali, I began crossing marijuana. . . . I was just the guide. Because I was getting people across, they offered me a job crossing some big backpacks for some drug traffickers. I said yes. . . . A commander in the PGR asked me . . . some guy who's now retired from the PGR here in Mexicali. The first time we went with four guys we picked up in the Los Alamos colonia.

But they caught us, and those guys spent a year and a half in jail. They didn't make it through with their packs. But I made it . . . my brother-in-law and I, because we were in front. We crossed and when we came to a field they were waiting for us. There was a line of some fifteen police. I got away because I was at the very front; I was the guide. I knew the terrain, and I ran. The migra sent dogs after me, and my brother-in-law and I went running through the field of asparagus. The plants were tall. There was a lot of water between the furrows, so we ran in the mud. My shoe came off and I went back for it, but a dog almost bit my face off. The dog spooked when I turned back because it thought I was going to do something to it. The agent told the dog to go ahead, to follow me. I grabbed my sneaker and ran across the asparagus field. From a distance, I saw that they had everybody on the ground, and a lot more migra agents were arriving. There were a lot of agents with dogs. And they began hitting the people who were carrying the backpacks full of marijuana . . . each one had thirty kilos in his pack. And they started to hit them and knock them to the ground. I could hardly breathe, I was so upset.

Those fellows were guides from downtown, from hotels that I know. I started them working here in Mexicali. Not all of them, because half of them were from the other guys [the drug traffickers]. I was really worried because these were my guides, and I did everything I could to help them and their families. My sister-in-law and I always kept in touch with them by cell phone, and the guides' friends and family would call. My sister-in-law is a very good client of the cell phone company. . . . They give her free telephones . . . and then get a kickback. They're really crafty because my sister-in-law does a lot of business, she's really big in people smuggling.

Why did you decide to keep working as a people smuggler and not cross drugs?

Because it's really risky. . . . People know right away when you're smuggling drugs. Everybody knows everything in this business. That's how the federal police from the PFP[13] learned that I was crossing marijuana with some guys, and they asked me to cross cocaine. They said they'd give me a hundred kilos of cocaine to cross. And I wanted to . . . because he was a friend of mine, but my other friends didn't want to. . . . They thought it was a double-cross, that they were going to cheat us. Well, since my friends didn't want to, the PFP commander ratted them out and wouldn't let us work anymore. They caught them crossing marijuana, and they locked them up with some migrants. . . . He told me he was going to mess them up, and he was going to mess me up too if I didn't break away from them.

Were you ever afraid?

Yeah, I was afraid. That's why I want to take my children to Tijuana and make some money. They think I work in a barbecue joint. I'm separated, I'm divorced, but I go to see the kids every day. If it weren't for them, I'd already be on the other side. I've always known that this is dangerous. They gave me five years' probation in the United States, and I can't cross anybody over the border for five years because they found out that I was a guide. Once they found out, they apprehended me twenty-two times. That's my record, twenty-two times, from when I began as a kid up until they caught me five years ago. So they apprehended me twenty-two times, but they never arrested me. And those twenty-two times I let myself be caught, because my pickup guy didn't show up for my people. The last time they caught me with two women . . . it was in 2002.

Twenty-two apprehensions. That's not many, not many at all. Lots of people who haven't been working long [as people smugglers] have already been caught a hundred or two hundred times. They've even gone to jail and everything. They've never sentenced me to jail time in the United States. The last time they caught me, I just told them, so that they'd let me go, that

I was the boyfriend of one of the women they caught me with. They caught
me with two girls from Michoacán. The migra didn't know that I was the
guide. . . . We tell the people coming from southern Mexico, "Don't say that
I'm the guide. Say that I'm your boyfriend, that we know each other, that
we're running away from there and we're going to get married." The girls
were always willing to do that. But that time, even though I'd told her, she
got nervous when they caught us and said that we'd known each other for
four months, and I said we'd been together for eight months or a year. . . .
So, well, the agents went to check the computer . . . and well, he saw that it
was all lies. . . . He told me, "You're a guide!" I said, "No, I'm not the guide."
"Well, how long have you known her?" And I said, "A year!" And he began to
laugh—ha, ha, ha—and said, "She told me four months." . . . He showed me
the computer and said, "Look at your photo; you're the guide!" But he didn't
arrest me; they just took my fingerprints and another photograph. And they
took me to the Mexican side of the border. That was five years ago. . . . I've
worked since then, but very low profile. I don't want to enter [the United
States] because I'm on probation, and the next time they catch me they'll put
me in jail. So I've been moving people on the Mexican side of the border.

The Wheel of Fortune

Have you never thought about leaving all this?

Sure, I want to get out of this business, but I just want to make some
money and retire. . . . Maybe $20,000 or $30,000. I don't know; maybe . . . we
could buy people ourselves . . . and we could work for ourselves . . . make a
bunch of money and retire.

How long would it take you to put that much money together?

It could be pretty quick, one or two months. My sister-in-law earns about
$15,000 a day. The day they caught me . . . it was $1,500 times eight. . . . How
much is that? It's $12,000, just in a little while. Because she doesn't share with
anybody. . . . She just has to have money set aside for when she gets caught.
They got her last Christmas. She had to pay the PGR $30,000 to get out. She
spent nine days in the Tijuana penitentiary. . . . Who's going to pay the PGR
$30,000 in a single roundup? . . . Now she's back at work . . . even though they
accused her of kidnapping because she had some migrants in her house.

And during all these years, did you set some money aside as savings?

No, I just have a big piece of land in Tijuana. I spent my money having
fun; I was always looking for a good time. . . . I had a lot of money, but when

the smuggling paths dried up, I had to manage my money carefully, bit by bit. My sister told me to buy taxis, buy apartments, like everybody did. . . . They're all well off, except me. That's what I get for not listening to my sister. . . . Oh . . . tomorrow, next week! And all the money I earned, I spent it all. I'd take five friends and we'd go out and have fun, but the lowlifes downtown would get all our money. You know what they're like.

Who are the lowlifes?

In the discotheques in Tijuana, there are a lot of crooks out to separate you from your money. They do it all the time. Lots of thugs and scammers who would take our money. That's why we had bodyguards, as they say. We'd go in big groups so nobody could mess with us, because they watch to see who's spending money and they grab him. And I'm from Tijuana . . . and even I'm afraid of them [*he laughs*].

I'm from Tijuana, and I grew up in San Ysidro. But I've always liked to cross people. . . . I've been in drug-trafficking gangs. . . . I grew up among them. They used me to cross drugs to the United States when I was a little kid. I didn't know. . . . I was little, about six years old. We were two brothers and one half-brother. . . . My older brother would tell us, "We're going to play soccer on the other side." And we'd put on our shorts and soccer jerseys, and take our new soccer balls. . . . And there we go crossing the line in a car loaded with cocaine, and we didn't know. My brother was the guide, the one who was crossing the drugs. One time that we crossed, we went into the McDonald's parking lot, unlocked the car, and went in to get some hamburgers. When we came out, the car wasn't there anymore. There was another car, and they'd left the keys in the tire rim. So you see, they'd take us in one car and we'd come back in another one. And that's how I grew up. . . . Little by little I realized that they were using me and now, as an adult, I see how they used us.

They killed my brother. . . . All that's over now. They killed him there, in Colonia Postal, near the technical college. Just his house was left, a house with a black bow. Arellano's people killed him. They got him and his boss. They [Arellano's people] were always hanging around with people from the Ruiz Cortines colonia, even with deputies from the PRI.[14] . . . And they killed them all, about eighteen people, right there in Señor Frogs [a bar]. I don't know if you remember when Franco Ríos was in Tijuana.[15] I'd go to his house, and I saw that his people were stealing PGR badges. I remember when a woman realized what was going on, and he told her, "Don't mess with me, you old bitch, because I'm going to kidnap your son; I'm going to kill him." And that's what happened. He kidnapped the woman's son and said he was a drug trafficker. They kidnapped him, shot him, and then dumped his body in Playas de Tijuana. That's where he showed up dead.

This was also when they killed my brother and his boss. My brother

always carried $5,000 in his pocket. He was always a little crazy. The
whole team, some twenty or thirty of them, all carried "deer's eye" charms
on chains. They'd go to Guatemala to get "*platanillo.*" I didn't know what
platanillo was; I thought it was a kind of banana. Now I know that Platanillo
is the place where they get cocaine. They'd tell me, "We went to Guatemala
and we were in the mountains." They'd tell me they were checking on the
platanillos and that they brought them down from the mountains on bicycles.
The members of the organization wore unusual blue caps that said, "Film
transport from Culiacán to Tijuana." I think it was a code. My brother was six
years older than I was.

And your other brothers . . . do they work in the same business?

No, my other brother manages a clothing factory in Tijuana. He's with
someone, married. He studied electronics, English, and computing. So he was
one of the innocents. Because he stayed in school, he knows electronics and
all that. He got ahead working, and he lives across the border. And one of my
sisters also has a clothing factory in Tijuana.

All my brothers and sisters have papers. They always tell me to take it
easy, to go there [Tijuana] to work. They tell me, "What are you afraid of?
Come here, build your house! We've all got a house except you!" They tease
me. But I don't want to go like that. I want to go with some money in my
pocket. That's why I'd like to be with the people, because the season for
crossing people is about to begin, and I've got my hideouts and everything
ready!

This month a lot of people will begin arriving from the South. You start
to see movement in March, April, and May. Those months are the time when
people come. And it lasts until September, October, or November, when it
tapers off. Lots of people, recommended people, are calling me and asking,
"Are you still crossing people?" No, well, yes . . . I'm still here.

9

A Young Mexican American

Mexican Immigrants' Descendants in the United States

According to Alejandro Portes and Rubén Rumbaut (2006, 244), the history of the United States is less the history of its immigrants than it is the history of the descendants of those immigrants, because of the latter's importance in the evolution of U.S. society. Immigrants' descendants are generally understood to comprise the U.S.-born children of immigrants.[1] However, there is strong evidence suggesting that growing up in the United States, regardless of one's place of birth, has important consequences in the process of integration, especially when the new arrival is young and undergoes the early stages of socialization in the new country. Making the distinction between being born in the United States and only growing up there draws a dividing line between the second generation (U.S. born) and what is commonly called the 1.5 generation (U.S. raised).[2]

The heirs of immigration display a wide variety in their life experiences. Nevertheless, it is possible to sketch the trajectory of the 1.5 and second generations in broad strokes. The importance of second-generation Latinos in the demographic dynamics of the United States has grown in the past decade, and that trend appears destined to continue. Suro and Passel (2003, 2–3) estimate that between the years 2000 and 2020, the number of U.S.-born Latinos will increase at a faster rate than the comparable figure for Latinos born outside the country. By 2030, the number of Latinos in U.S. schools will double and their numbers in the labor force will triple.

Illustration: Returning to Mexico via Tijuana. *(Photograph by Alfonso Caraveo Castro.)*

Being born in or growing up in the United States and holding U.S. citizenship differentiates the 1.5 and second generations socially, culturally, and politically from the first immigrant generation. Suro and Passel (2003, 8–9) found that the second generation is more bilingual, attains higher educational levels, and earns higher incomes than the first generation. Further, a higher percentage of the second generation marry outside their own ethnic or racial group, and this trend appears to continue into the third immigrant generation.

The relevance of the second and third generations is also apparent within the Mexican-origin population in the United States, which nearly quintupled between 1980 and 2010. In 2003, there were 26.7 million individuals of Mexican origin in the United States, of whom nearly 60 percent were second- and third-generation descendants of immigrants (Zúñiga, Leite, and Nava 2005). The process of integrating Mexicans into U.S. society and culture has generated heated controversy, fed by Mexico's geographic proximity to the United States, the large size of the immigrant population, the use of Spanish among this community, the illegal component within this population, and its historical longevity (Huntington 2005, 227–229), not to mention the persisting negative stereotype associated with being a Mexican in the United States and the fact that this population crosscuts easily defined racial categories (López and Stanton-Salazar 2001, 61). A recurring element in this discussion is the Mexican cultural matrix rooted in Catholic tradition vis-à-vis the Anglo-Protestant tradition.

These elements gain even greater relevance in the integration of descendants of Mexicans in California, given their proximity to a highly interactive border and the presence of Mexican communities in California since the nineteenth century. Since the 1960s, the proportion of second-generation Latino children in this border state has skyrocketed; at the same time, their average age has dropped significantly.[3] Even though the Mexican-origin population constitutes the largest minority group in the state, second-generation Mexican children do not outperform other, Asia-origin minorities in academic achievement or English-language proficiency (López and Stanton-Salazar 2001).

Not only do the pathways of integration differ by generation in the Mexican-origin population; they also differ according to a set of contextual elements, such as human capital, family structure, and the means of incorporation for each generation. Using these elements, Portes and Rumbaut (2006, 265) identify different trajectories in the modes of incorporation for each generation. Human, social, and cultural capital appear to be key to defining the terms of integration for the second generation. Of particular importance are parents' education and the existence of ethnicity-based community linkages. Other authors suggest that these contextual elements in fact point to the family's position in the class structure (see Zhou 1997, 987), which ultimately plays a more important role in children's adaptation by determining the kind of neighborhood in which they live, the quality of the schools where they receive their education, and the cohort of companions with whom they interact. The distinct paths to integration have their correlates in young people's identity, in an alchemy that combines parents' life experiences with the dominant currents of thought in U.S. society.

To East LA: Study as a Privilege

It's morning, on a weekend, on a college campus on the eastern edge of Los Angeles. Young people are heading out in different directions to meet their friends. The classrooms are silent; dormitories are abandoned. Only a few foreign students remain. The campus's low-rise buildings are grouped amid broad green lawns bordered by maple trees. The college offers an undergraduate degree, and it is one of a network of top-ranked private colleges catering to the elite, on the model of the University of Oxford. The racial and ethnic diversity of the students is striking, but all share the privilege of studying at an elite school made notable by the quality of its teaching and its small class size. But not all students originate from the same social class, something one might expect in light of the school's elevated cost—more than $50,000 a year. Many are first- or second-generation children of immigrants and come from varied socioeconomic backgrounds. They owe their privileged positions here to a system of undergraduate scholarships and student loans.

Emilio is in his senior year at the college, thanks to an academic scholarship. Diverging from his customary pattern, this weekend he is not visiting his family in Chula Vista. He will spend the weekend near the Mexican border. Emilio and his friend get in the car, turn the radio up, and prepare for the 119-mile trip to Tijuana. After two hours of freeway driving, here is the Mexican border with its gates wide open to everyone, no travel documents required. "Welcome to Mexico" reads the banner bridging the six traffic lanes leading into the city. A stoplight monotonously flashes red or green while customs agents and soldiers wait on the Mexican side to examine vehicles that a red light has randomly selected for inspection.

Emilio is twenty-two years old, slim, and nearly six feet tall. He doesn't sport earrings or bracelets. His attire is simply jeans, a T-shirt, and tennis shoes. Dark curls fall on his forehead in disarray. We are in Playas de Tijuana, where he spent some of his childhood years. Emilio seems happy; when he smiles, his metal braces catch the light. His eyes sparkle when he looks at us, but his face grows serious when he talks in fluent, educated Spanish about his life.

Early Childhood in Tijuana: Paradise with Trash

My father was born in Los Angeles, California, and my mother in Mazatlán, Sinaloa. My father grew up as an only child in east LA. His grades in school weren't very good. He was young, at that age when you don't know what to do with your life. In the 1970s, he went to Mexico City to attend a private high school in Coyoacán. My grandparents had some businesses; they weren't rich, but they had enough money to send him. After he finished high school in Mexico City, he went to Guadalajara to study medicine at the university. While he was studying, my dad went to Mazatlán on holiday and met my mother. They got married in Mazatlán in 1983 and went to live in Guadalajara, the plan being for my dad to finish medical school. My mother was twenty-two years old; my dad, twenty-five.

I was born there, in Guadalajara, in 1986, three years after my parents met, and my sister was born in 1987. My parents led a quiet life. They lived alone in a small apartment. My father studied, and my mother stayed home to take care of my sister and me.

When I was a year old, my family moved to Mazatlán. We didn't live in Guadalajara long enough for me to get a sense of it. I've never gone back, though they say it's a beautiful city. My mother always says that when she sees pictures of Guadalajara, she remembers all of it: the architecture, the art, the culture. She says that if she had to live in Mexico, she'd like to live in Guadalajara.

Where do you remember spending your childhood?

My memories of childhood are here, in Tijuana. We moved to Tijuana in 1988; I was still very young. My parents say that the city was very dirty back then. Its appearance was not an incentive that made you want to live here. They say there was a lot of trash in the streets. We first came to stay at my father's grandmother's house, near downtown. It wasn't a very safe area, but I don't remember seeing the poverty and misery that I see today. A year later we moved to a little house on Grieta Street in Playas de Tijuana. According to my mother, it was a more family-friendly neighborhood. That's really where I grew up. I don't remember so much abject poverty. I studied at the Cumbres Institute, where there weren't any poor children, but I used to hear that there were poor people.

Why did your family move to Tijuana?

Lots of reasons. My dad is a U.S. citizen, and he wanted to explore job opportunities in the United States, but he wasn't ready yet to move there directly. So he decided to move to a border city like Tijuana, to test the waters. The advantage of Tijuana was that he already knew it because he'd lived here when he was younger. He looked for a new line of work, because the career in medicine hadn't worked out for him in Mexico. As far as I know, he didn't like medicine and he wanted to start over. Originally the plan was to stay in Guadalajara to practice medicine, but that didn't work for family and economic reasons. He graduated, but he couldn't go on to specialize. While we were living in Tijuana, an opportunity opened up for him in San Diego, and he wanted to begin again.

So you began your education in Tijuana?

Yes. I studied at the Cumbres Institute in Tijuana until third grade. It's an elite private school, for boys only. The only thing I remember is that my parents sacrificed in order to pay the tuition. I don't know if it's still one of the most expensive schools, but it was then. I remember that there were kids there from wealthy families. Sons of businessmen and established families.

My friends at Cumbres lived in the Hipódromo and Agua Caliente neighborhoods, where the high-society people lived. There were poor neighborhoods too, like Mesa, with lots of violence. I remember a city that was socially divided, with marked differences between rich and poor.

Did you have contact with poor people, or did you see them only from a distance?

I don't remember any really poor people. We didn't have any family members here, only friends. The only relative was my great-grandmother, and she wasn't poor, because she'd inherited money from some businesses.

I didn't go to a sports or country club, because my parents didn't have that kind of money, but I played a lot in the street with my friends. That's one thing I remember, that I played a lot of soccer in the street when I was a kid.

Playas was always like paradise to me. I think I blocked out the realities of Tijuana, because for me the city was like a dream. It was the perfect place to be a kid. I had an unspoiled childhood, playing with the kids, with groups of friends in the street. I had a childhood like a typical Mexican kid. Playing in the street, hanging around with friends. I couldn't have asked for more. I was very happy.

What kind of work were your parents doing during that time?

My mother studied psychology, but she gave up her studies to stay home and take care of my sister and me. My dad worked at the Veterans Health Administration Hospital in San Diego. When he first started there, I think he worked in equipment inventory and maintenance.

He crossed the border every day. He got up at three o'clock in the morning and crossed the border in a car that was always breaking down. Sometimes he had to take a taxi to the line, then cross the border on foot and take the trolley to downtown San Diego. From there he took a bus to La Jolla, to the hospital. It took him about three hours to get there. That's why he got up at three in the morning, and he came home very late, about seven o'clock in the evening. What I remember is that he didn't spend much time with us because he was so tired when he got home. He just ate dinner, had a drink, and went to bed at eight or nine o'clock. That was his daily routine.

We'd cross the border too. Like everybody else in Tijuana, we'd cross to

go shopping. My mother always liked to buy clothes in the United States.
Sometimes we'd visit relatives, my dad's uncles, who lived in National City.
My dad would take us to San Diego every weekend for a picnic in the park.
That's when I realized that there was more fun to be had in the United States
than in Tijuana.

Life on the Other Side of the Border: Chula Vista

The summer of 1995 was a very dramatic time for my family, because my
maternal grandfather got sick when he came to visit us from Mazatlán. He
caught a cold and cough. He had emphysema; he was a smoker. His brain
was dying for lack of oxygen because he couldn't clear his lungs of phlegm.
He spent most of the summer at death's door in the ISSSTE[4] hospital. It was
especially dramatic for me, because this was the first time I'd understood
the realities of life: death, bills, poverty—because his medical care was very
expensive.

Given all of this, the time came when my father couldn't afford to keep
us in private schools in Tijuana any longer. He was going into debt, paying
out lots of money. He wanted to see if the time was ripe for us to go to the
other side. Even before coming to Tijuana, he already had plans to move to
the United States. His idea was to go step by step. He's a U.S. citizen, but he
wanted to make sure first that we were prepared for a different life.

That's why we didn't move to the other side directly from Guadalajara.
First he wanted to get established in his job. I'm not sure, but I think he saw
better educational opportunities for us in the United States. He wanted to
take advantage of them, so he decided to move. What I remember is that one
night we began moving little by little, and suddenly we were on the other side!
But in fact it was gradual, because I was still living in Tijuana when I started
school in the United States, and I crossed the border every day. That just
lasted a month, and then we settled in an apartment in Chula Vista, where
I've lived ever since.

How did the change affect you?

It was rough, really rough. I was nine years old, and it was hard to get
used to a new way of life. I didn't speak English very well; I could understand
but not speak it. People in the United States are very individualistic, and I
didn't find the sense of community that there was in Playas, where all the
neighbors knew one another.

Life is very different in the United States; families keep their distance from
each other. People are friendly, but they maintain their distance. It's not like
Tijuana, where people welcome you into their homes. I noticed that, because I
didn't have any friends, any pals in the street anymore, like I had in Tijuana.

It was hard at school too. The language set me apart, because I couldn't speak English. My parents enrolled me in bilingual classes in a school in Chula Vista that was near my house and near the border, where there were lots of Hispanics. I wasn't ready for an English-only classroom yet; that's why they put me in a bilingual class. There were lots of kids there who spoke English, but they weren't working at grade level. They were children from Hispanic families that had been in the United States for a long time, but they always spoke Spanish at home. So I couldn't make many friends at school because of my lack of English. Even though I didn't isolate myself, it was hard to make friends like the ones I'd had in Tijuana.

Who were these kids?

Most were Hispanics, just a few Anglos. Many of them were the children of manual laborers or office workers. Their parents weren't well-off or educated or in well-paid jobs. In that sense, I could identify with them because they were just like me: children of working people.

I encountered one big difference here in the United States compared to Tijuana: materialism, the importance of buying things to make you feel good. I was never materialistic. My parents never owned their home, not in the States nor in Tijuana. It's not that they can't buy a house; it's that they don't want to be in debt. It's easy to get into debt in the United States, and that's another reason we didn't spend a lot of money on material things. I saw that the kids in the United States had nice clothes, nice toys, kids' stuff. I never had much of that because I wasn't looking for a way to feel better; I looked only for ways to entertain myself.

What was your view of this consumption?

In those days, I couldn't draw the logical connection. Why did so many of the kids want material things like computer games, for example? Now that I'm an adult, I think it's because those kids—I may be generalizing—don't have the amusements that we had in Tijuana, activities like playing together, playing soccer in the street. Yesterday I went to play soccer at the fields, and I realized that kids here [in Tijuana] still play sports outside, in the open air. You don't see that in the United States, maybe because many people are afraid, because there's lots of gang violence in the United States. That's always been a problem, and I think that's why parents don't want their children to spend much time in the street. They ride bicycles, but not like in Mexico, where it's a cultural thing, part of childhood, because everybody remembers playing in the street with your pals. I think this is why so many parents in the United States buy computer games for their children, so that they stay home and are entertained without going outside.

In California without a Mexican Family

How did your family life change in the United States?

As for family, I remember that my mother started working. She didn't start right away, only after I was a junior in high school. Then my father got a promotion, and things were going well for him at work. He was still at the same hospital he'd worked at while we lived in Tijuana. What I noticed right away is that the pace of life was faster, you know? For example, we lived in Chula Vista, and my dad worked in La Jolla, twenty-two miles away. My sister and I would walk to school; it was only a few blocks away. My mother would pick us up when school got out, and we'd go home. It was just like it had been in Tijuana. We were never out of touch with one another, because we didn't have any other family in the United States. My father didn't have many relatives in Los Angeles, and he wasn't in contact with the few relatives he did have. It's hard for our relatives in Mazatlán to visit us now, because of visa or money complications. So it's basically been the four of us here in the United States.

Your father was born in Los Angeles, right? What happened with his family?

Yes. My dad was born in east LA. I don't know the history of my paternal grandparents very well, only that they lived in Tijuana and went to Los Angeles to put up a business, and that's where they settled. In those days it was easy to cross to the other side and get a visa. For my dad, growing up in east LA was like growing up in Mexico, because it's the largest community of Mexicans. And even though there are Asians and African Americans there too, there's not much interaction with them. They're separate communities, with marked differences dividing them. So he felt like a Mexican with U.S. citizenship, because he was born in the United States. His only relatives that I know are the San Diego uncles, who now live in Tecate. From what I understand, my father didn't come from a big family. The few who are left are in Michoacán, and those on my mother's side are in Rosario, Sinaloa.

When I was growing up, I'd visit my maternal grandparents once a year. My paternal grandparents are deceased. I didn't grow up in the classic extended Mexican family. That makes me different from my Hispanic friends. Their families have lots of parties and visit each other a lot. Some of them have grandparents in Tijuana.

Once you were in San Diego, how did you do in school?

I did junior high and part of high school in the same neighborhood in Chula Vista. I studied one year at a public school, Hilltop Middle School. It was awful. That's where I saw the problems with public schools in the United States. There are good public schools, but that one was bad. It was hard on me because I wasn't being stimulated intellectually. My parents saw that I was falling behind, and just by chance my dad heard that they were going to open a charter school on the campus of the University of California, San Diego.

The idea is to give minority youths the opportunity to go to the university. Charter schools offer a different kind of education. The level of education is unmatched, and there are fewer students, so classes are more intimate. The education is more intensive than in a regular school, with classes from eight in the morning until four in the afternoon. I was in the first generation. That school was a miracle for me. My parents had been thinking about switching me to a private school, where they'd have had to pay a fortune.

Why do you think the public school wasn't working?

I don't know that much about the educational system. They didn't accept me in the accelerated program, because I failed the exam by one point. Yes, just one point! So they put me in the regular classes, and the math they were learning was multiplication and division. I was in the first year of junior high, and I said to myself, why am I learning this stuff? The environment didn't motivate us to excel. In contrast, the goal in the charter school is to gain admission to a good university. I had good grades, so it was clear that going to a university would be my next step. I applied to several schools in California, but I didn't want to go to a big school like Cal State or the University of California, San Diego, where there are thirty thousand students.

Luckily, I found some small colleges that are generally known only to the wealthy, to high society and academics: the Claremont Colleges. I applied to Claremont McKenna, and they accepted me and gave me a lot of financial support. This is a very prestigious school in academic circles and high society. Besides, it's close to San Diego, and I could go home every weekend. Being a student at McKenna opens a lot of doors and builds your network. It's a small school—just a thousand students. The atmosphere is like the Cumbres Institute, where everybody knows everybody and the intellectual level is out of this world.

The Land of Opportunities: Work Hard and Triumph

What advantages does this school offer you?

Opportunities, because if you work hard, doors will open for you. This is a characteristic of the United States. Many people speak badly about the United States, but it's true that if you study or work hard, more opportunities will come your way. This is an idea that I grew up with. There was a time when I told myself, "Okay, I'm Mexican, but I'm also North American. I can take advantage of the U.S. education, with all of its opportunities. I can get an education in the United States and then go to Mexico to work." I've always had the idea, though, that it's hard to work in Mexico because you need connections. My parents would tell me that there aren't many opportunities in Mexico. I've always had scholarships in the United States; I don't know if the same would be true in Mexico, if there's a chance that some family would give me money to go to school. I don't know how a student with economic constraints manages to get ahead. Are there scholarships? Because there's a lot of money in the United States. You just have to look for it. They need to see that you really apply yourself and that you're driven to succeed.

I was very young when I left Mexico, but my parents lived the university experience there, and they say it was hard. They say that in Mexico, if you have money you can get into good schools, but otherwise it's very difficult. Mexico is a society that defines you according to what you own and who you know.

You mentioned that many of your schoolmates in Chula Vista didn't have a chance to go to a better school, so they went to a community college. Why couldn't they, like you, go to a good school?

There are a number of reasons, but it's not because I'm different. First, there were only four of us in my family, so that made it easier. My parents were not the type to say, "Oh, I have to go visit the family." I never had to stop studying in order to go visit relatives, never. My friends would always say they had to go visit their grandmother in Tijuana over the weekend, and we had a test on Monday. There's the difference. I'd study on weekends, and my friends would go visit relatives in Tijuana. So, in that sense, to be a family of four, without lots of relatives, that helped me a bit, because it was hard if you couldn't focus on your studies. I think it also helped that my parents were educated, even though they weren't professional people. My mother studied psychology, though she didn't get her diploma. My father studied medicine and graduated. They are educated people though they didn't pursue those careers. So they've always said that it's important to study in order to get ahead in life. "Never worry about money, about a career; just get an education, and see what doors open for you. Always keep looking for what stimulates you intellectually." So I studied history. I could have studied economics, business, or something that would give me a steady job, but I decided to study a subject that makes me think. I've noticed that some Mexican parents who live in the United States tell their children to study a career that gives tangible results. A nice house, a fancy car, nice things. That's why many of my friends are studying engineering, economics, things they think will guarantee a life of comfort.

You don't think that's true in your case—they didn't educate you like that?

Ever since elementary school in Tijuana, in the Cumbres Institute, they taught me scholarly discipline, because it was a conservative school, Catholic and very strict. Ever since I was little, I would give up playing with my friends, going out, in order to study. I still do that today. I'm not a partygoer. I always put my studies first, because I know that's my foundation for the future.

Many Hispanic students in my community don't think like that. Their parents didn't instill this mind-set in them.

My father speaks English well, but my mother had to work hard to learn it. In contrast, many Hispanic parents who've been living in the United States longer still haven't assimilated to U.S. culture and still don't speak English. They live in Hispanic communities and speak only Spanish. My parents have more Anglo friends than Hispanic friends, and I think it's because they speak English.

My mother started from zero, because none of her studies in Mexico were recognized in the United States. She had to get her GED, the equivalent of a high school diploma. Then she took classes at Southwestern College, where lots of young people from my generation go to school. So my mother has always looked for ways to continue studying and to improve her English.

You can't say there's a North American culture in the United States— only principles that stand for the country and motivate its people. It's a place where, if you work hard, you'll have opportunities. Nothing is impossible if you work hard. That's what my parents instilled in us; I don't know if it's true for them too.

Identity in Balance: Mexican and North American

Do you think that individual effort and achievement are rewarded in the United States?

Yes, that's what defines the United States. Many people come to the United States because they know you can succeed here if you apply yourself and work hard. But I think that many Hispanic families haven't assimilated. They've found it hard to instill those principles in their children. My advantage is that my parents continue to seek out intellectual stimulation; they like to read. That helped me and my sister a lot.

Why do you think it's so hard for Hispanic families to assimilate?

I think it's hard to give up deep-rooted Mexican principles like family and religion. Not everyone in the United States is Catholic, so many people

tend to close themselves off in their own communities. Perhaps they don't
want their children to lose their Mexican identity. My parents did a good job
in balancing our identity, so that we're 100 percent North American, but we
have a Mexican identity as well. I have that balance.

How do you define your identity?

Mexican American. That is, I have dual citizenship, and I appreciate
the good in both cultures. We've already spoken about what's good in the
United States, about the opportunities that are available. Now, what's good
about being Mexican is to be sociable and to be part of a community. For
me, religion is very important; I identify strongly with that. My family is
Catholic, and I feel very Mexican when I go to Mass, because I'm with all of
my Mexican brothers. Religion has helped me a lot. I didn't give that up when
I came to the United States. There are other, less important things too, like
soccer; I've always been a soccer fan. Because I was born in Mexico, I want
to preserve my identity as a Mexican. I've never returned to Guadalajara,
but I know I was born there, so I've got an even better reason to identify as
Mexican—though I identify more strongly with Tijuana and Mazatlán than
with Guadalajara.

Are your closest friends now of any nationality in particular?

No, one thing my parents did very well was never put limits on
our friendships. Many of my friends are Anglos. My father works with
Anglos, Filipinos, Japanese, and Chinese. My mother is the receptionist
at my high school, and she has African American friends, Anglo friends,
everybody.

During my years at Claremont McKenna, where most students are
Anglos from prominent families, I've noticed that we Hispanics have trouble
interacting with people of other races. But I think I'm different in this
regard, because I make friends with Jews, Muslims, African Americans, with
everybody. I believe that we are all humans, and that racial and religious
differences are something we construct ourselves to differentiate people.
I try to be friendly with everyone, no matter their gender, race, or religion,
and I never tie myself to a single group of friends. One of my best friends
at Claremont McKenna is African American. I also lived with a Persian for
three years and with a guy from India. So I never pigeonhole myself in group
X. For example, I never identified with the "Claremont Cabrones," a group of
Hispanics at McKenna. It's like a fraternity. They have parties; it also acts like
a Hispanic network. I never thought about joining, because I don't need to
belong to a group to know that I'm Hispanic.

Why do you think they do that?

I don't know. Maybe to create a familiar environment, because many of them come from Hispanic families that are closely tied to their Hispanic communities, and they bring this same mind-set to college. I also come from a Hispanic environment, but a large part of my education took place in La Jolla. I never had that affinity with my community, not that close. I also think it comes from families that never assimilated completely to the environment in the United States, and they need to draw on their cultural resources in order not to feel isolated, because at McKenna you're surrounded by wealth, by the upper echelons of society.

Is the difficulty in getting to know new people or interacting with people from different backgrounds a matter of ethnicity or social class? Or is it an individual thing?

I think it's a bit of everything. There may be ethnic reasons, because growing up in an environment where you're always with Mexicans can affect the way you view relations with people of other races. But there may also be economic reasons, because you might be intimidated by somebody who's had everything life has to offer. At the same time, it also depends on individual factors, like how your parents brought you up to see U.S. society. In my case, my parents told me that there's no middle class in Mexico, only rich and poor. In contrast, in the United States, if you work hard you can move up the social ladder. When I see people with money, I always say that I'm going to be like them, because somebody in their family had to work hard to reach that level. My goal is to start on that road so that my children and grandchildren will be successful. I'll be the first in my family to do that. I'm not going to be an idealist and say there aren't any obstacles, but everything depends on how your parents brought you up and their educational level.

My sister is studying at Brown University, an Ivy League school in Rhode Island. That makes us different too, because many Hispanic fathers don't let their sons, much less a daughter, go three thousand miles away. But my sister wanted to go, and my father said, "No problem. We'll support you. Get an education."

Tijuana Relaxes Me!

There was a time when we distanced ourselves from Mexico. Who knows why? After leaving for the United States, I didn't come back to Tijuana from 1996 until 2000.

It was a long time. I don't know why. There wasn't any reason. In the beginning, my friends from Tijuana would visit me in San Diego. But I don't know what happened. Just one of those things. We grew apart, we followed different paths; that's all. I was too little to decide to come to Tijuana to visit my friends. I guess I wasn't motivated enough to press it, because I was trying to build another life in the United States.

When did you renew your relationship with the Mexican side of the border?

It was all because of a dentist. I think that concern about our teeth brought us to Tijuana. The dentist is a close family friend, and he has his own clinic downtown. And, of course, it's less expensive in Tijuana than in Chula Vista. My treatment would have cost $2,000 in Chula Vista, but it was half of that or even less in Tijuana. That's why many Hispanics come here; it's cheaper. I'm also seeing more Anglos, more North Americans, coming to Tijuana for dental care.

What do you think of the health system in the United States?

I'm fortunate because my father gets free health insurance since he works in a hospital. Many people don't have that opportunity. I have to go to the hospital tomorrow because I hurt my knee. They're going to do an MRI, and it will cost me only $20, instead of $2,000. The United States has always had health problems because there's no universal health care system. Not everybody has access to the same medical treatment, like there is in Europe, in Denmark or Sweden. It's all privatized in the United States, because of the idea that you can't get everything for free. You have to work hard to earn it.

I don't see that in Mexico. It's more a mind-set kind of thing, because there's nothing physical that separates us, Mexicans from Americans. It's really hard to see people suffering in Mexico. Why are people suffering here? Or why aren't the streets clean here, like over there? Why are the police here corrupt? We don't have many problems in the United States, but when there are mistakes, we overcome them. In contrast, when mistakes are made in Mexico, people care more about arguing over them than about solving them.

Now that you're a young man, what is your view of the Mexican border region?

I see it as a place for fun. We come on the weekend to relax. My mother likes to do her shopping in the Comercial Mexicana. She stocks up on Mexican products they don't sell over there. We like to eat Mexican food, and we love the Chinese food here. For me, Mexico is a paradise, pure relaxation. Of course, we hear about border violence in the news, about the drug trafficking. I think it's a cultural thing that won't disappear. That's why when I sometimes ask myself if I'd like to *live* in Mexico, I have to consider the violence. There's insecurity in the United States too, but the law is stronger, stricter there. In Mexico, you can bend the law with money; you can bribe the police. Details like these create the perception that life on the border is getting more difficult. Tijuana is no longer the paradise where I grew up. That makes me question whether I want to come back here to live.

Do you see differences between the poverty in San Diego and that in Tijuana?

Yes. In the United States, there are centers where you have a chance to rehabilitate yourself or get your life back. Mexican society is very stratified, and the people who have money won't help. I don't understand why Carlos Slim, the richest man in the world, doesn't give money to help the people. It astounds me that 50 percent of the Mexican population lives in poverty. The only people who get ahead are the ones with money and education. It's really hard for poor people; there's no way for them to get ahead.

How would you define the border? What does the border mean to you?

The border? Well . . . two cultures. To me, it's like an interaction between two cultures that attract each other. Tijuana is attracted to the United States, and vice versa. So it's a mutual attraction, between the Mexican and the North American cultures. For me, the border is a dividing line between progress and regression. Because you go to Tijuana and you realize that there are still things to be overcome. You enter the United States and you see a different world, a different way of thinking, of living, people behaving differently. For me, the border is the barrier that divides those two worlds, those two ways of looking at life.

Living One Day at a Time: The Future in the United States

Do you think the United States is a good place for your professional and family life?

To live there? Yes. That is, I doubt whether I'd like my children to go to a school like Cumbres in Mexico and then come to the United States. I don't know yet if that's what I want to do. When I have children, that's when we'll decide, depending on where I live. I'd like to live in San Diego, though I know life there is difficult; everything is very expensive. I like Boston, New York, or Washington too, because it's easier to buy a house there.

What excites you most in life?

To obtain knowledge. I can do without money, without power. But to be ignorant? I've seen that the people who move forward, the people we admire in history, place more importance on gaining knowledge than on money or power. To aspire to wealth and power is to remain a sheep all your life, because you're letting yourself be manipulated by what people think is important for success. If you're a critical person, you have to say these ideas are things that people impose. Are you going to let yourself be manipulated by that? That's how I see it. If one day I manage to have money and power, I'll take it, but I won't sacrifice my desire to be an intellectual, to be a "Renaissance man," a Leonardo da Vinci. I want to know everything, not to just anchor myself in one thing. I want to think about how to solve problems using different solutions. I don't want to limit my imagination.

And religion, is that something you want to preserve in your life?

Yes, sure. Religion is important to me. I believe in God, but I don't go to Mass very often. Because religion is personal for me, and that makes me different from other Hispanics from Mexico. I see many people in Mexico going to Mass for the wrong reasons. They don't go because they feel it in their hearts; they go because they think they are sinners. That's the Catholic mind-set: that we're sinners and we have to do penance in order to win God's love. I don't think like that. I accept that such beliefs exist, but I define Catholicism my own way. For me, religion is more spiritual. It's something that guides my daily life. It's not something for Sundays only. Going to church isn't a moral responsibility I must fulfill in order to feel better and more closely connected with God. I'm not saying it's wrong, but for me religion is something more spiritual, something that guides my emotions, that makes me think, everything.

How do you see your professional and personal life in the future? Would you like to get married?

Family life? Yes, I want to get married. To have an intellectual wife, a professional, somebody cool. To have children, not many, just two, like my father and mother. As to career, I don't know yet. I'm going to see what interests me. I'm a dreamer; I've got big dreams. They say you should dream big because great people dream big dreams. So I'm dreaming large scale. I see myself as the president of a European soccer club, like Real Madrid, for example. Not the owner, but in charge of the club's operations. Those clubs handle a lot of money. My mother says I'm an idealist, that I should "focus on something." I tell her that I'm too young still to focus on a single thing. I just want to become educated, that's all. After my doctorate, if I end up doing a doctorate, I'll continue in law or business. I'm not sure.

I'm one of those guys who live one day at a time. So I'm not going to set out a plan right now. I'm just going to continue getting an education. One thing is sure: I'm not going to study for four years at the university and then go directly to work. That's not for me. I'm not ready to go to work yet. I want to continue my studies and work while I'm getting an education. I know there's something great for me out there, but I don't know what it is. I study

European history, so perhaps I'll go to live in Europe. When I'm older, I'd like to return to Mexico and retire in Mazatlán. If I make some money, I'd like to buy a house in Mazatlán, so I could come with my family for vacations. I don't want to lose my contacts in Mexico. Obviously I'll be in contact with my Mexican friends forever, and I've got people here in Tijuana. So Mexico will always be in my heart, but I don't know where work will take me. I want to go east to study. I'd like to live in New York or Boston. Those cities fascinate me. So if I find my future wife there, then that's where I'll stay. I'm not putting any limitations on myself. I don't say, I want to marry a Mexican. I just want someone who accepts me as I am. So I don't know. I'll take whatever life hands me.

10

Guarding the American Dream

The Growth of the Border Patrol

The Border Patrol was established in 1924 as part of the U.S. government's efforts to stem the smuggling of alcohol into the United States during Prohibition and also to block the entry of undocumented immigrants into U.S. territory.[1] A year after its creation, the agency had just 450 officials to guard the long U.S. borders with Canada and Mexico. During the second half of the twentieth century, and especially toward the end of the century, this small, disjointed organization would be transformed into one of the principal U.S. policing agencies.

Two moments were particularly significant in the strengthening of the Border Patrol. The first came in 1993, when the U.S. government enhanced border controls following a sizable increase over the previous ten years in the flow of undocumented migrants across the Mexican border. The newly inaugurated Clinton administration decided to substantially augment the budget of the Immigration and Naturalization Service, which included the Border Patrol, and also to concentrate these new resources on specific sections of the border that had been identified as the primary corridors through which migrants were crossing (Cornelius 2001, 661).

The Border Patrol's budget rose steadily in the following years, nearly tripling between 1993 and 2001, from $120 million to $350 million (Office of Management and Budget 2009). Over the same period, the number of agents rose from thirty-eight hundred to ninety-two hundred (U.S. Department of Homeland Se-

Illustration: Waiting for border crossers, Tijuana. *(Photograph by Laura Velasco Ortiz.)*

curity 2003). In addition to increases in its funding and agent corps, the Border Patrol received advanced electronic monitoring technologies, such as remote motion sensors, infrared night-vision cameras, and a state-of-the-art information network. And finally, new physical barriers were installed at the most problematic points on the border (Guerette 2007).

Within this context, a new strategy of "prevention through deterrence" was instituted. No longer would the agents' objective be to arrest migrants after they had crossed the border. Instead, the border line would be fortified with fences and a strong presence of Border Patrol agents to prevent migrants from crossing in the first place. The first of these efforts was Operation Hold the Line, implemented in El Paso, Texas, in 1993. It involved reinforcing physical barriers and stationing large numbers of agents in key border-crossing areas. It was followed by similar operations in other zones with heavy migrant flows: Operation Gatekeeper in the San Diego sector in 1994, Operation Safeguard in the Tucson sector in 1994, and Operation Rio Grande in south Texas in 1997.

These operations indeed resulted in a reduction in the number of undocumented migrants entering at the newly fortified crossing points. However, another direct consequence was to shift the flow of migrants toward more dangerous points on the border line, where the distance from urban areas and the harsh climatic and topographical conditions made it harder for the Border Patrol to control the border but also where the risks to the migrants rose exponentially. As a result, the number of migrants who have died attempting to cross the border has escalated since these operations began (Nevins 2003). In 1994, there were 180 officially recorded deaths among would-be migrants; by 2000, the number had risen to 370 (Eschbach, Hagan, and Rodríguez 2003). According to migrant advocate Enrique Morones, by 2006 the number of deaths among undocumented border crossers was averaging 600 per year (Morones 2009). The three principal causes of mortality were extreme temperatures, resulting in sunstroke, hyperthermia, and heatstroke (35 percent); exhaustion (21 percent); and vehicle accidents (11 percent) (Guerette 2007, 138).

The terrorist attacks of September 11, 2001, mark the second significant moment in the strengthening and reorientation of the Border Patrol. As part of the most thoroughgoing reorganization of U.S. security policies since the end of World War II, a new agency, the Department of Homeland Security (DHS), was created in 2002, its mission being to prevent future terrorist attacks on U.S. soil. U.S. Customs and Border Protection (CBP) is a subagency of the DHS, and with this reorganization the Border Patrol came under the jurisdiction of the CBP. The Border Patrol's priorities were also redefined, so that defending U.S. territory against terrorist threats became its primary mission. In the words of David Aguilar, chief of the Border Patrol:

> *CBP, as the guardian of the Nation's borders, safeguards the homeland—foremost, by protecting the American public against terrorists and the instruments of terrorism; while at the same time enforcing the laws of the*

United States. . . . Contributing to all this is the Border Patrol's time-honored duty of interdicting illegal aliens and drugs and those who attempt to smuggle them across our borders between the Ports of Entry. We are concerned that illegal human smuggling routes may be exploited by terrorists to conduct attacks against the U.S. homeland. Reducing illegal migration across our borders may help in disrupting possible attempts by terrorists to enter our country. (Aguilar 2005, 1)

Following this redefinition, the Border Patrol received strong support for its enhanced duties. Between 2002 and 2008, its annual budget tripled to $3.5 billion and the number of agents doubled to eighteen thousand (Office of Management and Budget 2009). As a result, the Border Patrol has been transformed into the largest policing force in the United States, even surpassing the Federal Bureau of Investigation (FBI).

According to assessments by the DHS, the number of detentions of undocumented migrants has declined steadily since 2000, partly the result of enhanced border control, which is thought to be deterring potential crossers. In 2000, there were 1.6 million detentions, but in 2008 there were only 724,000 (Rytina and Simanski 2009). Nevertheless, DHS data confirm that the number of undocumented migrants residing in the United States rose by 37 percent over the same period, from 8.5 million in 2000 to 11.6 million in 2008. Of this population, an estimated 7 million (61 percent) are Mexicans. On average, some 390,000 undocumented migrants settled in the United States each year between 2000 and 2008, and of these, 290,000 are Mexican (Hoefer, Rytina, and Baker 2009). The Border Patrol's imposing presence on the U.S. border with Mexico has shifted migration trajectories and pushed migrants into new routes that are more costly and more dangerous, but it has not halted undocumented migration, which is dictated by the profound economic asymmetry between these two countries and labor demand in the United States.

A Mexican American in the Border Patrol

At the end of a spirited exchange of e-mails in which we outlined the reasons for our request, Agent Julius Alatorre agreed to meet with us in the San Diego offices of the Border Patrol. Before visiting with Agent Alatorre, we had been able, thanks to support from Grupo Beta (the police corps that works to protect migrants on the Mexican side of the border), to visit and acquaint ourselves with the main crossing points between Tijuana and Mexicali that are used by undocumented migrants entering the United States.

Major U.S. government investments in recent years have totally altered the landscape of the Tijuana–San Diego border region. Formidable engineering works have transformed the previously shady and winding ravines that trace the border line into systems of slopes and terraces, drainage canals, and broad roadways that rival the best public highways. What was once an unbroken landscape *has been glaringly interrupted by a strip fortified with a double row of metal walls, well illuminated by night and easily reached by the omnipresent vehicles of the Border Patrol.*

Toward the east, heading toward Mexicali, the physical barriers gradually taper off until the border line in the desert area around Laguna Salada is defined merely by a stretch of metal obstacles placed to prevent vehicles from crossing. Patrolling in this area is left to the remote motion sensors, the infrared cameras, and the desert's killing heat.

The offices of the Border Patrol are located east of Chula Vista, a city in San Diego County with a large Mexican and Mexican American population. It's an imposing two-story building, solid and somber. An employee greets us and asks us to be seated in the reception area while Agent Alatorre is informed of our arrival. Previously we had visited the offices of Grupo Beta in Tijuana and Tecate, which are in ramshackle buildings, furnished with secondhand furniture, and teeming with migrants hoping for the modest assistance the Mexican government makes available. The contrast with these offices' lavish furnishings, their organization, and their plentiful resources is overwhelming. When we arrive at the office of the Border Patrol spokesperson, we encounter a young, slender, energetic official who, in impeccable Spanish marked by an undeniably Mexican American accent, relates his experience.

A Mexican Family in San Diego

I was born in San Diego, California, on April 13, 1979. My parents are both Mexican. My father is from Milpas Viejas, Nayarit, and my mother is from San Ciro de Acosta, San Luis Potosí. They're migrants; they came to the United States in the mid-1970s. Like many Mexicans who emigrated to the United States, they came to work. . . . My dad's an executive chef now in a restaurant in downtown San Diego, and my mother is the head of housekeeping in a hotel, also in central San Diego.

In addition to my parents, I have a brother who is two years older than I, and a half-brother on my mother's side, who's four years older. I had a younger sister, three years younger than I am, but she died when she was three and I was six. My sister and I were born in the United States; my brother was born in Tijuana and then emigrated to the United States.

Our family has always been close, and my parents were always there for us. They worked extremely hard to provide their children with everything we needed. That's the environment we were raised in; our mom and dad worked very hard and were very dedicated to the family. The way my parents live their life has been an inspiration for me . . . to work to improve myself like they were doing when they came to the United States.

I got all of my education in San Diego. I went to elementary school in National City, at Central Elementary. I started in 1984, when I was five, and I finished in 1990. Then I went to junior high at National City Middle School and then to Sweetwater High from 1993 to 1997. After graduation, I went to a junior college, Southwestern College, for two years, but I soon realized that college wasn't for me, so I started working at hotels, in sales, and things like that.

For a while, I thought maybe I'd like to be a teacher, an elementary schoolteacher, because I like children, maybe because I lost my sister when we were little. For whatever reason, I really like kids. And I also like to teach, so I thought I'd make a good teacher. But the way the education system works in the United States, first you have to take general education classes in junior college, and I couldn't do it; I just couldn't limit myself to Gen. Ed. classes when what I wanted to do was take teacher preparation courses. So I decided, "This isn't for me; I want to study subjects that have a practical application in the workplace." I admit that it's good to know a little bit about everything, but back then I thought I was wasting my time. And besides, I was paying for school . . . so I went to work to help my parents. That's when I started considering the possibility of joining the police or the Border Patrol or something similar.

Preparing to Patrol the Border

But another six years went by. I left college in 1999 and I joined the Border Patrol in 2005, so I worked for six years, mostly in hotels, gaining experience that helped me grow mentally and physically. In hotel work, you deal with lots of people, people from impoverished backgrounds and rich people, and people from lots of different places. Interacting with them taught me how to relate to all types of people. I treat everyone the same, because we're all human, we're all equal.

What made you decide to join the Border Patrol?

Even though several years had passed since September 11, 2001, the events of that day started me thinking, "What can I do to prevent such things from happening again?" At the time, I was old enough to join the army, and lots of eighteen-year-olds do that, but I ultimately discarded the army option because it would have taken me away from my family and friends in San Diego for several years. So I put that idea out of my head, and I started focusing on the police or the Border Patrol. In 2003, I started reading about the Border Patrol and I said, "Okay, I'm ready; I'm ready to join." So I decided to take the entrance exam. Unfortunately, the Border Patrol wasn't hiring many people at the time, everything moved very slowly. . . . Even though I scored 100 on the exam, the admissions process took another two years.

I had friends in the Border Patrol, and they told me good things but also bad things about the job, and I began to worry that they'd send me somewhere like New Mexico, Texas, or Arizona. . . . That made me take a second look at the job, and I stopped the process. I said, "I'd be better off trying something else." And then I spoke to an agent at the Del Mar Fair.[2] I was at the fair one day and saw him and talked to him for a while. I told him about my situation: "You know, I took the exam and scored 100, and I've read up on the job, but I don't want to end up in New Mexico or Texas or Arizona. I want to stay in California." And he told me, "You know what? You blew it. . . . With your test scores, they'd offer you something that might not be your first choice, but if you really scored as high as you say, they'll let you go wherever you want." So I took the test again, and the admissions process took two years: physical exams, psychological tests, life history, and all that. . . . Two years later I finally got the call: "Okay, we're ready to hire you. You've got two options; you can go to Campo, California, or Boulevard, California." I'd never heard of Boulevard, but both locations were in this county, and I chose Campo.

What kind of training do agents get?

I went to the Academy for five months, and that experience changed me. It made me aware that I could do a lot more than I had thought. . . . I learned a lot at the Academy in terms of training but also in terms of personal growth. It all changed me. For example, I remember when we were certified to carry pepper spray, a compound you spray in people's eyes. To be certified, you have to pass through this whole routine. First they make you do push-ups and run around so you sweat and your pores open up. That way the gas will penetrate through the skin. Then they spray you with it, but that's not all. Afterwards you have to wrestle the physical trainer; you have to pin him on the ground, arrest him, and call in on the radio, "I'm in such and such a place; I need backup." You have to provide all the information you can think of at the time. . . . I still have vivid memories of that day. I hope I never have to go through that again, but situations like that made me realize that I really could do more, more than I thought.

I also met someone who became a great friend. We met at the Academy and were friends from the start. We came here for orientation, and then we went to El Paso, Texas, and from there to New Mexico, and we got along great from the very beginning. When we returned to the station here in California, we remained good friends and had been working for a couple of years. . . . It was really unfortunate. He was working in the field one day in temperatures around 100°F and with high humidity. He'd been following a group of people all day long, and the result was that he had a heart attack . . . [and] he died. My friend's death hit me hard. It changed my life; it put everything in a new perspective. I began to understand how fortunate we are to be alive and realized that we need to be careful but also be grateful for every day of life and for our health. . . . That friendship really changed me, and I feel fortunate to have been his friend.

We returned to the Academy in February 2006, and that was our formal initiation into the work of the Border Patrol. Out of a class of fifty, thirty-seven of us graduated. They assigned me to the Campo station. Some went to Boulevard, and others to Texas and New Mexico. Only one of the five women in the class made it through . . . probably because the physical requirements are the same for men and women. The training exercises are really strenuous, and not many women can take it. I'm proud of the fact that I was able to do them, so it must be really hard for the women.

After leaving the Academy, we returned here to the San Diego sector, where we continued our orientation. . . . They explained what they expected of us and told us what lay ahead over the next ten months of training. Instruction doesn't stop with the Academy; we continued with instruction in Spanish and in law one day a week. At the end, you have to take two exams, and if you fail either one your career with the Border Patrol is over. We also were getting field instruction from our trainers. They'd show us the routes that migrants were following and what you need to do to track and arrest them. But they also taught us how to prepare files, how to do data processing on the computer. They taught us all of that over ten months of instruction. After seven months, they separated us and paired each of us with a single agent, and he became our personal trainer for the remainder of the ten months. When that's over, they say, "Here are your keys; here's your Jeep; get to work."

As far as your personal life, a lot of what they teach you at the Academy or stuff you learn on the job is useful in your personal life. You learn how to deal with people, how to react in dangerous or emergency situations. . . . In the Academy, you learn to think and take action in seconds . . . so when you confront similar situations outside of work, we're trained to react quickly, almost without thinking. We also have the sense that because we're in that profession, we have a high level of responsibility even when we're not working or are away from the workplace. We feel that responsibility because we're trained to respond, so when there's an accident or some kind of emergency, we react immediately, almost automatically, "How can I get in there? What can I do to help?"

Between Terrorists and Hungry Children: An Official's Dilemmas

What tasks and activities does an agent perform?

The mission of the Border Patrol is to prevent terrorists or terrorist weapons from entering the United States. That's been the top priority since 2001, since the events of September 11. But we've never abandoned our traditional mission, which is to prevent the entry of undocumented people into the United States. So basically what we do is attempt to stop any terrorist or illegal trying to enter the country. We have to stop them at the border.

What the Border Patrol expects is that when we complete our instruction we're ready to perform the same work as an agent with five or ten years of experience. The most complicated aspect of our work is to patrol the routes, because in areas like Campo and Boulevard there aren't any access roads, just trails and dirt tracks. You have to rely on your memory and orient yourself by things along the way: "Here's the red rock, so I turn left here, and then a little ways ahead I turn right." So an agent needs to know the routes, and for that you have to go over them again and again until you've memorized them all.

When we've finished our field training, our work consists of pursuing smugglers, illegal immigrants, and drug traffickers. We always start at the border, next to the fence, driving along the fence and watching the ground, looking for footprints of illegal immigrants. "Hey, that wasn't there an hour ago. Somebody crossed here; someone jumped the fence and went that way." Then you radio in the information, and if there are agents to the north, they'll look for the same sign along the route and radio in whatever they find, footprints or signs that help us locate whoever is moving over the route.

It's a team effort. Even though an agent is on his own in the hills, communicating by radio allows us to work cooperatively, and that's how we're able to achieve our objective of locating and detaining smugglers and illegal immigrants who've crossed the border. Our radios are an invaluable tool. I'm not saying my radio is more important than my gun, but it's definitely one of our most important tools, and we use radios all the time to communicate with one another.

What's a Border Patrol agent's workday like?

No day is like any other. There's always something new. You always have new experiences. There's an inspection station at the station where I work, so one day I might drive there and spend the whole day inspecting cars traveling toward San Diego. But if we're working in the field, first we go to a morning meeting where our chiefs pass on any information they think might be useful, like if an individual or a group passed through the zone and we didn't find them, or whatever information they think we might be able to use.

Then we get in our vehicles and head for the border, because everything starts at the border. That's where we do our initial patrol, the first pass, to make sure everything is okay, that everything is in order, and then we start patrolling the area. We drive north for an hour, and then we head back to the border, and that's when we notice something—"Something happened here; this wasn't here before"—and we open communications. . . . All the agents have a certain section they have to cover, so everybody knows which area he's responsible for, and when he goes through his area he should be able to recognize if something is different, if something has changed that suggests people are around there. When he notices something, he'll radio the other agents in the area. "Did anybody come through the area? Did you notice this?" And based on our communications, we attempt to track the group that crossed through there, and that's how we spend our day in the mountains, in the hills.

The zone where I work extends from Imperial Beach to Boulevard, but I'm attached specifically to the station in Campo, which is over five thousand feet above sea level. It's very high, so you have to walk a lot and you have to be in good physical condition to do the job, because it's exhausting. I've found people in really inaccessible places, where you have to climb on your hands and knees, and when I reach them I ask, "Hey, how're you doing? Are you tired yet?" And they answer, "Yes, we're tired." And then I've thought, "It's lucky I'm getting paid for this, because I'm tired too."

In situations like that, being able to speak Spanish is a great advantage. I'm grateful for what my parents did for me, for the traditions they taught me and the way they brought me up. Whenever somebody tells me, "You speak Spanish very well; you sound just like us," I tell them, "Thanks, so do you; your Spanish is really good." Spanish is my first language, and that helps people to trust me.

But it also has a downside. It sometimes happens that you feel very bad for the people. For example, it's really hard when you come across a family, when you see people coming in wanting to work, to improve their lives, and they come with their children. Honorable people struggling to have a better life. . . . But I have to do my job. The laws apply to them as well as to me. I have to pursue them, and I knew that when I entered the Border Patrol. I knew that I'm human and they're human, and that there are appropriate ways to treat people. But being nice is one thing, and breaking the laws of the United States is a completely different thing. So I can be the nicest guy they'll meet in the field, but I still have to do my job; it's something I have to do. . . .

I remember one occasion, maybe in the first month after I left the Academy. It was February, and the weather was still very cold in Campo. It was raining and snowing. I think the temperature was around 30°, so it must have been snowing. They radioed me to say that there was a group of people beside a road, abandoned; their *coyote* [people smuggler] had abandoned them there. And when we got there, I found a family with little kids, five or six years old, and that was pretty overwhelming to see those kids scared, wet, trembling with cold. But I had to put sentiment aside in order to do my job. That really opened my eyes, because I realized that my job didn't just involve arresting terrorists or illegals. I also had to detain humble people, families. It affects me personally when I come across cases like that. But often those detentions are really rescue operations. In that case, those people were lucky that we were there to pick them up, take them to our station, give them food and blankets, and rescue them from that situation.

On another occasion I was with one of my trainers, just the two of us in a Jeep, and we drove down a road. The trainer was showing me the routes, and he said we were going to check out a road that was rarely used. "Agents hardly ever go in here, but we'll see where the road takes us." So we drove in and we found a man prostrate on the side of the road. All we could see was an outstretched hand, so we got out of the Jeep and we heard him say, "Help me. Help me." . . . That fellow was lucky because he was all by himself in an area where people generally don't go. The guy had given up hope; he was going to lie there until someone found him or until he died. Those are the kinds of cases that make me think we're doing good work. Many people here in San Diego, in Southern California, or in Tijuana don't have a good impression of us, the migras, and that's because of the stories told by the people smugglers and drug smugglers, folks like that. But in situations like the ones I was describing, I know that we're doing good work; I know that my reasons for being in the Border Patrol are honorable. They are to try to help, not just my country, my nation, but anyone I find who's in jeopardy. I'm there to help those people, and I'm proud to work for those people.

How dangerous is your work?

Personally, I've been lucky so far because I haven't found myself in extremely dangerous situations. But our work tends to be dangerous. We work a lot at night, with just a flashlight, and sometimes you can't even use that because we don't want to give away our position. So we have to work in the dark. We drive, we walk, we run in darkness. The zone where I work has lots of mountains, lots of ravines, and you can fall at any moment. Your vehicle can roll over, so generally speaking, our work is dangerous. . . . I remember the case of an agent who was at the inspection station, where the work is supposedly routine and safe. One day some smugglers crashed through; they ran over him and killed him. I've been lucky until now; I haven't been in any situations like that, but things happen and we always have to be alert. It's unfortunate, but several of our agents have died in the line of duty.

A Mexican American's American Dream

Have you held different positions in the Border Patrol?

Right now I'm serving as a spokesperson for the Border Patrol, but first and foremost I'm a Border Patrol agent. I'll be serving as a public information spokesperson at this office for two years, but after two years I go back on the line, as we say in the field. Or maybe another opportunity will present itself, and I might be an instructor or something like that. Meanwhile, I'm trying to do things to build my résumé so that someday, when I get the chance, I can present my case to my supervisor or the chief. . . . I want to be prepared for various areas of the job.

Before being in my current position, I worked in the legal area for a while, checking criminal histories, trying to build cases against people with criminal records here or in Mexico. I also worked in the Chula Vista Detention Center, dealing with criminals who'd entered the United States and had criminal histories.

I always try to improve myself, to learn new things. So when I heard they were looking for someone to fill the spokesperson position, I immediately saw a possibility. I thought it would be a good job for me, that I could help improve the image people have of us as Border Patrol agents, as migras, an image that doesn't always match reality.

Many people ask me, "You're a Mexican American, so why are you doing this job? Why are you trying to interdict people who only want a better life?" But I'm not trying to keep people from getting ahead in life; that's not what I do. When I joined the Border Patrol I realized that many of the people entering the United States are entering by illegal means because they have a criminal record for drug trafficking, murder, something like that, and these are the people we focus on and we try to put them back behind bars.

But there are also people who come only because they want to work, people who come to make a better life for themselves and their families. They make great sacrifices to come, and they come full of hope. I know they'll find some way to achieve their goal. If they want to improve their lives, they'll do it, whether here or in Mexico. If people are honest and respectful, and if they're motivated to achieve their goals, they'll succeed one way or another. I know it's very hard to get into the United States. Many people I've come across in the field ask me, "Hey, why don't they take down the fence? Why don't they just let everyone in who wants to come to the United States?" But the question is "Why are they coming to the United States? Why do they want to enter this country? Why are they fleeing their own country?" And it's because the situation in their home country has become so intolerable that they feel compelled to flee. Now, if we let everyone into the United States, everything bad that's happening in their countries would be happening here.

We serve as a filter to stop people who try to cross the border illegally, though we also recognize that people are going to cross legally or illegally as long as there are opportunities for them in the United States. They'll keep trying to get in. . . . It's a dream, the American Dream, that's calling them. It's a dream that's been around for many years, and it's not going to disappear soon. That's why we need to protect the United States, our country, to keep the American Dream attainable, protect our land and demand that people who want to come to the United States do so legally.

What's your relationship with Mexico?

I still have relatives in Mexico. A while back my father told me that some of my uncles had seen me in the news on Univisión or Televisa in Nayarit, and they said, "Hey, that's our nephew!" And they phoned my dad: "We saw

Julius on TV. He's doing a good job of it; he's a spokesperson for the migra."
That makes me proud, because some people might think my family would
disapprove of me, thinking that I'm trying to deny people the American
Dream. But it's not like that; it's completely different. Everybody in my family,
beginning with my parents, are very proud that I'm trying to get ahead, just
like they tried to improve life for our family. . . . And that's enough for me;
I don't need anything else. They are proud of what I'm doing, of the kind of
person I've become, and that's all I need.

Do you occasionally visit Mexico?

No, I don't go to Mexico. The situation there is really bad, especially on
the border. Everything you hear, not just in the news but from family and
friends as well . . . assassinations, shootings, kidnappings. . . . My mother
knows two people whose relatives were kidnapped, and they had to get a
lot of money together so the kidnappers would release them. The situation
in Mexico is really bad, and given the job I have now, appearing on TV and
in other media. . . . I realize that not everyone recognizes me, but if I go to
Tijuana and someone does recognize me, well, things could get really ugly.
And it's not just that; it's everything that's happened recently with the cartels,
the smugglers, the kidnappers. . . . Even if they didn't recognize me, I still
wouldn't feel safe crossing the border. Besides, my relatives in Mexico don't
live here on the border. They're farther south, in San Luis Potosí and Nayarit,
so I don't have any reason to cross.
   In the Border Patrol, they've warned us: If we don't have any reason to
enter Mexico, if it's not something we have to do, then we should avoid it at
all costs. Because if somebody realizes that we're migras, that could provoke
problems in Mexico or in the United States. Why risk it?

How do you see yourself in the future, maybe twenty years from now?

I was pretty young when I joined the Border Patrol, so I feel there are still
a lot of doors to open, and I want to go as far as I can. I've set my goals high;
that's because my parents taught me to set high goals and try to achieve the
best I can. It's the same in my personal life and my work life. That's why I'm
always trying to determine what's the best thing I can do with my life.
   Right now I'm trying to build a strong résumé, one that demonstrates
experience in several areas of work, so that I can advance to a position as
supervisor, assistant to the chief, chief. . . . I always want to open new doors
and keep moving forward, in my career and in my life. It's important for me to
know that if I stay in this profession, I'll be able to achieve my goals.

**Do you feel that, as a Mexican American, you have the same professional
and work opportunities as everyone else in the Border Patrol?**

There are better opportunities for somebody who's bilingual. There are many people like me in the Border Patrol, many Mexican Americans, and opportunities are better for us, because communication is very important in our work. And if I'm able to communicate in two languages, and if I'm also able to communicate with all kinds of people, that gives me an advantage in the job, and that increases my opportunities. . . . Do you know the name of the chief of the Border Patrol, the top man? His name is David Aguilar. . . . His name, just his name alone, demonstrates that my opportunities are the same or better than anyone else's.

To be Mexican American, to have grown up here in Southern California, in San Diego, that's helped me a lot, because if the doors weren't open, I'd open them with one language or the other, whatever the situation. I learned how to talk to people on the street, to uneducated people, to poor people, and to educated and privileged people too. And I'm at ease in any situation, dealing with anyone, whether Mexican or American, or from whatever country. Because of my background, because I grew up in this region and knew both sides of the Tijuana–San Diego border, I learned to see both sides of any story. Because I know that there are always at least two versions for every story, so I always keep that in mind in order to better understand people.

This border is replete with stories. The border is . . . yeah, there's a fence; in fact, in some places there are two fences. But sometimes the border is just a line painted on the ground, like in Imperial Beach. I'd say that, more than anything, the border is . . . a way of thinking. Those of us in the United States often fail to appreciate the opportunities we have on this side of the border, and people in Mexico dream about having the opportunities we have. I'm fortunate because I know both sides; that's why I feel lucky to be in the United States, to have been born here, and to have the opportunities I've have. When I encounter migrants who are trying to cross illegally, I understand their reasons for wanting to come to the United States. But I do my job; I enforce the law. Even so, I also admire those people, because I understand that there are two sides to every story.

Conclusion

Opportunity and Uncertainty

The Border as a Source of Social Stratification and Differentiation

A challenge for researchers in border studies is to comprehend how social and cultural differentiation processes linked to physical borders between nation-states in a globalized world operate in people's lives. According to Kearney (2008), scholars have yet to determine how geopolitical and sociocultural frontiers interrelate and what impact their linkage has on the stratification, differentiation, and exclusion of border region inhabitants. Analysts have rarely addressed this question in terms of the border between Mexico and the United States, perhaps the most asymmetrical and dynamic in the world, despite the increasingly complex interactions between these countries, which are as intense as they are extensive. This book contributes to the debate by illustrating some of the diverse life experiences linked to the border crossing and organizing them within the frame of structural processes that constitute the region's economic and social space.

Crossing the border is a life experience embedded in the relations of class, gender, and ethnicity that predominate in each side's classification system. The experience is nuanced, however, by autonomy and juxtaposition in such a way that the direction (from south to north or vice versa) and legal condition of crossing underscore the differentiation and stratification in the region. Kearney (2008) notes that the border filters people's social position and value on two levels—first, through a classification mechanism that defines, categorizes, and imprints the identities of people that the border both encloses and divides, and second, by upending the position and class relations of the individuals who cross. The act of crossing the border also influences the asymmetrical relationships of gender and ethnicity, which in the U.S. context take on connotations associated with the stereotypes of the Mexican feminine or masculine. This can be seen in the life histories of both men and women. For example, gender relations determine the job opportunities available to women commuters and the nature of the marital relationship between an undocumented male worker and a woman with U.S. citizenship.

In addition to the economic forces that have shaped the border throughout its history, during the latter decades of the twentieth century the region became particularly sensitive to national economic, immigration, and, more recently, national security and anti-terrorism policies. As the narratives in this book reveal, these factors exert differential impacts on lives on opposing sides of the border. This appears to confirm the hypothesis advanced by Alegría (2008), who questions the existence of a transborder economic region and postulates instead that what defines the dynamic on either side of the border is each country's respective national processes. The narratives also reveal the presence of a social differentiation mechanism linked to the defense and enforcement of the border, a mechanism that categorizes residents on each side within a transborder classification system (Kearney 2008).

However, recognizing the importance of national logics in the structuring of the border region does not imply rejecting hypotheses about the region's cultural integration and the resulting construction of transborder identities. This apparent contradiction can be resolved in two complementary ways. On one hand, globalization in the region has facilitated a growing articulation or juxtaposition of the global, the national, and the regional (Stephen 2007). That is, globalization involves national and local-level mechanisms, including relations grounded in regional asymmetries and the dense social interactions between individuals and communities on both sides. On the other hand, the process of regional integration is not homogeneous; it operates with particular intensity in certain social categories whose material life and symbolic referents are closely tied to flows across the border. Thus integration and differentiation are contradictory yet simultaneous processes that operate in a space characterized by a marked asymmetry between bordering nations. In this local political ecology, an enforcement infrastructure acquires crucial importance (Heyman 1994; Wilson and Donan 2000).

The narratives reveal multiple experiences of violence and insecurity linked to geographic displacement and border crossing, a phenomenon that seems to increase as border control efforts intensify. Once again, gender and ethnicity emerge as fundamental dimensions of this vulnerability. Domestic violence recurs again and again as a common experience for women, coming at the hands of family members, including father, mother, siblings, spouses, and children. Domestic violence is often the driving force in female mobility toward the border, a survival resource that is used to escape one's place of origin for a more distant location within Mexico or to cross the border and escape the impunity with which such violence can be carried out on the Mexican side. In general terms, both mobility and crossing can serve as resources for survival, but they can also represent a new source of vulnerability. The structural violence that is expressed in the individuals' lives in a physical or symbolic form becomes another framework for constraining opportunities, dramatically reducing options for action, as is the case with domestic violence, physical violence at the border crossing, and the ethnic discrimination that operates on both sides of the border. In Mexico, indigenous persons encounter an inherited violence of discrimination, and on the other side of the border, Mexicans (both indigenous and mestizo) experience discrimination as undesirable immigrants from the South.

We employed typologies to group the biographies selected for inclusion in this book along a continuum according to the nature of each person's relationship with the border crossing. This allowed us to document the richness and diversity of the narrators' ways of life and also to identify patterns that underlie an organic connection, both material and symbolic, with the region's border identity. The organization and analysis of the material combine a phenomenological approximation of life experiences with the narratives themselves, given that life narratives and oral tradition access both the social and subjective planes. We deliberately chose not to disturb the unitary vision that each narrator brings to his or her life story, and for that reason we do not interrupt with external interpretations. The editing and reorganization of the narratives for coherence in time and thematic content were aimed at sparking a certain tension, similar to that evoked by a work of fiction, in which a sense of expectation leads the reader to absorb the parts within the context of the complete narrative thread.[1]

The narratives collected here support Vila's (2000) thesis about the heterogeneity of border identities and call into question the dominant portrayal of border residents as people moving constantly across the border. Vila and other authors in this debate (Gloria Anzaldúa, Renato Rosaldo) emphasize the importance of a symbolic crossing of the border. In this book we have concentrated on the life experience of the crossing, a sphere where the border's geopolitical and sociocultural dimensions converge. The typology used to classify these life experiences allows us to capture the central place the border holds for the region's inhabitants and also to identify mechanisms through which the border condition is operationalized in their lives. With this approach we can link diverse individuals: those who rarely or never cross the border yet live with the impacts of its structural dimension, those who depend directly on the border crossing for their livelihood, and even those who have relegated this experience to the past, establishing new lives on the U.S. side but retaining the border crossing permanently inscribed as part of their personal history and identity.

The Border as Opportunity

According to Vila (2000), the dominant narrative in the border region is the hegemonic story of the United States as the land of opportunity. Portes and Rumbaut (2001) agree, asserting that Mexican migration to the United States is in part the product of the prestige of the "American way of life" outside that nation's boundaries. Yet, as the narratives presented here attest, not everyone who lives on the Mexican side crosses to the United States, and not all who cross manage to successfully assimilate into U.S. society. Furthermore, many of those who settle in the United States return at some later time to live on the Mexican side. As usual, reality is more complex than any model, and it is no simple task to identify the logic that underlies such heterogeneity.

Various authors have declared that the geopolitical frontier itself is a potent source of differentiation, confining the inhabitants of one side or the other within distinct social categories and filtering the position and value of those who cross and those who do not (Kearney 2008; Heyman 1994; Wilson and Donan 2000). The typology we propose enables us to differentiate experiences on a continuum of ways of life that extends from those that do not directly involve the border-crossing experience to those that are literally a product of it.

The theme of the border as a land of opportunity cuts across all social categories and all types of border experience. One of the most widespread images is the border crossing as a route to jobs that pay in dollars, that is, to wages that are substantially above those in Mexico and to consumption and recreation choices that are out of reach on the Mexican side. Nevertheless, these opportunities are not open to all; more than half of Tijuana residents do not have visas to cross the border legally. A crosser's legal status is a source of differentiation because a would-be visa holder must provide proof of sufficient income and a history of residence in Tijuana in order to obtain a visa. This might suggest that a legal crossing is exclusively a question of social class. But the situation is not so simple. For example, because of the long history of Mexican migration to the United States, there are now substantial numbers of migrants who entered the United States illegally during the second half of the twentieth century, obtained U.S. resident visas at some later point, and now reside in Tijuana. This is true of many agricultural workers who, through their employment in the United States, were able to raise their standard of living relative to other residents on the Mexican side of the border. Yet even though their incomes are notably higher than those of most Tijuana workers, and their status is higher because they have U.S. jobs and residency permits, they live in the city's poorer neighborhoods and display a lifestyle similar to that of their neighbors. Such situations illustrate the complexity of a subtle and dynamic stratification tied to both the structural and the symbolic dimensions of the border.

But the border does not only mean job opportunities with dollar-denominated wages. Its lucrative clandestine markets, such as trafficking in drugs and people, also yield dollars. The illegal trafficking of drugs and people drives very specific ways of life and family dynamics. For undocumented migrants, people smugglers, drug traffickers, and immigration officials on both sides of the border, the daily routine is reckoned in terms of illegal crossings and interdiction efforts. This everyday experience of the border, whether recurrent or sporadic, legal or illegal, is a hub from which other ways of life radiate outward and infiltrate border neighborhoods on both sides of the line, where cross-border activities spread their influence via the labor market, consumption patterns, and family networks.

The relevance of our typology rests on the extended narrative that crossing the border from south to north signifies a broadening of life opportunities, whether perceived in the future, the present, or the past. The fact that crossing the border is highly selective—because of differential access to transborder family networks, one's economic situation, or involvement in an inherently dangerous occupation—reinforces the idea that crossing opens up opportunities that can reach even into contiguous spaces within border cities through the multiplier effects of family and social relationships, through family dynamics and local consumption. The view that crossing the border connotes opportunities that justify the associated suffering and risk is perhaps the clearest lived expression of the structural asymmetry that characterizes the border between Mexico and the United States.

The Border Never Crossed

Though the prospect of crossing northward over the border is a powerful magnet, attracting hundreds of thousands of people, a large fraction of those who manage to reach the shadow of the border remain on the Mexican side, either because they failed in their crossing attempt or because they never attempted to cross. Thus the first kind of life experience of the border refers to residents in the Mexican border zone who do not cross into the United States but whose lives are framed by the area's border condition.

For Rosalía, a Mixtec woman who works as a day laborer in agriculture in San Quintín, the border never crossed is a vague referent that nonetheless determines a good portion of her life, since she has been employed for the past twenty-two years by an agricultural export company, working long, hard days for meager wages as she helps supply the California market with fruits and vegetables. This kind of work is one of the clearest examples of the wage asymmetry that drives the commercial relationship between the opposing sides of the border. Further, her family situation is also strongly permeated by the border reality: Eventually she receives indirect news about the husband who abandoned her. He crosses to the United States regularly to work, but he provides no support for his children. The eldest son, meanwhile, feels a strong attachment to the border region and seems little disposed to accompany Rosalía on her longed-for return to her place of origin.

This is also the case with Elena, a homeworker, laborer, and social activist who, burdened with a history of family conflict, has spent most of her years in Tijuana trying to support a household and escape gender subordination. For these women, industrial homework and jobs in the maquiladoras are two of the employment options available in this city of rapid growth and high dependency on the California economy. The maquiladoras in particular have been a key element determining the shape of labor markets in recent decades, defining work opportunities and lifestyles for thousands of border families.

Rosa has not crossed the border either, and one can infer from her narrative that she has no plans to do so. She came to Tijuana to escape the domestic violence to which she was subjected in her home community, and she has worked for more than twenty years as a prostitute in the streets of the Zona Norte, a dense social space where tourists coming from north of the border congregate in search of sex entertainments, and migrants coming from the South seek lodging and companionship.

In these narratives, the border region is experienced as a place that offers a chance to improve one's situation, not directly by crossing to the United States but through the dynamic of the Mexican border zone itself, where people find employment, housing, and, eventually, government supports that apparently are not present in their places of origin. For cases in this category, opportunity lies on the Mexican side, and crossing the border is seen as only a distant and vague notion nourished by accounts from friends, family members, and clients. For such dissimilar cases as a prostitute, a homeworker, and a farmworker, the border exerts a decisive presence in the structuring of their respective professions, but the border crossing is not envisioned as a personal option.

The Border as Backdrop

The border is a huge market driven by insatiable consumer appetites, and someone who is very astute or hardworking can exploit it to achieve a better life. This seems to be the motto of those who have found their niche in the informal markets of the border. This second type of life experience of the border includes people who cross the line only occasionally but whose lives are structured around the kinds of legal and illegal commercial transactions that are paradigmatic of border regions.

Juan's and Ofelia's narratives present very dissimilar cases in terms of the content of their respective experiences of the border, but they are alike in that both have a direct relationship with border transactions. Their lives unfold on the Mexican side, but unlike the preceding type of case, this does not preclude an eventual crossing to the United States.

Juan's story illustrates with unusual clarity one of the most notable characteristics of the regional reality at the beginning of the twenty-first century: the social tension and insecurity resulting from the ongoing war between drug cartels vying for control of territory and distribution routes within the framework of a large U.S. market for illicit drugs and rising consumption levels in Mexico.

In the midst of this violent conflict over control of the market, exacerbated by government enforcement efforts, the life of a narco-trafficker offers a timely testimony about this sordid and violent face of the border, and about the contradictions inherent in a purely police and military perspective on one of the greatest social and cultural challenges that the border region has ever faced.

For her part, Ofelia, an indigenous Mixtec street vendor peddling artisan crafts on the streets of Tijuana, structures her work life around the legal market of border tourism. Her narrative recounts a long and arduous settlement process in Tijuana, during which she still manages to establish cross-border family and social networks.

In these very different cases, the possibility of crossing the border from time to time is an option because this group has social or family networks on the other side. Thus, their image of the United States is informed by a greater familiarity, and both the crossing itself and border transactions surface regularly in their narratives. This type of border life experience suggests that physical proximity alone is not sufficient to enable crossing; additional economic and social requisites must be met, especially access to transborder family networks. In the cases grouped in this type, the idea of crossing the border structures one's itinerary, beginning with the decision to leave one's place of origin, whether to plunge into the illegal drug trade or to trace the route of transnational agricultural labor to the job markets that employ the poorest of Mexico's poor, including its indigenous people.

The Daily Border

Crossing the border daily is the paradigmatic transborder life experience; the border crossing is the strategic resource that unifies the life stories of those who cross every day. Of course, connections with the border take diverse forms, since the conditions and motivations associated with the crossing admit innumerable possibilities. This is a broad category, and there are many possible cases that could have been included here. However, the ones we have selected are clearly representative.

Eloísa's narrative follows the life of a commuter, defined by residence on the Mexican side of the border and employment on the U.S. side, an arrangement that optimizes the benefits of the wage differential between the two nations. Such commuters work in the less-skilled jobs that are stereotyped in the United States as appropriate for Mexicans. The case of the Panther describes the life of a people smuggler, for whom undocumented migration is a business and the lives of the undocumented migrants are merchandise to be bought, sold, and sometimes forfeited. The Border Acrobat is a master undocumented migrant, whose existence consists of a continual coming and going from one side of the border to the other without documents appropriate to either side, living a transborder life plagued by loss and fear but conducted with dry humor and optimism.

These are transborder lives in the full sense of the word, given that their very existence depends on moving from one side to the other. Constant cross-border mobility demands a marked ability to adapt, more so than for the other groups discussed here, as well as certain cultural skills—such as speaking some English and knowing how to navigate the normative differences between the two societies—and access to family or social networks on both sides of the border. The legal status of crossing also introduces an important difference between the two types of frequent crossers: traffickers of people or drugs, and migrants seeking work or reunification with family members. Social networks are more important for individuals crossing without documents than for documented crossers, even those presenting false papers.

This kind of border life usually presupposes residence on the Mexican side, but it is highly susceptible to economic fluctuations on either side of the border and to changes in national security policies, prompting these individuals to move continually from one side to the other. The vision that prevails in this group is somewhat ambiguous: Residence in Mexico is a practical choice, but it is also an affective one. Mexico is seen as a place of personal warmth and freedom, attributes not found in the United States.

The diversity in transborder experiences gives nuance to the dominant image of the so-called cosmopolitan border inhabitant who moves freely on both sides, sometimes with dual citizenship, and it reveals the category of undocumented border inhabitant, whose existence transpires in the social and legal interstices between the two countries and who lives a marginalized life in both. These lives without documents and in constant cross-border movement are transformed into merchandise in the hands of the people smugglers, who negotiate the border asymmetry, transporting migrants for fees calibrated to the increased levels of border control and networks of corruption. The high value that migrants attribute to a successful border crossing justifies the risks they assume along the way, including the possibility of dying, and it explains the fortitude they demonstrate when, once successfully across the border, they become subject to discrimination and abuse. They have been migrants since childhood. In the absence of a home that provides certainty for the present or hope for the future, their "homes" are the nostalgic evocations of the far-distant past of their earliest years.

The Border Left Behind

The fourth and final type of life experience on the border stems from international migration and settlement in the United States. The lives of the 1.5 and second generations of Mexican migration are clear examples of this type. In their life stories, the border is the Mexican one, and it is behind them, not in front of them. Though their life experience is clearly rooted in what is Mexican—through family or work—their life horizons lie before them, in their country of residence, the United States. The Mexican border does not offer opportunity; instead, it contains elements of their origins and past, which they take pride in having overcome. The cases in this category are two young people who place high value on their future in the United States, confirming the popular view on the Mexican side of the border that the United States is a land of opportunity.

Emilio, a university student at an elite California college, has a relationship with Mexico that is simultaneously affectionate and critical. For years, his father was a commuter, residing in Tijuana and working in San Diego, but once the family relocated to the United States, Emilio grew up and was educated as a U.S. citizen. Though proud of his origins, he has fully absorbed the values of the society in which he resides. His connection with Mexico is strong, but it is very precisely defined: The United States means work, responsibility, and progress, while Mexico evokes images of relaxation, fun, and friendships. In the case of Julius Alatorre, this assimilation of values finds its maximum expression; this son of striving Mexican immigrants has become an agent of the Border Patrol. His task is to pursue and detain anyone entering the United States without legal documents, a mission that he undertakes with conviction and pride.

The life trajectories of both these individuals unfold in the border region, yet there are significant differences in their reasons for and frequency of crossing to Mexico. They offer two visions of the Mexican frontier: as an unsafe place and as a hospitable and fun-filled place. These narratives do not speak of freedom on the Mexican side but emphasize the area's disorderliness, filth, and corruption. A constant in these cases, which seems to generalize across this category, is a continual comparison between one's current life and that of one's parents. That is, the parents represent Mexico; they embody a continuation with Mexico at the same time that they are the referent against which one evaluates his or her personal achievements or failures in the United States.

The Border as Uncertainty: A Border State of Mind

Although opportunity is the dominant theme in the narratives of border residents, a second image consistently forces its way into these life histories, and it is uncertainty. Uncertainty emerges here with a strong emotive force linked to the spatial-temporal changes that occur in one's biographical trajectory, in social spaces such as places of residence and work, and in the ruptures and discontinuities in interpersonal relations, as in family life and romantic attachments. These changes are recalled as breaks in a life history that hold affective significance, and they reveal a state of mind that some narrators recognize as characteristic of contemporary life (Beck 2002).

The contradictory impulses toward mobility and stability that characterize life in the border region seem to lie at the base of the uncertainty that permeates these life histories, which are marked by geographic displacement and the pursuit of opportunity. The inherent risks in moving from south to north, especially for the undocumented, presuppose levels and expressions of uncertainty that are specific to a transborder life, in contrast to patterns that are less dependent on coming and going across the border.

For those who spend their lives on the Mexican side working in maquiladoras, export agriculture, or prostitution, uncertainty arises principally from fluctuations in a labor market that is increasingly flexible, precarious, and underregulated and from an exceedingly unstable family life in which relationships with partners, parents, and children (depending on one's stage in the life cycle) are always subject to tensions created by a shifting, unpredictable, and often untenable environment.

Violence is not only present in public space; it also appears in domestic life and tends to surface in the earlier life stages and with a strong gender connotation. This is the case for innumerable women who have come to the border to escape domestic violence, abandonment, or stigma, to immerse themselves in new contexts in which it is precisely the absence or instability of family ties that make them vulnerable to new sources of violence.

Further, even when residence and employment on the Mexican side are dependable enough to obviate the need for crossing the border, an individual's migration history and economic situation can produce a high level of instability because of the conditions of migration, the precariousness of employment, and a fragmented and unsettled family life. Nevertheless, living in a city where one's legal status is not questioned offers a horizon of permanence that offsets the uncertainty arising from other factors.

The more intense one's relationship with the border crossing, the higher the level of uncertainty. If we recall Jorge Durand's (1994) metaphor of the border as a revolving door that expands or shrinks depending on national and global economic and political forces, it is easy to understand that to the degree one's life is tied to the border crossing, there will be instability or uncertainty linked to the border's fluidity. This is very clear for people whose life experiences are closely linked to the border, whether on a sporadic or a daily basis. These individuals are more likely to feel the impacts of fluctuations at the border, which range from minor day-to-day variations, such as the length or speed of the crossing queue, to major ones, such as the construction of formidable border fences and the issuing of anti-terrorism alerts that temporarily exacerbate crossing conditions even for individuals who meet all legal requirements.

As these narratives reveal, for those whose livelihood depends on crossing the border, the lack of crossing documents is a source of uncertainty that affects all aspects of life. And for those involved in illegal activities, such as human smuggling or drug trafficking, there is a high degree of uncertainty in the very nature of their occupations, which depend on adherence to strict rules of loyalty and discretion within their domain of corruption. Both factors—the lack of crossing documents and involvement in illegal activities—increase uncertainty to the point that basic personal safety comes under threat, and individuals in these situations risk being robbed, arrested, injured, or even killed.

Paradoxically, because of the lifestyles associated with illegal activities, such individuals have no financial advantages when compared, for instance, with their parents. A life devoted to trafficking in drugs or people does not yield material gains above those achieved by the women who work in agriculture, the maquiladoras, or prostitution. Ultimately, the life of a people smuggler or narco-trafficker is permeated by uncertainty and precariousness. What little certainty these individuals may enjoy comes from the strength and solidarity of their transborder family relationships. For example, the webs of corruption surrounding smugglers' activities on both sides of the border confer some degree of safety in the border crossing, so that a smuggler's chances of being apprehended are lower than those of an undocumented migrant, who lacks the support of nearby family and social networks. Thus, even though a smuggler may fail in his efforts, the likelihood that he will be caught is relatively low and thus his uncertainty is also somewhat diminished.

Whether one's livelihood derives from legal or illegal enterprises, this kind of border life unfolds within a network of transborder family relationships that facilitates crossing and finding employment on the other side. These narratives demonstrate that activities such as human smuggling or drug trafficking are not individual undertakings. Rather, they are embedded in a social web of family and neighborhood ties that encompasses both sides of the border.

The continual crossings give rise to a conception of the border as highly fluid, sufficiently so, in fact, to permit the formation of interethnic couples. Yet the frequent crossings also highlight the impermeability of the border through the stereotypes, held on both sides, of people from Mexico and the United States. The distinct structures and lifestyles on opposing sides ultimately extract a cost in a transborder life. A legal or illegal crossing to the United States is a resource that is used over and over again by the subset of the population that has transborder networks and certain cultural skills, such as bilingualism, that allow them to switch identities. If things go wrong on this side, there is always the option to work on the other side, even though, for different reasons, the life horizon for all three—the commuter, the Acrobat, and the Panther—is in Mexico, not the United States. Vila's (2000) metaphor of "reinforcing borders" seems plausible for these individuals, for whom crossing the physical border does not necessarily lead to an embrace of the "American lifestyle" but rather tends to reinforce their cultural differences.

Among the individuals who are flourishing on the U.S. side, products of international migration from Mexico and settlement in the United States—the cases of a border left behind—uncertainty does not arise from the border with Mexico, much less from the border crossing itself, but rather from their chances for integration into U.S. society. For them, the process of integration, especially in school and the workplace, is the primary source of uncertainty. Even for these legal residents or citizens of the United States, the border still holds important meaning stemming from their ethnic-national origin, which impresses itself on their possibilities for integration.

In all these cases of the "border left behind" life experience, one's current condition is constantly compared with that of one's parents. Parents represent continuity with Mexico and are the reference point for an ongoing comparison when one assigns value to personal achievements or failures in the United States. One's ethnic-national origin is a spatial-temporal point that serves as a basis for placing a value on life in the United States. The narrative of the parents' history of struggle confers certainty that life in this new country is better. However, we need only look at the thousands who are constantly being turned away from U.S. territory or who have arrived but live permanently outside the law or remain invisible on the margins of the prosperous U.S. society to see that life is not better for everyone who attempts to cross the border.

But even this evidence seems to support the symbolic value of a stable life on the U.S. side of the border among those who have successfully achieved it. When compared with those who debate whether or not to cross the border, when compared with past generations or family members who have remained in Mexico, those who have settled in the United States have succeeded in surmounting not only the geographical border but, perhaps more important, the symbolic border as well. Thus, though the majority of Mexican migrants occupy the lowest rungs in the U.S. job structure, getting a job and establishing a home in the United States will continue to be valued as an achievement and a qualitative leap forward in one's standard of living.

Notes

Foreword

1. Additional information on the Association of Borderlands Studies and the *Journal of Borderlands Studies* is available at http://www.absborderlands.org and http://www.absborderlands.org/2JBS.html (accessed November 10, 2009).

2. O. Martínez 1994, 27.

3. Ibid., 5.

4. Anderson and Gerber 2008, 11.

5. For general information on the border, see the publications list of El Colegio de la Frontera Norte in Tijuana, available at http://www.colef.mx/publicaciones/ (accessed November 10, 2009), along with the following: Migration Information Source 2006; Americas Program, Center for International Policy, Texas–New Mexico Border Series, available at http://americas.irc-online.org/am/5856 (accessed November 10, 2009); Peach and Williams 2003; Environmental Protection Agency 2009; Center for Latin American Studies 2008. The Center for Latin American Studies Web site provides additional information complementary to Anderson and Gerber 2008.

6. Ganster and Lorey 2008, 2.

7. Population figures for 1940 and 2005 have been rounded from those in Ganster and Lorey 2008, 71, 126–127.

8. O. Martínez 1994, 303.

9. U.S. Department of Commerce, Office of Trade and Industry Information, 2008 Exports of NAICS, available at http://tse.export.gov (accessed November 10, 2009).

10. O. Martínez 1994, 304. See also Vila 2005.

11. M. L. Martinez 2002, 53–54.

12. Ganster and Lorey 2008, xvi, 1.

13. Ruiz 1998, 219.

14. *CIA World Factbook 2010*, available at https://www.cia.gov/library/publications/ the-world-factbook/index.html (accessed November 10, 2010).

15. Anderson and Gerber 2008, 141–145.

16. In 1854, the United States purchased from Mexico a thirty-thousand-square-mile territory that forms contemporary southern Arizona and southwest New Mexico. Known as the Gadsden Purchase in the United States and the sale of La Mesilla in Mexico, the acquisition took place in order to provide the United States with a potential southern transcontinental rail route. The border was further modified in 1963, when the United States and Mexico settled the El Chamizal dispute, involving a small amount of land between El Paso, Texas, and Ciudad Juárez, Chihuahua.

17. Truett 2006, 15. For a nineteenth-century articulation of this narrative, see Bancroft 1883–1890).

18. See Hunt 1853, 20; Gregory 1997, 20–21; and Deverell 2004, 7.

19. González Iñárritu 2007.

20. Henderson 2007, xxi.

21. U.S. Bureau of the Census 2009.

22. For a succinct account of Mexican railway, mining, and agricultural change in the late nineteenth and early twentieth centuries, see Gonzales 2002, chap. 2. For the transformation of the frontier into the border, see Katz 1981, 7. For the population share of the border states and territories, see Secretaría de Economía, Dirección General de Estadística 1956, 7–8. For the share of foreign investment in Chihuahua, Coahuila, Nuevo León, and Sonora, see Ganster and Lorey 2008, 40.

23. Ganster and Lorey 2008, 35.

24. See McCaa 2003.

25. Ganster and Lorey 2008, 41; Kuntz Ficker 2004.

26. See Reisler 1976.

27. Ngai 2004, 67.

28. See Hoffman 1974.

29. On the Bracero Program, see Ngai 2004, chap. 4; Calavita 1992; García y Griego 1996, 45–85; and the exhibition at the Museum of American History titled "Cosecha amarga, cosecha dulce: El programa bracero, 1942–1964," available at http://american history.si.edu/exhibitions/small_exhibition.cfm?key=1267&exkey=770 (accessed November 10, 2009).

30. U.S. Bureau of the Census, Foreign Trade Statistics, available at http://www. census.gov/foreign-trade/balance/c2010.html, and U.S. Bureau of the Census, *Statistical Abstract of the United States 2009*, available at http://www.census.gov/prod/www/abs/ statab.html (accessed November 10, 2009).

31. Fernández-Kelly and Massey 2007.

32. See Castañeda 2007; Massey, Durand, and Malone 2002; and Passel and Cohn 2008.

33. Verini 2008.

34. According to Guillermo Valdés, director of the Centro de Investigación y Seguridad Nacional, Mexico's national security agency, as many as twenty-eight thousand may have died in armed clashes since the Mexican government began its offensive against the drug cartels in late 2006. *Los Angeles Times* 2010. For a brief account of the background of drug trafficking in Mexico, see Astorga 2004.

35. McKinley 2009.

36. Carlsen 2008.

37. On prostitution in Tijuana, see Katsulis 2008.

Introduction

1. In 2008, the minimum daily wage in Baja California was 52.59 pesos, the highest in the country, while in parts of southwestern Mexico it was only 49.5 pesos. See http://www.sat.gob.mx/sitio_internet/asistencia_contribuyente/informacion_frecuente/salarios_minimos/45_10809.html (accessed July 15, 2009).

2. The Minuteman Project was founded in 2004 with the aim of monitoring the flow of undocumented immigrants across the U.S.-Mexican border. For more information, see http://www.minutemanproject.com/ (accessed September 3, 2010).

3. This book does not include any case from among the U.S. citizens of various ethnic and national origins who reside on the Mexican side of the border because of its low cost of living but may work on the U.S. side. This group includes retirees who live along the Baja California coast and a number of professionals and self-employed persons.

4. This account is based on three interviews, including two with Rosalía (a pseudonym), conducted on October 18, 2004, and April 4, 2006. The third interview was with Darío (a pseudonym), also on April 4, 2006. All the interviews took place in the Nuevo San Juan Copala Colonia in the San Quintín Valley.

5. The narrative about Elena (a pseudonym) is based on an interview conducted on July 8, 2008, in the Infonavit Colonia, Tijuana.

6. The story of Rosa (a pseudonym) is based on two interviews, on June 14, 2008, in Colonia Libertad, and on May 1, 2009, in the Zona Norte, Tijuana.

7. The narrative about Juan (a pseudonym) is based on an interview conducted on July 12, 2008, in a colonia in Tijuana.

8. The account of Ofelia Santos (her real name) is based on two interviews. The first took place on March 10, 1994, in Colonia Obrera, and the second on July 14, 2005, in the Plaza Santa Cecilia in downtown Tijuana.

9. The story of Eloísa (a pseudonym) is based on an interview conducted on June 9, 2008, in the Playas de Tijuana neighborhood of Tijuana.

10. The story of Porfirio (a pseudonym) derives from an interview on April 25, 2008, at the Casa del Migrante in Tijuana.

11. This account of the Mexicali Panther (a pseudonym) draws on an interview conducted on May 1, 2008, in Mexicali, Baja California.

12. The narrative of Emilio (a pseudonym) is based on an interview conducted on June 8, 2008, in Playas de Tijuana.

13. The story of Julius Alatorre (his real name) is based on an interview conducted on June 5, 2008, at the San Diego office of the Border Patrol.

Chapter 1

1. The area known as the San Quintín Valley comprises four precincts (*delegaciones*). From south to north, these are Punta Colonet, Camalú, Vicente Guerrero, and San Quintín.

2. The three languages belong to the Mixtec-Zapotec linguistic family (Basauri 1990, 93).

3. Although an attempt was made to include all regional companies, this was not possible because some declined to be interviewed. It was ultimately possible to conduct interviews at thirteen of the twenty companies identified by El Consejo Estatal de Población (COESPO) in 2003. Together they demonstrate a range of diversity in size and market orientation (national-transnational) that yield data very pertinent to this book. For further details, see COESPO-COLEF 2003c.

4. Data from Sectetaría de Agrícultura y Ganadería (SAGARPA) confirm these patterns.

5. According to Llamadas 2000 and Cruz 2004.

6. Presidential communiqué no. 2040, San Quintín, Baja California, February 25, 2000, available at http://zedillo. presidencia.gob.mx/pages/vocero/boletines/com2040. html (accessed May 25, 2006).

7. Data drawn from grower registries of vegetable and fruit production in greenhouses and shade-cloth installations.

8. There is no quantitative information available on the resident population in this type of housing. Our numbers are drawn from direct observation.

9. According to some managers, international certifiers have pressed strongly for the closure of the camps because they are a potential source of contamination of agricultural products.

10. The name Nuevo San Juan Copala is a source of discord among its inhabitants, given that the official name of the colonia is Las Misiones. See note 23, below.

11. The Triquis are one of the seventeen indigenous peoples who live in Oaxaca. As López Bárcenas (2009:23) indicates, the territory the Triquis inhabit is like an island in the middle of a Mixtec ocean.

12. The Mixtec region covers part of the states of Puebla, Guerrero, and Oaxaca.

13. Beginning in the 1950s, concurrent with migration to the United States under the Bracero Program, the Mixtecs and Triquis established a migration route to northeastern Mexico (Sonora, Sinaloa, and Baja California) to work as day laborers in export agriculture.

14. The García brothers own the San Vicente Agricultural Ranch in the Camalú precinct.

15. In some towns in the Oaxacan Mixteca, all of one's elders are addressed as "uncle" or "aunt" although there may be no blood relationship. This may indicate the prevalence of a single large family or strong bonds of ethnic kinship.

16. This is a reference to summertime, when darkness does not fall until seven or eight o'clock at night.

17. Some community leaders organized a land invasion by migrants from San Juan Copala and other peoples from Oaxaca who lived in the Aguaje del Burro camp. That land was then subdivided into lots that were distributed among those who participated in the invasion.

18. The Agricultural Day Laborers Program is a federal program within Mexico's Ministry of Social Development.

19. She is referring to placing plastic sheeting over the furrows so that seeds can later be sown in the plastic-protected furrows. The idea is to simulate a greenhouse effect for the seeds and then protect the growing plant, as well as to facilitate drip irrigation. In doing this operation, the worker places a large roll of plastic at one end of the row and pulls it across to cover an entire furrow. After the plants have grown, the worker has to pull the plastic off the row with the plants in it, keeping the roots intact.

20. They call it the "boss's hospital" because it is where workers employed on the García brothers' ranch receive their medical care.

21. A *cundina* is a collective savings group based on mutual trust. It is used extensively in Mexico. The term may have been derived from the verb *cundir,* which means to reproduce or expand. In some other parts of Mexico, they are called *tandas.* In both cases, each member of a group of individuals contributes a certain amount of money at specified intervals, and each receives a payout in turn.

22. Her daughters lived in San Quintín without birth certificates until she was able to return to her town, San José de las Flores, and register them with their father present so that the children could take their father's surname.

23. San Juan Copala is the name of a Triqui municipality in Juxtlahuaca District, Oaxaca, and it is the place of origin of many of the residents of this colonia.

Chapter 2

1. "A maquiladora plant is understood to be an economic enterprise that performs part of its final production process, generally product assembly, inside Mexican national territory and does so under an export assembly contract that commits the mother company, located abroad, to perform an industrial process or service to transform, produce, or repair goods brought in from outside the country, and involving the temporary import of parts, pieces, and components, which, once completed, are exported" (INEGI, cited in Centro de Estudios de las Finanzas Públicas de la Cámara de Diputados 2003, 2).

2. In the 1990s, business publications identified Tijuana as the "television capital of the world" because half the televisions sold in the United States were assembled in Tijuana. By 1998, Tijuana maquilas were producing more than 9 million TV sets annually (Contreras and Carrillo 2003).

3. Instituto del Fondo Nacional de la Vivienda para los Trabajadores (National Workers' Housing Fund Institute).

4. Elena's husband had access to an Infonavit loan program, enabling him to buy the house in which she now lives.

5. In 1996, the exchange rate was approximately 8 pesos to the dollar; 1,200 pesos would have been equal to about US$150.

6. About US$250.

7. Instituto Nacional de Estadística y Geografía (National Institute of Statistics and Geography).

8. Consulta Mitofsky and Gallup are two major opinion polling firms.

9. Factor X is a feminist nongovernmental organization that works with female maquiladora workers in Tijuana.

10. This is a reference to the name of the Colonia Infonavit Latinos.

Chapter 3

1. The tolerance zone is located in the northern part of Tijuana. It covers two city blocks, from First Street to Coahuila Street and from Constitution Avenue to Niños Héroes. These are the official borders, though in practice the zone extends farther, covering five blocks.

2. The government planned to redevelop the zone and move the women who were working on area streets to enclosed spaces. See Cornejo 2002.

3. This is according to the municipal subdirector of health. See *El Mexicano* 2006.

4. According to Acevedo, Piñera, and Ortiz (1985), bars and track betting were outlawed in the United States in 1911, and the "dry law" (Volstead Act), approved in 1919, outlawed the distilling and sale of alcohol in the United States. These measures led to a boom in "prohibitionist enterprises" in Baja California, especially in the nascent town of Tijuana.

5. This image has persisted over time. Not long ago, French singer Manu Chao had a global hit with a song whose chorus included the lines "Welcome to Tijuana / Welcome to Tijuana / Tequila, sex, and marijuana."

6. Officials from the National Action Party (Partido Acción Nacional, or PAN).

Chapter 4

1. At the 1981 exchange rate of 25 pesos to the dollar, 20,000 pesos equaled US$800.

2. San Luis Río Colorado is across the border from Yuma, Arizona, about forty miles from Mexicali, the capital of Baja California.

3. A medium-security state prison located in the La Mesa precinct, within the greater Tijuana urban area.

4. He is referring to the Islas Marías, a federal penal colony on the islands of the same name in the Pacific Ocean off the coast of Nayarit.

5. El Hongo is a settlement on the Tijuana-Mexicali highway, twenty-two miles east of Tecate.

Chapter 5

1. In 2005, Baja California had 33,604 inhabitants five years of age or older who were speakers of an indigenous language. The same figure for Coahuila is 5,842, for Sinaloa 30,459, and for Tamaulipas 20,221 (INEGI 2005).

2. In 1942, the United States and Mexico signed the second Bracero Program treaty, an agreement allowing thousands of Mexicans to enter the United States to work in agriculture and on the railroads. That program continued until 1964 (GAO 1988).

3. The Simpson-Rodino Law is the colloquial name for the 1986 Immigration Reform and Control Act (IRCA), whose purpose was to reduce "illegal" immigration to the United States. One of its measures was the fining of employers who hired undocumented workers. Another was an increase in federal resources for the Border Patrol. Most important, workers who were able to prove that they had lived in the United States continuously since 1982 could have their U.S. residency regularized. The reform also had a special program for agricultural workers (Vernez 1990, 3), and most of the Mixtec migrants took advantage of it.

4. In the towns in Oaxaca's Mixteca region, as in many other rural areas in Mexico, the people use liters to measure corn and other grains (1 liter of corn equals 690 grams).

5. A reference to the Bracero Program, which operated in the United States from 1942 through 1964.

6. Luis Echeverría Álvarez was president from 1976 to 1982. Ofelia refers to 1975 as "the Echeverría years," perhaps because long before the election, the "official" presidential candidate (that is, the candidate selected by the Partido Institucional Revolucionario [Institutional Revolutionary Party, or PRI], which historically always won the election) had begun a massive campaign to raise his profile among the country's voters. The same may be the case below, when she associates a local politician, Xico Leyva Mortera, with the year of his campaign (1977) rather than the years of his administration (1978–1980).

7. Colonia Obrera, or "Workers' Neighborhood," is where Ofelia and her family live, and it was the first settlement of migrants who came from the Mixteca region in Oaxaca.

8. Xicotencatl Leyva Mortera was municipal president of Tijuana from 1978 to 1980. See note 6, above.

9. Víctor Clark-Alfaro is a human rights activist and founder and director of the Centro Binacional de Derechos Humanos (Binational Human Rights Center) in Tijuana.

10. *Gringo* is a slang word for a North American, usually but not necessarily a white person. Though not pejorative in itself, it can be used pejoratively. *Gringa* is the feminine form.

11. By "professors," Ofelia means a group of teachers who arrived during the 1970s from the Mixteca region, the result of an initiative by municipal president Federico Valdez to bring bilingual Spanish-Mixtec teachers to Tijuana.

12. Central Revolucionaria de Obreros y Campesinos (Workers' and Campesinos' Revolutionary Central) is part of the PRI (Partido Revolucionario Institucional).

13. *Mija* is an abbreviated way of saying *mi hija* (my daughter), a widely used form of address, but one that also has strong paternalistic overtones and that tends to infantilize the person addressed. *Mijo* is the masculine form.

14. Federico Valdez was municipal president from 1986 to 1989.

15. Men who sell silver medals in Avenida Revolución.

16. Confederación de Trabajadores de México (Mexican Workers' Confederation), the largest PRI-controlled union.

17. In 1993, the government cut three zeros from the peso. Thus, 300,000 "old pesos" became 300 "new pesos," equivalent to approximately US$97.

18. In Mexico, under the corporatist system, a leader will be given permits that he or she can then distribute to the workers in his or her network.

19. Members of the Partido Acción Nacional (National Action Party, or PAN). In 1989, the PAN won the elections in the state of Baja California. For the first time in Mexico, a party other than the PRI governed a state. In 2000, the PRI lost power at the federal level.

20. The Programa Nacional de Solidaridad (National Solidarity Program) was created by President Carlos Salinas de Gortari (1988–1994), and it was the most important social program during his administration.

21. *Pochos* are persons of Mexican descent but inept in their use of Spanish.

22. This was in 1994, when the neo-Zapatista rebellion occurred in Chiapas.

23. With direct and indirect questions, we deduced that Ofelia used the verb *comprender* in the sense of "to discover" or "to mutually exchange ideas"; it also implies respect and understanding between two people concerning the meaning of a fact, an object, or an action.

24. According to Ofelia, one cannot "feel" for one's children without loving them. Sometimes they make you mad, other times sad, and sometimes joyful, but if one feels for them, then they are important.

25. In 2005, Ofelia had to go to San Diego continually because one of her sons was in jail there. San Diego police had arrested him when they caught him selling drugs on the street in that city. Months later, another of her sons—the eldest—was found dead in Tijuana. A work colleague said he had been kidnapped because of a disagreement between narco-traffickers on the Mexican side of the border. Ofelia didn't want to talk much about this.

Chapter 6

1. According to data from the Banco de México, there were 51.4 million border crossings at Tijuana in 2004 (Bringas 2004).

2. According to Alegría (2002, 39), the average wage for a factory worker in San Diego in 1998 was nine times higher than the corresponding wage in Tijuana.

3. U.S. Customs and Border Protection provides SENTRI passes (Secure Electronic Network for Travelers Rapid Inspection) to preapproved, low-risk travelers to expedite their land border crossings.

4. Their data include commuters from both Tijuana and Rosarito.

5. According to Alegría (2002), there is disagreement over the idea of a single "binational" labor market or two labor markets in which a specific type of worker is able to gain advantage.

6. Escala Rabadán and Vega Briones present a suggestive analysis of the perceptions held by a group of commuters living in Tijuana and Rosarito (2005, 161).

7. Eloísa may be misremembering the year in which her father closed his souvenir shop, because she later states that he went to work for the Rosarito municipal government in 1987.

8. The Colegio de Bachilleres.

9. Universidad Autónoma de Baja California, or Autonomous University of Baja California.

10. Secure Nursing Service, in the United States.

11. Instituto Tecnológico de Estudios Superiores de Occidente, or Western Technological Institute for Advanced Studies.

Chapter 7

1. In 2003, the functions formerly fulfilled by the Immigration and Naturalization Service were transferred to Immigration and Customs Enforcement (ICE), part of the U.S. Department of Homeland Security.

2. At the same time as the Bracero Program, in the 1950s, the U.S. government instituted "Operation Wetback," which deported more than 500,000 people and caused others to flee.

3. The *bordo* is the area where the channelized Tijuana River crosses the border from Tijuana to San Diego. Because the riverbed cuts across the border, there is a break in the border fence there, and the area is protected only by Border Patrol agents.

4. These are public areas (street corners, parks, town squares) where employers go to hire workers, typically undocumented migrants.

5. *Gabacho* is a Chicano pejorative term for an English-speaking non-Hispanic person.

6. *Güera* (*güero* is the masculine form) is a Spanish slang term for a fair-skinned or light-haired person. It is not derogatory but can be used that way.

7. A *coyote* is someone who smuggles immigrants across the border and into the United States for a fee.

Chapter 8

1. These were Operation Blockade in El Paso, Texas (1993); Operation Gatekeeper in Southern California (1994); Operation Lifesaver in Arizona and California (1998); and Operation Rio Grande in Brownsville and Laredo, Texas (1997).

2. Between 1994 and 1996, the Immigration and Naturalization Service's annual budget for the Southwestern Region rose from $400 million to $800 million, and the number of Border Patrol agents increased from 4,200 to 9,212 (Nevins 2002).

3. Estimates of the number of undocumented migrants are based on three sources: deportation data from Mexico's Instituto Nacional de Migración and the Encuesta de

Migración Internacional en la Frontera Norte (EMIF) and detention statistics from the U.S. Bureau of Immigration and Citizenship Services, formerly the U.S. Immigration and Naturalization Service. All these sources registered a reduction between 1993 and 2006. Nevertheless, because these numbers do not include people who are in the United States clandestinely through other means, such as overstaying a visa or entering with false documents, we cannot be certain that the flow has decreased significantly.

4. The Colegio de la Frontera Norte has been conducting the EMIF survey since 1993. It measures various flows, including deportations, and it covers three regions along the border: the east (Matamoros, Nuevo Laredo, and Piedras Negras), the center (Ciudad Juárez and Nogales), and the west (Mexicali and Tijuana). For this chapter, we analyzed EMIF data from 1998 to 2006; we thank Francisco Barraza for his assistance with the analysis.

5. The EMIF data yield the following percentages of deported individuals who had employed guides to assist them in crossing into the United States: for 1993–1994, 12.3 percent; 1994–1995, 8.9 percent; 1996–1997, 11 percent; 1998–1999, 17.8 percent; 1999–2000, 18.3 percent; 2000–2001, 17.5 percent; 2001–2002, 13.8 percent; 2002–2003, 20.9 percent; 2003–2004, 24.3 percent; and 2004–2005, 45.1 percent.

6. Moreno Mena is the coordinator of the Red de Derechos Humanos de los Migrantes.

7. As Pedro P. reported, "My business is based on trust, on the recommendation of people I have passed to the other side. Folks come to me because I have a reputation for skill and reliability. . . . I would never do anything that would put my name at risk" (Hellman 1994, 177).

8. All cost figures for people-smuggling fees, smugglers' earnings, and so on in this chapter are in U.S. dollars.

9. Highway 98 is in Imperial County, a significant distance from the Tecate border crossing. We suspect that our informant had a memory lapse and that the highway in question is actually Highway 94, which connects Tecate and San Diego.

10. He discusses the number of people he was crossing in terms of his work relationship with his sister-in-law, because she is the entrepreneur who "buys" the groups of would-be migrants.

11. The reference is to Mexico's Federal Investigation Agency (Agencia Federal de Investigación), a policing organization.

12. The Procuraduría General de la República is the government agency charged with investigating and prosecuting federal crimes.

13. The Federal Preventive Police (Policía Federal Preventiva).

14. The Institutional Revolutionary Party (Partido Revolucionario Institucional, or PRI), a political party long dominant (until very recently) in Mexico.

15. Francisco Franco Ríos was the attorney general in Baja California beginning in 1992, during the administration of Ernesto Ruffo. According to journalist Carlos Ramírez (2001, 2), members of the military police testified in 1993 that Franco had been selling state judicial police credentials, at $10,000 each, to the bodyguards of the leaders of drug cartels.

Chapter 9

1. Suro and Passel (2003, 2) define the second generation as "born in the United States with at least one foreign born parent. U.S. citizens by birth." This is also the definition followed in the U.S. Bureau of the Census's 2005 Current Population Survey. For

the Census definition, see http://www.census.gov/population/www/socdemo/foreign/cps 2006.html#gen (accessed September 3, 2010).

2. Portes and Rumbaut (2006, 246) define the 1.5 generation as children who were under age thirteen when they came to the United States. David López and Ricardo Stanton-Salazar (2001, 65) distinguish U.S.-born children from children who grew up in the United States, dividing the latter group into gradations of 1.75 (under five years of age), 1.5 (six to twelve years), and 1.25 (older than thirteen), depending on age at arrival.

3. In 1960, the average age for the second generation was twenty-five years; in 2000, it was ten years (López and Stanton-Salazar 2001, 50).

4. He refers to the Instituto de Seguridad y Servicios Sociales de los Trabajadores del Estado (Security and Social Services Institute for State Workers).

Chapter 10

1. "The Eighteenth Amendment to the United States Constitution, prohibiting the importation, transport, manufacture or sale of alcoholic beverages, went into effect on January 16, 1920. With the passage of this amendment and the numerical limits placed on immigration to the United States by the Immigration Acts of 1921 and 1924, border enforcement received renewed attention from the government" (U.S. Department of Homeland Security 2003).

2. The San Diego County Fair.

Conclusion

1. The narrative thread is the connecting argument in a biographical history and carries the core theme (Vila 2000).

References

Acevedo, C., D. Piñera, and F. J. Ortiz. 1985. "Semblanza de Tijuana, 1915–1930." In *Historia de Tijuana: Semblanza general,* edited by D. Piñera. Tijuana, Mexico: Centro de Investigaciones Históricas, Universidad Nacional Autónoma de México–Universidad Autónoma de Baja California/XI Ayuntamiento de Tijuana.

Aguilar, David. 2005. "The Southern Border in Crisis: Resources and Strategies to Improve National Security." Statement of David Aguilar, Chief, Office of Border Patrol, U.S. Customs and Border Protection, Department of Homeland Security, before the U.S. Senate, Committee on the Judiciary, Subcommittee on Terrorism, Technology, and Homeland Security and Subcommittee on Immigration, Border Security, and Citizenship, 109th Congress, 1st session, June 7, 2005. Washington, DC: U.S. Government Printing Office.

Alegría, Tito. 1989. "La ciudad y los procesos transfronterizos entre México y Estados Unidos." *Frontera Norte* 2 (4): 53–90.

———. 1990. "Ciudad y trasmigración en la frontera de México con Estados Unidos." *Frontera Norte* 2 (4): 50–93.

———. 2002. "Demand and Supply of Mexican Cross-Border Workers." *Journal of Borderlands Studies* 17 (1): 37–55.

———. 2008. "¿Existen las metrópolis transfronterizas? El caso de Tijuana." In *Ciudades en la frontera: Aproximaciones críticas a los complejos urbanos transfronterizos,* edited by Haroldo Dilla Alfonso, 128–165. Santo Domingo, Dominican Republic: Editorial Manatí.

Alonso, José Antonio. 2002. *Maquila domiciliaria y subcontratación en México en la era de la globalización neoliberal.* Mexico City: Plaza y Valdés/El Colegio de Tlaxcala.

Alonso Meneses, Guillermo. 2007. "¿Terrorismo gringo? Antropología de la globalización y la migración clandestina en la frontera México-Estados Unidos." In *Antropología de las fronteras: Alteridad, historia e identidad más allá de la línea,* edited by Miguel Olmos Aguilera, 153–188. Mexico City: El Colegio de la Frontera Norte and Miguel Ángel Porrúa.

Anderson, Joan B., and James Gerber. 2008. *Fifty Years of Change on the U.S.-Mexico Border: Growth, Development, and Quality of Life.* Austin: University of Texas Press.

Anguiano, María Eugenia. 2005. "Cross-Border Interactions." In *The Ties That Bind Us: Mexican Migrants in San Diego County,* edited by Richard Kiy and Christopher Woodruff. La Jolla, CA: Center for U.S.-Mexican Studies, University of California, San Diego.

Anzaldúa, Gloria. 1987. *Borderlands/La frontera: The New Mestiza.* San Francisco: Spinsters/Aunt Lute.

Astorga, Luis. 2004. "Mexico: Drugs and Politics." In *The Political Economy of the Drug Industry: Latin America and the International System,* edited by Menno Vellinga, 85–102. Gainesville: University Press of Florida.

Bancroft, Hubert Howe. 1883–1890. *History of California.* Vols. 18–24 of *The Works of Hubert Howe Bancroft.* San Francisco: A. L. Bancroft.

Barajas, María del Rocío, and Kathryn Kopinak. 2003. "La fuerza de trabajo en la maquiladora: Ubicación de sus espacios laborales y de reproducción en Tijuana." *Región y Sociedad* 26:5–30.

Basauri, Carlos. 1990. *La población indígena de México.* Vol. 1. Mexico City: Instituto Nacional Indigenista.

Bauman, Zygmunt. 1999. *La globalización: Consecuencias humanas.* Mexico City: FCE.

Becerril González, Juan Gabino. 1996. "Reporte de trabajo de campo." Master's thesis. El Colegio de la Frontera Norte, Tijuana, Mexico.

Beck, Ulrich. 2002. *La sociedad del riesgo global.* Barcelona: Siglo Veintiuno.

Bringas, Nora. 2004. "Turismo fronterizo: Caracterización y posibilidades de desarrollo." Research report. Mexico City: El Colegio de la Frontera Norte–El Centro de Estudios Superiores de Turismo.

Bringas Rábago, Nora L., and Ruth Gaxiola Aldama. 2010. "Con el estigma a cuestas: Turismo sexual masculino en Tijuana." In *Turismo sexual en México: Hombres que se vinculan con hombres; Una perspectiva multidisciplinaria,* edited by Álvaro López and Anne Van Broeck. Mexico City: CONACYT/Universidad Nacional Autónoma de México.

Brouwer, Kimberly C., Patricia Case, Rebeca Ramos, Carlos Magis-Rodríguez, Jesús Bucardo, Thomas L. Patterson, and Steffanie A. Strathdee. 2006. "Trends in Production, Trafficking, and Consumption of Methamphetamine and Cocaine in Mexico." *Substance Use and Misuse* 41 (5): 707–727.

Browning, Harley, and René Zenteno. 1993. "The Diverse Nature of the Mexican Northern Border: The Case of Urban Employment." *Frontera Norte* 5 (9): 11–32.

Bustamante, Jorge. 2001. "Proposition 187 and Operation Gatekeeper: Cases for the Sociology of International Migrations and Human Rights." *Migraciones Internacionales* 1:7–34.

Calavita, Kitty. 1992. *Inside the State: The Bracero Program, Immigration, and the I.N.S.* New York: Routledge.

Carlsen, Laura. 2008. "A Primer on Plan Mexico." Americas Program Special Report, Center for International Policy. Available at http://www.cipamericas.org/archives /1474 (accessed November 10, 2009).

Carrillo, Jorge, ed. 1993. *Mercados de trabajo en la industria maquiladora.* Mexico City: El Colegio de la Frontera Norte/Plaza y Valdés.

Castañeda, Jorge. 2007. *Ex Mex: From Migrants to Immigrants.* New York: New Press.

Center for Latin American Studies, San Diego State University. 2008. "Fifty Years of Change on the U.S.-Mexico Border: Growth, Development, and Quality of Life." Available at http://latinamericanstudies.sdsu.edu/BorderData.html (accessed November 10, 2009).

Centro de Estudios de las Finanzas Públicas de la Cámara de Diputados. 2003. "Consideraciones generales sobre el régimen fiscal aplicable a las maquiladoras para 2003." Mexico City.

Chabat, Jorge. 2002. "Mexico's War on Drugs: No Margin for Maneuver." *Annals of the American Academy of Political and Social Science* 582:134–148.

Clark, Víctor. 1988. *Los mixtecos en la frontera (Baja California).* Cuaderno de Ciencias Sociales 4 (10). Mexicali, Mexico: Instituto de Investigaciones Sociales, Universidad Autónoma de Baja California.

El Colegio de la Frontera Norte–El Consejo Nacional de Ciencia y Tecnología (COLEF-CONACYT). 2003. "Migración, trabajo agrícola y etnicidad." Research project employing data from Mexico's *XII Censo General de Población y Vivienda* (INEGI, 2000).

Consejo Estatal de Población (COESPO). 2008. "Perfil sociodemográfico Tijuana 2008." In *Apuntes de población de Baja California.* Vol. 5. Mexicali, Mexico: Consejo Estatal de Población.

Consejo Estatal de Población–El Colegio de la Frontera Norte (COESPO-COLEF). 2003a. Encuesta a jornaleros agrícolas en campamentos del valle de San Quintín.

———. 2003b. "Encuesta sociodemográfica y de migración en la región de San Quintín, B.C." In *Estudio integral de migración en la región de San Quintín, B.C.,* edited by Rodolfo Cruz, María Eugenia Anguiano, Rodolfo Corona, Ana María Chávez, Telesforo Ramírez, and Laura Velasco. Manuscript. El Colegio de la Frontera Norte–Consejo Estatal de Población, Tijuana, Mexico.

———. 2003c. "Encuesta a empresas agrícolas en el valle de San Quintín, B.C." In *Estudio integral de migración en la región de San Quintín, B.C.,* edited by Rodolfo Cruz, María Eugenia Anguiano, Rodolfo Corona, Ana María Chávez, Telesforo Ramírez, and Laura Velasco. Manuscript. El Colegio de la Frontera Norte–Consejo Estatal de Población, Tijuana, Mexico.

Contreras, Oscar. 2000. *Empresas globales, actores locales: Producción flexible y aprendizaje industrial en las maquiladoras.* Mexico City: El Colegio de México.

———. 2010. *Empresas transnacionales, aprendizaje tecnológico y desarrollo local: Un estudio de caso en el noroeste de México.* Mexico City: Universidad Nacional Autónoma de México.

Contreras, Oscar, and Jorge Carrillo, eds. 2003. *Hecho en Norteamérica: Cinco estudios sobre la integración industrial de México en América del Norte.* Mexico City: Cal y Arena/El Colegio de Sonora.

Cook, Roberta. 2006. "NAFTA Trends in Fresh Fruit and Vegetable Marketing." Davis: Department of Agricultural and Resource Economics, University of California, Davis, January. Available at http://giannini.ucop.edu/CookGFJan06.pdf (accessed June 2, 2006).

Cornejo, Jorge Alberto. 2002. "Cuando las magdalenas devolvieron las pedradas." *La Jornada,* July 4.

Cornelius, Wayne A. 2001. "Death at the Border: Efficacy and Unintended Consequences of US Immigration Control Policy." *Population and Development Review*
27 (4): 661–685.

Coubés, Marie Laure. 2003. "Evolución del empleo fronterizo en los noventa: Efectos
del TLCAN y de la devaluación sobre la estructura ocupacional." *Frontera Norte*
30:34–64.

Cruz, Andrés (director of the Escuela Revolución Mexicana, Nuevo San Juan Copala,
San Quintín Valley). 2004. Interview by the authors, Valle de San Quintín, Baja
California, April 15.

Dear, Michael, and Andrew Burridge. 2005. "Cultural Integration and Hybridization at
the United States–Mexico Borderlands." *Cahiers de Géographie du Québec* 49 (138):
301–318.

Deverell, William. 2004. *Whitewashed Adobe: The Rise of Los Angeles and the Remaking
of the Mexican Past*. Berkeley: University of California Press.

Dilthey, Wilhelm. 1994. *Teoría de las concepciones del mundo*. Barcelona: Altaya.

Durand, Jorge. 1994. *Más allá de la línea: Patrones migratorios entre México y Estados
Unidos*. Mexico City: CONACULTA.

Durin, Severine. 2008. "Los indígenas, un nuevo sujeto de atención institucional en
el Área Metropolitana de Monterrey (1995–2006)." In *El norte de México: Entre
fronteras*, edited by Juan Luis Sariego. Mexico City: Colección Escuela Nacional de
Antropología e Historia–Chihuahua/Escuela Nacional de Antropología e Historia/
Instituto Nacional de Antropología e Historia/CONACYT.

Echánove, Flavia. 2009. "Insertándose en las cadenas globales de mercancías: El caso
de la agricultura por contrato en productos no tradicionales." In *México–Estados
Unidos: Los desafíos de la integración,* coordinated by Oscar Contreras. Reporte de
investigación para el Programa Interinstitucional de Estudios sobre la Región de
América del Norte.

EMIF (Encuesta de Migración Internacional en la Frontera Norte). 1993–2003. Annual
Reports. Mexico City: Secretaría del Trabajo y Previsión Social, Consejo Nacional
de Población, Instituto Nacional de Migración/El Colegio de la Frontera Norte.
Available at http://www.conapo.gob.mx/mig_int/series/0506.xls (accessed January
10, 2009).

———. 1998–2006. "Flujo de deportados." Tijuana, Mexico: Secretaría del Trabajo y
Previsión Social, CONAPO/El Colegio de la Frontera Norte.

Environmental Protection Agency. 2009. "What Is Border 2012 Achieving?" (June 23).
Available at http://www.epa.gov/border2012/framework/index.html (accessed November 10, 2009).

Escala Rabadán, Luis, and Germán Vega Briones. 2005. "Living and Working as Cross-
Border Commuters in the Tijuana–San Diego Region." In *The Ties That Bind Us:
Mexican Migrants in San Diego County,* edited by Richard Kiy and Christopher
Woodruff. La Jolla, CA: Center for U.S.-Mexican Studies, University of California,
San Diego.

Eschbach, Karl, Jacqueline Hagan, and Néstor Rodríguez. 2003. "Deaths during Undoc-
umented Migration: Trends and Policy Implications in the New Era of Homeland
Security." In *In Defense of the Alien,* edited by the National Legal Conference on
Immigration and Refugee Policy. New York: Center for Migration Studies.

Fernández-Kelly, Patricia, and Douglas S. Massey. 2007. "Borders for Whom? The Role
of NAFTA in Mexico-U.S. Migration." *Annals of the American Academy of Political
and Social Science* 610 (March): 98–118.

Finckenauer, James O., Joseph R. Fuentes, and George L. Ward. 2001. "Mexico and the United States of America: Neighbours Confront Drug Trafficking." *Forum on Crime and Society* [United Nations Centre for International Crime Prevention] 1 (2): 1–18.

Flores Atilano, Juan José. 2000. *Entre lo propio y lo ajeno: La identidad étnico local de los jornaleros mixtecos.* Mexico City: Instituto Nacional Indigenista/Programa de las Naciones Unidas para el Desarrollo.

Ganster, Paul, and David E. Lorey. 2008. *The U.S.-Mexican Border into the Twenty-first Century.* 2nd ed. Lanham, MD: Rowman and Littlefield.

GAO (U.S. General Accounting Office). 1988. *Studies of the Immigration Reform and Control Act's Impact on Mexico.* Briefing Report to the Honorable Dennis DeConcini, U.S. Senate. Available at http://www.eric.ed.gov/PDFS/ED299083.pdf (accessed October 12, 2009).

García y Griego, Manuel. 1996. "The Importation of Mexican Contract Laborers to the United States, 1942–1964." In *Between Two Worlds: Mexican Immigrants in the United States,* edited by David Gutiérrez. Wilmington, DE: Scholarly Resources.

Garduño, Roberto. 2009. "La narcoguerra/XII." *La Jornada,* March 12.

Gay, Robert. 2005. *Lucia: Testimonies of a Brazilian Drug Dealer's Woman.* Philadelphia: Temple University Press.

Gonzales, Michael J. 2002. *The Mexican Revolution, 1910–1940.* Albuquerque: University of New Mexico Press.

González Iñárritu, Alejandro, dir. 2007. *Babel.* 143 min. Paramount Home Entertainment, DVD.

González-Ruiz, Samuel. 2001. "Fighting Drug Cartels on the Mexico–United States Border." *Forum on Crime and Society* [United Nations Centre for International Crime Prevention] 1 (2): 19–30.

Grávalos, Esther, and Alejandro García. 2001. "Seminis Vegetable Seeds." *AgBioForum* 4 (1): 40–45. Available at http://www.agbioforum.org/v4n1/v4n1a07-gravalos.htm (accessed May 30, 2006).

Gregory, James N. 1997. "The Shaping of California History." In *Major Problems in California History,* edited by Sucheng Chan and Spencer Olin. Boston: Houghton Mifflin.

Guerette, Rob T. 2007. *Migrant Death: Border Safety and Situational Crime Prevention on the U.S.-Mexico Divide.* New York: LFB Scholarly Publishing.

Hellman, Judith Adler. 1994. *Mexican Lives.* New York: New Press.

Henderson, Timothy J. 2007. *A Glorious Defeat: Mexico and Its War with the United States.* New York: Hill and Wang.

Heyman, Josiah McC. 1994. "The Mexico–United Status Border in Anthropology: A Critique and Reformulation." *Journal of Political Ecology* 1:43–65.

Hoefer, Michael, Nancy Rytina, and Bryan C. Baker. 2009. "Estimates of the Unauthorized Immigrant Population Residing in the United States: January 2008." *Population Estimates.* Washington, DC: DHS Office of Immigration Statistics.

Hoffman, Abraham. 1974. *Unwanted Mexicans in the Great Depression: Repatriation Pressures, 1929–1939.* Tucson: University of Arizona Press.

Hunt, Timothy Dwight. 1853. *Address before the New England Society of San Francisco.* San Francisco: Cooke, Kenny.

Huntington, Samuel. 2005. "Mexican Immigration and Hispanization." In *Who Are We? The Challenges to America's National Identity,* by Samuel Huntington. New York: Simon and Schuster.

Ibarra, Israel. 2008. "Disminuye el 70% contratación de prostitutas." *El Mexicano,* December 10.

INCB (International Narcotics Control Board). 2009. *Report of the International Narcotics Control Board for 2008.* New York: United Nations.

INEGI (Instituto Nacional de Estadística y Geografía). 2000. *XII Censo General de Población y Vivienda 2000.* Mexico City: INEGI.

———. 2005. *II Conteo de Población y Vivienda 2005.* Mexico City: INEGI. Available at http://www.inegi.gob.mx/est/contenidos/espanol/rutinas/ept.asp?t=mlen03&c=3328 (accessed August 27, 2008).

———. 2009. *Industria maquiladora de exportación.* Economic Information Database (Banco de Información Económica). Available at http://dgcnesyp.inegi.org.mx/cgi-win/bdieintsi.exe (accessed March 23, 2009).

INI (Instituto Nacional Indigenista). 1993. *Migración indígena y economía informal: Comercio ambulante en Baja California.* Subdirección de Investigación. Delegación Estatal de Baja California, Mexico.

Katsulis, Yasmina. 2008. *Sex Work and the City: The Social Geography of Health and Safety in Tijuana, Mexico.* Austin: University of Texas Press.

Katz, Friedrich. 1981. *The Secret War in Mexico: Europe, the United States, and the Mexican Revolution.* Chicago: University of Chicago Press.

Kearney, Michael. 2003. "Fronteras y limites del estado y el yo al final del imperio." *Alteridades* 13 (25): 47–62.

———. 2008. "La doble misión de las fronteras como clasificadoras y como filtros de valor." In *Migración, fronteras e identidades étnicas transnacionales,* edited by Laura Velasco. Mexico City: El Colegio de la Frontera Norte/Miguel Ángel Porrúa.

Kuntz Ficker, Sandra. 2004. "The Export Boom of the Mexican Revolution: Characteristics and Contributing Factors." *Journal of Latin American Studies* 36:267–296.

Llamadas, Juan Manuel (coordinator of the Programa de Jornaleros Agrícolas in the San Quintín Valley, Delegación de San Quintín). 2000. Interview by Laura Velasco, Marie Laure Coubés, and Christián Zlolniski, Valle de San Quintín, Baja California, November 30.

López, David E., and Ricardo Stanton-Salazar. 2001. "Mexican Americans: A Second Generation at Risk." In *Ethnicities: Children of Immigrants in America,* edited by Rubén G. Rumbaut and Alejandro Portes. Berkeley/New York: University of California Press/Russell Sage Foundation.

López Bárcenas, Francisco. 2009. *San Juan Copala: Dominación política y resistencia popular; De las rebeliones de Hilarión a la formación del municipio autónomo.* Universidad Autónoma Metropolitana/Xochimilco. Mexico City: MC Editores.

López Estrada, Silvia. 2003. "Work, Gender and Space in a Dynamic Economy: Women's Home-Based Work in Tijuana, Mexico." *Journal of Developing Societies* 18 (2–3): 169–195.

———. 2005. "Trabajo a domicilio, pequeños talleres y precariedad laboral en Piedras Negras y Torreón." Research report. Tijuana, Mexico: El Colegio de la Frontera Norte.

Los Angeles Times. 2010. "Death Toll in Mexico's Drug War Raised to 28,000" (August 3). Available at http://latimesblogs.latimes.com/laplaza/2010/08/death-toll-drug-war-mexico.html (accessed September 9, 2010).

Martinez, Manuel Luis. 2002. "Telling the Difference between the Border and the Borderlands." In *Globalization on the Line: Culture, Capital, and Citizenship at U.S. Borders,* edited by Claudia Sadowski-Smith. New York: Palgrave.

Martínez, Mariana. 2009. "¿Traerá 2009 alto a la violencia?" *La Prensa San Diego,* January 9.

Martínez, Oscar J. 1994. *Border People: Life and Society in the U.S.-Mexico Borderlands.* Tucson: University of Arizona Press.

Massey, Douglas S., Jorge Durand, and Nolan J. Malone. 2002. *Beyond Smoke and Mirrors: Mexican Immigration in an Era of Economic Integration.* New York: Russell Sage Foundation.

McCaa, Robert. 2003. "Missing Millions: The Demographic Costs of the Mexican Revolution." *Mexican Studies/Estudios Mexicanos* 19:367–400.

McKinley, James C., Jr. 2009. "U.S. Is a Vast Arms Bazaar for Mexican Cartels." *New York Times,* February 26. Available at http://www.nytimes.com (accessed November 10, 2009).

El Mexicano. 2006. "Revisa Municipio salud de prostitutas en sus trabajos." Available at http://www.el-mexicano.com.mx/noticias/estatal/2006/02/17/revisa-municipio -salud-de-prostitutas-en-sus-trabajos.aspx (accessed February 17, 2006).

Migration Information Source. 2006. "The U.S.-Mexico Border" (June 1). Available at http://www.migrationinformation.org/Feature/display.cfm?id=407#1 (accessed November 10, 2009)

Miró, Ramón J., and Glenn E. Curtis. 2003. "Organized Crime and Terrorist Activity in Mexico, 1999–2002." Report 20540-4840, prepared by the Federal Research Division, Library of Congress, under an Interagency Agreement with the U. S. Government. Available at http://loc.gov/rrf/frd/pdf_files/OrgCrime_Mexico.pdf (accessed March 2, 2009).

Moreno Mena, José. 2008. Interview by Laura Velasco Ortiz, Mexicali, Baja California, May 1.

Morones, Enrique. 2009. "Dangerous Journey: The Plight of Mexican Migrants to the U.S." Conference presentation, Center for U.S.-Mexican Studies, University of California, San Diego, January 28.

Nevins, Joseph. 2003. "Thinking out of Bounds: A Critical Analysis of Academic and Human Rights Writing on Migrant Deaths in the U.S.-Mexico Border Region." *Migraciones Internacionales* 2 (2): 171–190.

Ngai, Mae M. 2004. *Impossible Subjects: Illegal Aliens and the Making of Modern America.* Princeton, NJ: Princeton University Press.

Office of Management and Budget, Executive Office of the President of the United States. 2009. *Budget of the United States Government.* Available at http://www. whitehouse.gov/omb/budget/fy2009/homeland.html (accessed June 15, 2009).

Passel, Jeffrey. 2006. "The Size and Characteristics of the Unauthorized Migrant Population in the US: Estimates Based on the March 2005 Current Population Survey." Research report. Pew Hispanic Center. Available at http://pewhispanic.org/files /reports/61.pdf (accessed March 31, 2009).

Passel, Jeffrey S., and D'Vera Cohn. 2008. *Trends in Unauthorized Immigration: Undocumented Inflow Now Trails Legal Inflow.* Washington, DC: Pew Hispanic Center.

Peach, J., and J. Williams. 2003. "Population Dynamics of the U.S.-Mexican Border Region." Southwest Center for Environmental Research and Policy. Available at http:// www.scerp.org/population.htm (accessed November 10, 2009).

Pérez Maya, Lorena. 1990. "Ser mazahua en Ciudad Juárez." *México Indígena* 4:15–22.

Pérez Sáinz, Juan Pablo, Manuela Camus, and Santiago Bastos. 1992. *Todito, todito es trabajo: Indígenas y empleo en la Ciudad de Guatemala.* Guatemala City: FLACSO.

Portes, Alejandro, and Rubén G. Rumbaut. 2001. *Legacies: The Story of the Immigrant*

Second Generation. Berkeley/New York: University of California Press/Russell Sage Foundation.

———. 2006. "Growing Up American: The New Second Generation." In *Immigrant America: A Portrait.* Berkeley: University of California Press.

Ramírez, Carlos. 2001. "Indicador Político." *El Universal,* June 12.

Rea, Hugo. 2004. "Prometen solución en una semana a sexoservidoras." *El Mexicano,* September 28.

Reisler, Mark. 1976. *By the Sweat of Their Brow: Mexican Immigrant Labor in the United States, 1900–1940.* Westport, CT: Greenwood Press.

Romano, E., S. Cano, E. Lauer, A. Jiménez, R. B. Voas, and J. E. Lange. 2004. "Tijuana Alcohol Control Policies: A Response to Cross-Border High-Risk Drinking by Young Americans." *Prevention Science* 5 (2): 127–134.

Rosaldo, Renato. 1997. "Cultural Citizenship, Inequality and Multiculturalism." In *Latino Cultural Citizenship: Claiming Identity, Space and Rights,* edited by William V. Flores and Rina Benmayor. Boston: Beacon Press.

Ruiz, Ramón Eduardo. 1998. *On the Rim of Mexico: Encounters of the Rich and Poor.* Boulder, CO: Westview Press.

Rytina, Nancy, and John Simanski. 2009. "Apprehensions by the U.S. Border Patrol: 2005–2008." Fact sheet. Washington, DC: DHS Office of Immigration Statistics.

Salinas, Daniel. 2008. "Giros negros, ganan batalla masajes." *Frontera,* February 28.

Secretaría de Economía, Dirección General de Estadística. 1956. *Estadísticas sociales del Porfiriato, 1877–1910.* Mexico City.

Stephen, Lynn. 2007. *Transborder Lives: Indigenous Oaxacans in Mexico, California, and Oregon.* Durham, NC: Duke University Press.

Suro, Roberto, and Jeffrey S. Passel. 2003. "The Rise of the Second Generation: Changing Patterns in Hispanic Population Growth." Pew Hispanic Center Study. Washington, DC: Pew Hispanic Center.

Tierney, William. 2000. "Undaunted Courage: Life History and the Postmodern Challenge." In *Handbook of Qualitative Research,* edited by Norman Denzin and Ivonna S. Lincoln. Thousand Oaks, CA: Sage Publications.

Truett, Samuel. 2006. *Fugitive Landscapes: The Forgotten History of the U.S.-Mexico Borderlands.* New Haven, CT: Yale University Press.

El Universo [Guayaquil, Ecuador]. 2008. "El mundo: Crisis económica causa estragos en prostitución." Available at http://www.eluniverso.com/2008/12/21/1/1128/8A563379D632431E8265B2E5A47422F7.html (accessed December 21, 2008).

U.S. Bureau of the Census. 2009. "Top Ten Countries with Which the U.S. Trades" (August). Available at http://www.census.gov/foreign-trade/top/dst/2009/08/balance.html (accessed November 10, 2009).

U.S. Department of Homeland Security. 2003. *Border Patrol History.* Available at http://www.cbp.gov/xp/cgov/border_security/border_patrol/border_patrol_ohs/history.xml (accessed June 15, 2009).

Valenzuela, José Manuel. 2003. "Centralidad de las fronteras: Procesos socioculturales en la frontera México–Estados Unidos." In *Por las fronteras del Norte: Una aproximación cultural a la frontera México–Estados Unidos,* edited by José Manuel Valenzuela. Mexico City: Fondo de Cultura Económica.

Velasco Ortiz, Laura. 1995. "Migración femenina y estrategias de sobrevivencia de la unidad doméstica: El caso de los mixtecos en Tijuana." In *Mujeres, migración y maquila en la Frontera Norte,* edited by Soledad González, Olivia Ruiz, Laura Velasco, and

Ofelia Woo. Mexico City: El Programa Interdisciplinario de Estudios de la Mujer, El Colegio de México/El Colegio de la Frontera Norte.

————. 2000. "Migración, género y etnicidad: Mujeres indígenas en la frontera de Baja California y California." *Revista Mexicana de Sociología* 62 (1): 145–171.

————, coord. 2010. *Tijuana indígena: Un estudio de las condiciones socioeconómicas y de integración de los indígenas inmigrantes.* Mexico City: Consejo Nacional para el Desarrollo de los Pueblos Indígenas.

Verini, James. 2008. "Arming the Drug Wars." Condé Nast Portfolio.com (July). Available at http://www.portfolio.com/news-markets/international-news/portfolio/2008/06/16/Examining-the-US-Mexico-Gun-Trade/ (accessed November 10, 2009).

Vernez, George, ed. 1990. *Immigration and International Relations: Proceedings of a Conference on the International Effects of the 1986 Immigration Reform and Control Act (IRCA).* Washington, DC: Urban Institute Press and Rand Corporation.

Vila, Pablo. 2000. *Crossing Borders, Reinforcing Borders: Social Categories, Metaphors, and Narrative Identities on the U.S.-Mexico Frontier.* Austin: University of Texas Press.

————. 2005. *Border Identifications: Narratives of Religion, Gender, and Class on the U.S.-Mexico Border.* Austin: University of Texas Press.

Wilson, Thomas, and Hasting Donan. 2000. *Border Identities: Nation and State at International Frontiers.* Cambridge: Cambridge University Press.

Zhou, Min. 1997. "Segmented Assimilation: Issues, Controversies, and Recent Research on the New Second Generation." In "Immigrant Adaptation and Native-Born Responses in the Making of Americans." Special issue, *International Migration Review* 31 (4): 975–1008.

Zúñiga, Elena, Paula Leite, and Alma Rosa Nava. 2005. *La nueva era de las migraciones.* Mexico City: Consejo Nacional de Población.

Index

LAURA VELASCO ORTIZ is a Professor in the Department of Cultural Studies at El Colegio de la Frontera Norte. She is the author of *Mixtec Transnational Identity*, an updated translation of her book *El regreso de la comunidad: Migración indígena y agentes étnicos. Los mixtecos en la frontera México–Estados Unidos.*

OSCAR F. CONTRERAS is a Professor in the Department of Social Studies at El Colegio de la Frontera Norte. He is the author of many articles and books, most recently *Aprendizaje tecnológico y desarrollo local: La industria automotriz en el norte de México.*